Licensing (Scotland) Act 2005

AUSTRALIA
Law Book Co.
Sydney

CANADA and USA
Carswell
Toronto

HONG KONG
Sweet & Maxwell Asia

NEW ZEALAND
Brookers
Wellington

SINGAPORE and MALAYSIA
Sweet & Maxwell Asia
Singapore and Kuala Lumpur

Licensing (Scotland) Act 2005

by

Jack Cummins, M.A., LL.B.
Solicitor,
Partner in Hill Brown Licensing,
Editor, Scottish Licensing Law and Practice

THOMSON
™
W. GREEN

Published in 2006 by
W. Green & Son Ltd
21 Alva Street
Edinburgh EH2 4PS

www.wgreen.thomson.com

*Printed and bound in Great Britain by
Atheneum Press, Gateshead, Tyne & Wear*

No natural forests were destroyed to make this product;
only farmed timber was used and replanted

A CIP catalogue record for this book is available from
the British Library.

ISBN-10 0-414-01657-2
ISBN-13 978-0-414-01657-6

© W. Green & Son Ltd 2006

Crown Copyright legislation is reproduced under the terms of Crown Copyright Policy Guidance issued by HMSO. All rights reserved. No part of this publication may be reproduced or transmitted in any form, or by any means stored in any retrieval system of any nature without prior written permission, except for permitted fair dealing under the Copyright, Designs and Patents Act 1988, or in accordance with the terms of a licence issued by the Copyright Licensing Agency in respect of photocopying and/or reprographic reproduction. Application for permission for other use of copyright material including permission to reproduce extracts in other published work shall be made to the publishers. Full acknowledgment of author, publisher and source must be given.

PREFACE

Those of us in licensing practice 29 years ago may recall their sense of relief when W. Green produced the first edition of their annotations to the Licensing (Scotland) Act 1976. Messrs Allan and Chapman provided a welcome navigational starting point for novice and specialist alike, cast adrift on the uncharted seas of that statute's novel provisions.

The learned authors could not have anticipated the innumerable problems to which the drafting of the Act would give rise, nor the unremitting stream of judicial decisions which it unleashed; and, for the past 22 years, practitioners have owed a debt of gratitude to Sir Crispin Agnew and Heather Baillie, who have kept the original work in tune by digesting the amending legislation and weaving those decisions into the text.

Now the cobwebs of the 1976 Act are about to be blown away. We shall require to work with a statute which benefits from a clear, modern drafting style, even if the "jigsaw" approach to certain sections places unreasonable demands on the reader's capacity for mental gymnastics (see, for example, s.54). Of course, the Act's policy direction will not be to the taste of every palate: for example, "any person" may object to a premises licence application, although only one source supported the Scottish Executive's stance when evidence was given to the Local Government and Transport Committee; and the decision to set maximum hours for off-sales (from 10 am to 10 pm), taken during a chaotic Stage 3 debate, was simply perverse. As I suggest in the notes to Sch.3, para.5, imported English legislative provisions may not take root in Scottish jurisprudential soil and are likely to give rise to difficulty.

Perhaps a little optimistically, Messrs Allan and Chapman considered that the retention of provisions contained in the Licensing (Scotland) Act 1959 allowed them to follow in substantial measure the commentary to the eighth edition of Purves's *Scottish Licensing Laws*. In approaching the Licensing (Scotland) Act 2005 I have started with a substantially blank canvas. No doubt the work will grow over the years as the Act's provisions are subjected to judicial scrutiny. At the time of writing, regulations are about to be published for consultation purposes and will be laid before the Parliament for approval in February 2007. These will include provisions relative to the transition to the new system, due to begin in February 2008. The Scottish Executive has wisely decided to allow a period of some 18 months so that we may be spared the administrative chaos experienced by our counterparts in England and Wales, where the transition period lasted only six months.

I am grateful to Sheriff Principal Gordon Nicholson, CBE, QC who generously allowed me to take his mind on a number of matters; and Janet Hood, Head of BII Scotland, who was kind enough to comment on a number of annotations. In the usual way, I take responsibility for the finished work.

Glasgow
Jack Cummins
September 2006

ABBREVIATIONS

"this Act", "the Act": Licensing (Scotland) Act 2005 (asp.16)
"the 1976 Act": Licensing (Scotland) Act 1976 (c.66)
"the 2003 Act": Licensing Act 2003 (c.17)
"the DCMS Guidance": Guidance issued by the Department for Culture, Media and Sport under the 2003 Act (revised June 2006)
"the Explanatory Notes": the Explanatory Notes published by the Scottish Executive to accompany the Act
"EHCR": European Convention on Human Rights
"Agnew and Baillie": Agnew and Baillie, *Licensing (Scotland) Act 1976* (5th edn, W. Green, Edinburgh, 2002)
"Clayson": The Clayson Committee, chaired by Dr Christopher Clayson, "Report of the Departmental Committee on Scottish Licensing Law" (Cmnd 5354)
"Cummins": *Licensing Law in Scotland* (2nd edn, Lexis Nexis UK, London, 2000)
"Gordon": *The Criminal Law of Scotland* (3rd edn, by Christie, Vol.1, W.Green, Edinburgh, 2005)
"Nicholson": The Nicholson Committee, chaired by Sheriff Principal Gordon Nicholson, CBE, Q.C., "Review of Liquor Licensing Law in Scotland"
"Daniels": "The Report of the Working Group on Off-sales in the Community"
"White Paper": "The Licensing (Scotland) Bill: A consultation on Liquor Licensing"
"Policy Memorandum": The Policy Memorandum prepared by the Scottish Executive relative to the Licensing (Scotland) Bill

INTRODUCTION

The path to reform

Clayson and the Licensing (Scotland) Act 1976

At the start of the 21st century, the effects of alcohol misuse are one of Scotland's most pressing concerns. It results in an annual cost to the health service of £96m and an estimated overall cost to society of £1.1bn. Deaths due directly to excessive alcohol consumption more than doubled between 1990 and 2000. The number of people admitted to hospital with alcohol-related conditions rose by 37,909 in the period from 1990 to 2005 to a total of 51,599.

Against that disconcerting background, it could scarcely be satisfactory that the law regulating the sale and consumption of alcohol in Scotland is almost exclusively contained in an Act which came into force 29 years ago.

The Licensing (Scotland) Act 1976 is largely the fruit of recommendations made by the Departmental Committee on Scottish Licensing Law chaired by Dr Christopher Clayson, whose report was published in August 1973 (Cmnd.5354). The 1976 Act transferred responsibility for the administration of liquor licensing from licensing courts to licensing boards comprised of local councillors; half-yearly meetings were replaced by sittings in January, March, June and October; refreshment and entertainment licences were introduced; the terminal evening permitted hour was moved from 10 pm to 11 pm; permitted hours became capable of much wider extension; public houses could now apply for permission to open on Sundays; the currency of licences was extended from one to three years, with provision for their suspension; licence holding by non-natural persons was introduced; and the virtually unfettered discretion of the licensing courts was replaced by grounds for the refusal of new licence, transfer and renewal applications, with a right of appeal to the sheriff and thereafter to the Court of Session.

In his preface to the eighth edition of *Purves's Scottish Licensing Laws*, Sheriff A.G. Walker was able to suggest that the Licensing (Scotland) Act 1959, as a consolidating measure, produced a "coherent whole" by knitting together the tattered remnants of various statutes. The 1976 Act has not attracted such unalloyed approval. It defied the Biblical injunction by pouring new wine into old skins (the authors of the original commentary to the Act confidently borrowed parts of the Purves text)[1]; and the re-enactment of provisions contained in the earlier Acts created repugnancies: see, for example, *Hart v City of Edinburgh District Licensing Board*, 1987 S.L.T. (Sh.Ct.) and Cummins, p.6. Infelicitous drafting in legislation where "precision and simplicity are all"[2] has produced an unremitting stream of judicial decisions, some of which have served to underscore weaknesses

---

[1] Allan and Chapman, *Licensing (Scotland) Act 1976* (1st edn, W. Green, Edinburgh, 1977).
[2] *Carter v Bradbeer* [1975] 1 W.L.R. 1204 at 1221, *per* Lord Edmund-Davies.

overcome only by the most arcane of reasoning.[3] It has also been observed that "a clear pattern or consistent philosophy" in the Act is difficult to detect.[4]

Legislative intervention in the past three decades has attempted "quick fixes" or patchwork solutions. The Law Reform (Miscellaneous Provisions) (Scotland) Act 1990 introduced provision for children's certificates; attempted to stiffen the criteria to be applied by licensing boards when considering extended hours applications; simplified the approach to overprovision by removing a requirement to examine "facilities"[5]; made easier the procedure for obtaining Sunday permitted hours in refreshment-licensed and public house premises; introduced standard permitted weekday hours from 11 am to 11 pm; and provided for the opening of off-sale licensed premises on Sundays. A new system of two-step licence transfers created substantial difficulties for those involved in the purchase and sale of licensed premises; and the Licensing (Amendment) (Scotland) Act 1992 re-instated the option of an application for a one-step permanent transfer.

The Licensing (Scotland) (Amendment) Act 1996 allows licensing boards to impose so-called "health and safety" conditions to protect drug-takers at "rave" events,[6] a step precipitated by drug-related deaths at an Ayr nightclub.

Most importantly, the present legislation has failed to keep pace with changing social trends and drinking habits, and provides no effective means of addressing health and public order problems associated with alcohol abuse.

The foregoing criticism of licensing in its present state is by no means an adverse reflection on the system proposed by Clayson. On the contrary, it may be considered that, if the Committee's report had been more closely followed, the need for reform would have been less acute. The proliferation of regular extensions of the permitted hours would have been avoided if Parliament had more faithfully enacted the Clayson recommendations. The Committee advocated standard hours for on-licensed premises between 11 am and 11 pm (Report, para.9.56) but did not feel "justified in recommending a later terminal hour" for hotel bars, public houses and refreshment licences" (Report, para.9.74).[7] It was, however, accepted that "a later time may be justified in areas which cater for holidaymakers" (Report, para.9.74).

In an interview with *The Glasgow Herald* (as it was) in 1991, Dr Clayson said:

---

[3] See commentary to *Docherty v Leitch*, 1998 S.L.T. 374; [1997] 8 S.L.L.P. 13 at [1997] 8 S.L.L.P. 2.

[4] *Argyll Arms (McManus) Ltd v Lorn etc Divisional Licensing Board*, 1988 S.L.T. 290 at 292. Nicholson proposed that certain "guiding principles" should be embodied in the new Act as "licensing principles" (Report, paras 2.21 *et seq*). These objectives are the "licensing objectives": 2005 Act, s.4.

[5] Following the House of Lords decision in *Caledonian Nightclubs Ltd*, 1996 S.L.T. 451; [1996] 4 S.L.L.P. 11, it was suggested that the new approach allowed overprovision to be determined on a rough-and-ready basis, providing licensing boards with a discretion which was virtually unassailable: see commentary to *Caledonian Nightclubs Ltd* at [1996] 4 S.L.L.P. 20; and Paul Romano, "Explaining Overprovision" [1996] 5 S.L.L.P. 16.

[6] Although the Lord Advocate was at pains to emphasise that the Government was not intent on accommodating drug misuse: *Hansard*, June 3, 1996, col.1086.

[7] Permitted hours for entertainment-licensed premises were also to run from 11 am to 11 pm, with a period of 30 minutes allowed for the service of liquor before and after the entertainment (Report, para.9.81).

"I am mystified as to why licensing authorities who are elected representatives should have allowed these hours to extend so far in the first place. My Committee's original proposal was for the hours to run from 11 am to 11 pm [Report, para.9.56]. Exceptions were to be rigidly controlled. An extension was to be quite exceptional, for special occasions. If only the Government had accepted that ... They did not enact the critical recommendation."[8]

The new children's certificate proposed by Clayson did not see the light of day until 1991.[9] The Committee had in view an exception to the exclusion of children under 14 from the bar of licensed premises where the prohibition was not required "from the point of view of the interests of the public or their general convenience" (Report, para.11.18), expressing the hope that licensing authorities "will not frustrate our general intention by adopting too restrictive a policy" (Report, para.11.17). While licensing boards would have been enjoined to assess the suitability of premises[10] and enjoy a discretion to attach conditions to the grant of certificates, no terminal hour was proposed, a disappointed applicant would have been entitled to appeal to the sheriff, and access to bars by children under 14 would not have been conditional upon the taking of a meal.

Unhappily, when children's certificates were introduced some 17 years after Clayson, their availability was not received enthusiastically in many parts of Scotland because of the conditions attached by licensing boards, which were either unduly onerous or simply risible; and which were all the more remarkable since breach of a condition is a criminal offence. For example, Kyle and Carrick District Licensing Board (as was) imposed a condition that "if the part of the premises under application is a public house as opposed to a lounge bar, the applicant, as far as possible, shall ensure that small children are not subjected to offensive language" (admitting of the possibility that large and small children may be subjected to offensive language in a lounge bar and large children in a public house).[11] The absence of any right of appeal against the attachment of conditions resulted in licence holders availing themselves of other options[12]; and the 8 pm terminal hour was considered to be unnecessarily restrictive.[13]

Anxieties generated by delays in the disposal of appeals under the 1976 Act[14] might have been avoided or at least minimised if effect had been given to the Clayson recommendation that there should be instituted a right of

---

[8] Nicholson noted that extensions to the permitted hours had become the norm, rather than the exception, contrary to Clayson's intentions (C, paras 1.9, 2.1, 5.2), but considered that it would not be appropriate to propose a return to "very limited permitted hours" (Report, para. 2.14).
[9] Law Reform (Miscellaneous Provisions) (Scotland) Act 1990, s.49.
[10] The Committee had in view factors such as "the type of clientele, the provision of seats and tables, any record of misconduct or disorder, the availability of food and drink other than alcoholic liquor, toilet facilities, and the number of people likely to use the premises at any one time" (Report, para.11.15).
[11] This condition has not been maintained by the successor board, South Ayrshire Licensing Board.
[12] As, for example, by making provision for children in separate restaurant areas.
[13] See Nicholson, para.13.5.
[14] See notes to the 2005 Act, s.1.31; and Nicholson, para.11.5. See also "Delays in licensing appeals", 2003 S.L.T. (News) 233.

appeal to the sheriff principal; provision for which is now made in the 2005 Act.

Opinions will always differ as to whether the misuse of alcohol is fuelled principally by increased opportunities for its purchase and consumption or by other factors such as pricing and endemic cultural attitudes. When she was in charge of licensing reform, Justice Minister Cathy Jamieson expressed concern at the rise in the number of off-sale licences over the past 50 years (2,188 in 1945, 6,249 in 2002).[15] In a Scottish Executive press release Ms Jamieson said that: "Many communities have concerns about the concentration of off-licences in what quickly become hotspots for boozed-up young people ... One or two off-licences may be a useful asset for a community. Too many can become a scourge."

Recently, however, the price at which alcohol is sold has became a matter of sizeable concern;[16] and it may be considered that the Clayson Report, which rejected overprovision as a ground for refusal, was uncannily astute, almost prophetic, in its analysis of the relationship between licensing law and alcohol misuse. In the view of the Committee, increasing disposable income was likely to fuel a rise in total alcohol consumption; and consumption was "related to the financial resources available for the purpose rather than the extent of opportunities to purchase or consume" (Report, paras 1.36, 1.37). In a speech delivered to the Royal Medico-Chirurgical Society of Glasgow in 1975,[17] Dr Clayson noted that alcohol expenditure in the United Kingdom was increasing by an average of £253m. each year. By 1991, annual expenditure had reached £23.5bn; and by 2002 that figure had risen to £38.4bn. While expenditure has risen inexorably, alcohol prices have fallen substantially. It has been estimated that, in real terms, adjusting prices for rises in inflation and earnings, the cost of an average bottle of whisky in the off-trade has fallen in the past 30 years from £31.12 to £13.99, and a bottle of wine from £14.00 to £4.99. Inevitably, health experts have called for substantial price increases to prevent a cirrhosis epidemic.

The Nicholson and Daniels Committees

Speaking at the National Conference for Licensing Boards in 1997, Henry McLeish, who was Minister for Home Affairs at the Scottish Office, told delegates that he was unaware that the 1976 Act had fallen into disrepute but promised to consider representations from those with practical experience of the licensing system. Despite continuing disenchantment with the shortcomings of the legislation and the arrival of devolution, in April 2000 the then Justice Minister Jim Wallace told the Parliament that the Scottish Executive had "no plans at present to review or amend the Licensing (Scotland) Act 1976, or to introduce a new Licensing (Scotland) Bill" (although the Home Office had just published plans for the reform of licensing law in England and Wales).[18]

---

[15] Note, however, that in recent years the trend has been one of decline: in 1998, 6,337 off-sale licences were in force; the figure for 2004 is 6,103.
[16] The 2005 Act introduces controls on so-called "irresponsible promotions" (Schs 3 and 4).
[17] Reproduced in *Scottish Medical Journal*: Scot. Med. J. 1976, 21:175.
[18] "Time for Reform: Proposals for the Modernisation of our Licensing Laws" (CM 496).

Later that year, Donald Gorrie MSP urged to Executive to set up a "Clayson-style" commission as a precursor to a radical overhaul of licensing law.[19] By early 2001 the Executive was sufficiently galvanised to announce the establishment of an independent committee "with a wide-ranging remit" to carry out a comprehensive review. Eventually, on 28 June 2001, Justice Minister Jim Wallace announced the appointment of a committee under the chairmanship of Sheriff Principal Gordon Nicholson, CBE, Q.C. (as he now is), with the following terms of reference: "To review all aspects of liquor licensing law and practice in Scotland, with particular reference to the implications for health and public order; to recommend changes in the public interest; and to report accordingly."

The Committee's report took into account views expressed by over 200 respondents who participated in a consultation exercise and 23 organisations whose representatives gave oral evidence. It was completed in February 2003 but its publication did not take place until August of that year because of the Scottish Parliamentary elections. The Scottish Executive proceeded to consult on the Report and received over 160 responses.

In September 2003, the Scottish Executive appointed Peter Daniels, Chief Executive of East Renfrewshire Council, to chair a short-life working group, whose terms of reference were as follows:

"In the light of evidence from Sheriff Principal Nicholson's Review of Liquor Licensing, and from consultation on the Antisocial Behaviour Bill, to consider the issues surrounding the regulation of off-licences and to make recommendations to Ministers on:

- the scope for better engagement and consultation at community level on the grant of licences; and
- management and enforcement mechanisms which will help to prevent off-licences being a focus for antisocial behaviour."

The Daniels Report was published in February 2004. It was "in broad agreement" with the licensing system envisaged by Nicholson, but considered that the predecessor report "may not go far enough" in its proposals to improve upon the 1976 Act's provisions in relation to objections (Daniels Report, paras 3.5 *et seq*.; Nicholson Report, paras 6.13 *et seq*.). Daniels proposed broader enfranchisement, with the scope of those entitled to object to a new premises licence extended "to anyone who can demonstrate a real and material interest" (Report, para.3.13). It appears to have been considered that the determination of such an interest was likely to prove problematic in practice; and the 2005 Act (s.22) permits "any person" to object.

The Executive's tentative legislative intentions were set out in a White Paper published in May 2004. The Licensing (Scotland) Bill was published on March 1, 2005 and received Royal Assent on December 21, 2005.

---

[19] Mr Gorrie also set out 16 proposals for reform, almost all of which have been incorporated in the 2005 Act.

The Licensing (Scotland) Act 2005

Licensing boards

Nicholson considered whether, under a new system, licensing boards should be retained in their present form. In the Committee's view two questions arose:

- Do licensing boards satisfy the "independent and impartial tribunal test" for the purpose of art.6 of the ECHR?
- Ought they to be replaced by a more representative tribunal?

The first question is considered below, *sub voce* "Human Rights". There was little likelihood that the second question would be answered in the affirmative. Such an approach enjoyed little support and would, no doubt, have been politically unacceptable. Nicholson proposed a continuation of the present provisions since, on the whole, the present system had worked "fairly well"; and the Committee saw "considerable force in the argument that councillors are well suited to being members of boards on account of their local knowledge and their democratic accountability to the electorate" (Report, para.3.3). There was, however, a sound case for reducing the size of boards. Appearing before a large board could be intimidating experience for objectors, and many boards had told the Committee that members often found it difficult to attend meetings. The Report recommended that a licensing board should comprise a maximum of 15 members or 10 members in a division area, but the number of members sitting to consider applications should not exceed five. The Act provides that a licensing board is to consist of not fewer than five nor more than 10 members (Sch.1, para.1(1)); the quorum for a board meeting is one half of the number of members, subject to a minimum of three. The Report also recommended training for board members (Report, 3.10), provision for which is made in the Act (Sch.1, para.11); but a proposal that the offence of "canvassing" should be extended to embrace objectors was rejected on the view that a sufficient safeguard was provided by the code of conduct established by the Ethical Standards in Public Life etc. (Scotland) Act 2000.

Policy statements

Section 6 obliges licensing boards to prepare and publish triennial policy statements and to ensure that the policy seeks to promote the licensing objectives. Statements must, in particular, include a statement as to the extent to which the board considers there to be overprovision of licensed premises or licensed premises "of a particular description" in any locality (s.7). Nicholson considered that the promulgation of a policy was likely to be "highly beneficial": it could give "a broad indication of special terms and conditions which a board might consider appropriate in relation to particular forms of licensed business" and the proposed approach to authorised licensing hours (Report, para.6.39).

Local licensing forums

The formulation of the policy statement is to take place in consultation with the local licensing forum, a creation of the Act (s.10), whose duty will be to:

- keep under review the operation of the Act in the board's area, with particular reference to the exercise of the board's functions; and
- give advice and make recommendations to the board as the forum considers appropriate.

The members of a forum will be appointed by the council, who must seek to ensure so far as possible that the forum's composition is representative of the interests of licence holders; the chief constable; persons having health, education or social work functions; young people; and residents in the area (Sch.2, para.2).

Disposal of business

The 1976 Act provides limited assistance as to the manner in which licensing boards should conduct their business. Certain functions may be delegated; and some decisions must be taken at a meeting of the board, in certain cases a quarterly meeting (s.5). They are bound to "consider" applications (s.15(1)) and objections (s.16(5)) and to "have regard" to observations made by the chief constable (s.16A(5)). There are various references to hearings (e.g. in ss.13(1) and 15(2)), but even where no express right to be heard is conferred it will usually be implied.[20] Although a board must, of course, conduct its proceedings in a quasi-judicial manner, it had been suggested that it has the freedom to perform its functions as it pleases "in so far as it is not bound by statute".[21]

The 2005 Act dispenses with quarterly meetings. Where a hearing is required under any provision of the Act, it simply requires to be held at a meeting of the board (s.133(1)). The procedure to be followed may be set out in regulations, making provision for, inter alia, the rules of evidence which are to apply (s.133(2), (3)). The hearing of evidence by boards would mark a substantial departure from current practice. In *Catscratch Ltd v City of Glasgow Licensing Board (No. 2)*, 2002 S.L.T. 503; [2001] 20 S.L.L.P. 10 the Lord Ordinary considered that the hearing of evidence would be unnecessarily cumbersome in a relatively routine application (for the regular extension of permitted hours) where objection had been taken by local residents, provided that the applicant's case had been properly stated; and the test for the purposes of Art.6 of the EHCR raised the same issues, requiring a similar conclusion to be drawn.[22]

---

[20] *C.R.S. Leisure Ltd v Dumbarton District Licensing Board*, 1990 S.L.T. 200.
[21] *Fitzpatrick v Glasgow District Licensing Board*, 1978 S.L.T. (Sh.Ct.) 63.
[22] See also *J.A.E. (Glasgow) Ltd v City of Glasgow District Licensing Board*, 1994 S.L.T. 1164.

The licensing objectives

Central to the new licensing system are five "licensing objectives" set out in s.4, similar to the objectives contained in the Licensing Act 2003, save for the reference to public health: (a) preventing crime and disorder; (b) securing public safety; (c) preventing public nuisance; (d) protecting and improving public health; and (e) protecting children from harm.

The pursuit of these objectives:

- is a cardinal feature of licensing board policy statements (s.6(3));
- provides the basis for the refusal of an application for the grant of a premises licence (ss.23(5)) or an occasional licence (s.59(6));
- provides the basis for the attachment of conditions to a premises licence (s.27(6)) or an occasional licence (s.60(4);
- may lead to the imposition of sanctions upon the holder of a personal licence (s.84);
- may form a competent ground for the review of a premises licence (s.36(3)).

The scope of the licensing system

In terms of the 1976 Act, any person who "trafficks in any alcoholic liquor in any premises or place without holding a licence in that behalf" commits an offence (s.90). Section 9(1) of the Act provides that a licensing board may "grant a licence to any person for the sale by retail or supply of alcoholic liquor by that person; and a licence so granted "shall be in respect of premises specified therein" (s.9(2)). "Premises" could include not only a permanent structure but also marquees and defined outside areas[23] (which would normally be licensed by means of an occasional licence granted under s.33). Licences have been granted for permanently moored craft.[24] The 2005 Act prohibits the sale of alcohol on any "premises", except premises which are the subject of a premises licence. "Premises" means "any place and includes a vehicle, vessel or moveable structure" (s.147(1)).

The changes wrought and provisions retained by this Act may be summarised thus:

"Premises"	The 1976 Act	This Act
Seamen's canteens	Special licensing provisions (ss.40–46)	No special provisions[25]
Service canteens held "under the authority of the Secretary of State"	No licence required (s.138(1)(a))	"Exempt premises": no licence required when occupied for the purposes of the armed forces: ss.1(2), 124(1)(e)
Wholesale premises	Largely exempt (ss.90A, 138(2)(b))	Distinction between "wholesale" and "retail" sales abolished[26]
Theatres erected before January 1, 1904	No licence required: treated as if an entertainment licence were in force	Exemption abolished[27]

---

[23] *Hutcheon v Cadenhead* (1892) 19 R. (J.) 32.
[24] *Cf. Gate v Bath Justices* (1893) 147 J.P. 289.
[25] In terms of a Nicholson recommendation (Report, para.4.28).
[26] See below *sub voce "Selling to trade"*.

	(ss.121, 138(1)(b))	
Aircraft	No licence required while airborne (s.138(1)(c))	"Exempt premises" while engaged on a journey: s.124(1)(c)
Hovercraft	No specific provision; but presumably treated as "passenger vessels" (see below)	"Exempt premises" while engaged on a journey: s.124(1)(c)
Railway vehicles	No licence required provided "passengers can be supplied with food" (s.138(1)(c))	"Exempt premises" while engaged on a journey: s.124(1)(c)
Vessels	No licence required "while in the course of being navigated" (s.138(1)(c))[28]	"Exempt premises" but only while engaged on an international journey or a journey forming part of a ferry service (s.124(1)(d))[29]
"Moveable structures"	Normally licensed by means of an occasional licence (s.33)	Treated as "premises": s.126
"Moving vehicles"	Not licenseable	Treated as premises: s.126
Premises situated at motorway service stations	Licence may not be granted (s.28)	"Excluded premises": licence may not be granted: s.123
Premises used as a garage	Licence may be granted	"Excluded premises": licence may not be granted except in certain circumstances: s.123

"Exempt premises"

Exempt premises are not entirely disconnected from the licensing system. For the purposes of Part 8 of the Act, which sets out a large number of offences, these premises are "relevant premises" when used for the sale of alcohol (s.122). Thus, for example, any "responsible person" (s.122) who knowingly allows alcohol to be sold to a person under 18 on, say, an aircraft commits an offence (s.103(1)); a notice requires to be displayed relative to the prohibited purchase of alcohol by a person under 18 (s.110); and (no doubt bizarrely) a person who behaves in a disorderly manner and refuses or fails to leave a ferry boat, hovercraft, train or aircraft engaged on a journey is liable to prosecution (s.116(1)).

The offence of selling alcohol to persons under the age of 18 is no longer restricted to licensed premises (see s.102).

"Selling to trade"

In terms of the 1976 Act, no licence is required for the sale of alcohol "from premises which are used exclusively for wholesale trading (whether solely of alcoholic liquor or not" (s.90A). The difference between wholesale and retail sales is determined by reference to the quantity sold in a single transaction.[30]

---

[27] Nicholson considered that a continuation of the 1976 Act's treatment of these theatres would be "bizarre" (Report, para.14.44).
[28] Subject to certain restrictions on the sale of alcohol on Sundays: s.93.
[29] Otherwise provision for the licensing of vessels is contained in s.126.
[30] In terms of the Alcoholic Liquor Duties Act 1979 (c.4), s.4(1): "'wholesale', in relation to dealing in alcoholic liquor, means the sale at any one time to one person of quantities not less

This Act abandons the distinction between the two types of sale and introduces in its place the concept of "selling to trade": that is to say, the "selling of alcohol or other goods to a person for the purposes of that person's trade" (s.147(2)). The quantity of alcohol sold is now irrelevant. A licence is not required for the sale of alcohol "to trade" (s.1(2)); but "a person who sells alcohol to trade otherwise than from premises which are used exclusively for the purpose of the selling of goods (whether solely alcohol or not) to trade commits an offence" (s.117).

In the result:

- The sale of alcohol to members of the public who are not trade customers will require to be authorised by the grant of a premises licence, irrespective of the amount sold.
- The sale of alcohol in any quantity to trade customers from premises only used for trade purchases will not require to be authorised by a licence.
- A licence will be required for premises in which alcohol is only sold to traders but other commodities are sold for non-trade purposes.
- A premises licence appears to be required for bulk sales of alcohol to a members' club.[31]

(These new arrangements apply equally, of course, to internet and other "remote" sales of alcohol: see below, *sub voce "E-commerce".*)

Premises used for the selling of alcohol to trade are "relevant premises" for the purposes of the offences provisions contained in Part 8 of the Act.

Clubs

A distinction falls to be drawn between, on the one hand, proprietary clubs, conducted as commercial business, and which will normally be the subject of an entertainment licence granted under the 1976 Act (and, in future, a premises licence issued under the 2005 Act); and, on the other, bona fide members' clubs in which the supply of alcohol is authorised by means of a certificate of registration granted by the sheriff (1976 Act, Part VII).

This Act brings members' clubs within the mainstream licensing system, a reform for which there was, in the opinion of Nicholson "an overwhelming case" (Report, para.9.4). The supply of alcohol in members' clubs will now treated as a "sale" (s.3) requiring to be authorised by a premises licence. Certain clubs will be the subject of dispensations; but much of the detail as to the manner in which clubs of different types will be treated rests on regulations which have yet to be published.

Premises licences

The Act abandons the current seven fixed licence categories within which many modern licensed developments have struggled to accommodate

---

than the following, namely—(a) in the case of spirits, wine or made-wine, 9 litres or 1 case; or (b) in the case of beer or cider, 20 litres or 2 cases."
[31] See notes to s.1(2), (3).

themselves. For example, a department store selling wines and spirits for consumption off the premises and containing a shoppers' restaurant could only operate under the authority of a public house licence: neither a refreshment licence nor a restaurant licence permit off-sales, while the consumption of alcohol on premises which are off-sale licensed is prohibited.

The new premises licence introduced by the Act will provide both licensing boards and the trade with unprecedented flexibility, as well as affording boards a much higher degree of control over the manner in which premises are operated. Application for a licence may be made by "any person,[32] other than an individual under the age of 18" (s.20(1)). The application requires to be supported by:

- an operating plan;
- planning and building control certificates; and, where food is to be supplied on the premises, a food hygiene certificate; and
- a layout plan.

The operating plan will set out the applicant's proposals, including (a) the times during which it is intended to (i) sell alcohol for consumption on or off the premises; (ii) conduct any other activities; and (b) the arrangements (if any) for the admission of children (s.20). The licensing board must consider the application at a hearing (s.23) and, unless a ground for refusal applies, the application must be granted. "Any person" may object to the application or make certain representations, save that the chief constable may only (a) recommend refusal where the applicant has been convicted of a "relevant offence or a foreign offence";[33] or (b) object on the ground that the applicant, or a connected person, is involved in "serious organised crime" (s.22).[34] The chief constable is obliged to furnish the licensing board with a report detailing "all cases of antisocial behaviour" identified with the preceding 12 months "as having taken place on, or in the vicinity of" the application premises (s.21(3)).

A premises licences will have an indefinite duration but may be suspended, revoked, or varied (s.39).[35] It may be transferred on application by its holder (s.33) or, in certain circumstances,[36] by a third party (s.34) (the reasons for this dichotomy is not clear).

Grounds for refusal

The grounds for refusal are set out in s.23(5) and may be summarised as follows:

(1) The premises are "excluded premises", that is to say, they are situated at a motorway service station or, subject to certain exceptions, used as a garage (s.123).

---

[32] Including a non-natural person such as a limited company, council, partnership or club.
[33] The nature of relevant and foreign offences has yet to be prescribed: see s.129.
[34] See below *sub voce "Objections and Representations"*.
[35] A licence may be varied on application by the holder (s.29); or varied by the licensing board following a premises licence review (s.39).
[36] For example, where the licence holder has died.

(2) The application must be refused because:
  (i) an application for the same premises was refused in the preceding year, unless a direction was made at the time of the earlier refusal allowing the submission of a further application in the ensuing year[37]; or unless the board is satisfied that there has been a material change of circumstances since the earlier refusal (s.64(2))[38];
  (ii) grant of the application would allow the sale of alcohol on the premises during a continuous period of 24 hours or more (unless there are "exceptional circumstances" justifying such a grant) (s.64(2));
  (iii) the off-sales hours proposed in the application are such that alcohol would be sold for consumption of the premises before 10 am, after 10 pm or both on any day (s.65(3)).
(3) Grant of the application would be inconsistent with one or more of the licensing objectives.
(4) The licensing board considers that the premises are unsuitable for the sale of alcohol, having regard to the nature of the proposed activities to be carried on in the premises, their location, character and condition and the persons likely to frequent the premises.
(5) Grant of the application would result in the overprovision in the locality of licensed premises, or licensed premises of the same or similar description as the subject premises, with not only the number, but also the capacity, of existing premises to be taken into account for the first time.

Conditions

The 1976 Act provides licensing boards with very limited opportunities to attach conditions. Licences may be granted subject to a condition preventing the sale of spirits (s.29); conditions may be attached to entertainment licences (including conditions placing restrictions on the permitted hours) "in order to secure that the sale or supply of alcohol is ancillary to the entertainment" (s.101(2)); licensing board byelaws may set out "conditions which may be attached to licences for the improvement of standards of, and conduct in, licensed premises" (s.38(1)(f));[39] conditions designed to protect the health and safety of customers must be attached by a licensing board where premises may be used for so-called "rave" events (ss.18A, 18B); a licence may be made "seasonal" (s.62); and such conditions as the board thinks fit may be attached to the grant of an occasional or regular extension of permitted hours (s.64(5)).

These eclectic controls have not been sufficient to prevent changes in licensed premises which would not have been approved if proposed at the time an application was granted. Nicholson postulated the examples of a small shop which seeks an off-sale licence ostensibly to provide a modest range of beers, wine and spirits for the convenience of those purchasing

---

[37] *Cf* 1976 Act, s.14.
[38] *Cf* Civic Government (Scotland) Act 1982, Sch.1, para.6.
[39] A byelaw cannot provide that a certain type of activity is only permitted with the prior consent of the board: *Applegate Inns Ltd v North Lanarkshire Licensing Board* [1997] 6 S.L.L.P. 6.

groceries but which afterwards "is turned into a large off-sales emporium"[40]; and a hotel in which, by degrees, the provision of letting bedrooms becomes secondary to expanded bar facilities (Report, para.4.2). Difficulties have also been encountered with public house premises providing adult entertainment.[41] The 2005 Act ensures that licensing boards not only have a clear view of the manner in which the premises will be operated but also prevents so-called "licensing by stealth" by providing that alcohol is to be sold, and any other activity carried on, only in accordance with the operating plan (Sch.3, paras 2, 3).[42]

Extensive provision is also made for the attachment of conditions. These may be divided into four categories (s.27):

(1) Mandatory conditions set out Sch.3 designed to ensure a consistent national approach in relation to, *inter alia*, the control of irresponsible alcohol promotions. Additional conditions may be prescribed (s.27(2)) "as new practices develop within the licensed trade or as new public order issues arise".[43]

(2) Conditions which must be attached to premises licences authorising trading for a continuous period beginning on one day and ending after 1 am the following day. These conditions have yet to be prescribed, but must be prescribed.

(3) "Pool" conditions which Scottish Ministers may prescribe and which licensing boards will have a discretion to attach.[44]

(4) Conditions which licensing boards may impose as being "necessary or expedient for the purposes of any of the licensing objectives".

Conditions of type (4) may not be inconsistent with types (1) and (3); may not (a) have the effect of making those conditions "more onerous or restrictive"; and may not "relate to a matter (such as planning, building control or food hygiene) which is regulated under another enactment" (s.27(7)). The last constraint no doubt derives from a concern that licensing boards may, as in the past, use liquor licensing to pursue non-licensing objectives.[45]

In addition, the licensing board may, with the consent of the applicant, modify an operating plan where they would otherwise be minded to refuse the application (s.23(7)); and, while compliance with the modified operating

---

[40] Holders of off-sale licences need not obtain the consent of the licensing board for alterations to their premises) 1976 Act, s.35).
[41] While conditions circumscribing entertainment may be attached to entertainment licences (1976 Act, s.101(2)) there is no similar provision in relation to public houses licences, except through the mechanism of byelaws (s.38).
[42] Nicholson considered that "a licensing board should be able to be reasonably satisfied that the kind of operation for which a licence is being sought will remain substantially unchanged once the licence has been granted" (Report, para.4.3).
[43] According to the Scottish Executive's memorandum to the Subordinate Legislation Committee.
[44] For possible examples, see notes to s.27(5).
[45] See, for example: *Bantop Ltd v City of Glasgow Licensing Board*, 1990 S.L.T. 366 (Board took into account unsatisfactory hygiene conditions when considering an application for the regular extension of permitted hours); and *La Belle Angele v City of Edinburgh Licensing Board*, 2001 S.L.T. 801; [2000] 17 S.L.L.P. 10 (flyposting was not "public nuisance" for the purpose of s.64 of the 1976 Act).

plan becomes a condition of the licence, the modificatory power is not subject to the safeguards set out in s.27(7). The Act's approach in this area is not entirely consonant with that of Nicholson. The Report considered that, as part of a "pro-active" approach, licensing boards ought to be able to modify operating plans even in the absence of formal objections or representations, creating "a theoretical risk" that a board could pursue a policy at odds with the licensing regime proposes by the Committee (Report, para.4.14 *et seq.*). It also noted that:

> "[A]ll licensing boards will be required to conduct their business consistently with declared policies (which themselves will require to comply with the 'licensing principles'); *and all decisions taken by licensing boards would, under our proposals, be subject to an appeal.*" (Emphasis supplied.)

In terms of recommendation 12(c):

> "A decision by a licensing board *to modify, or add to*, a term in an operating plan or schedule, and a decision not to do so notwithstanding objections or representations to that effect, should be subject to appeal." (Emphasis supplied.)

In terms of the Act's approach, a modification to which an applicant *agreed* could scarcely be the subject of a subsequent challenge;[46] and faced with a modification which is unpalatable, an applicant may nevertheless consider that acceding to the board's proposal is preferable to the refusal of an application and the prospect of a lengthy and expensive appeal. On the other hand, the modification power may operate to the benefit of applicants content to accept alterations to their proposals which do not fundamentally disturb their business plans; and there have been occasions on which applications have been refused because a board was not content to proceed on the basis of undertakings of doubtful validity.[47]

Provisional, temporary premises and occasional licences

A premises licence may be granted provisionally (s.45) and comes into effect when confirmed (s.46). The provisional procedures broadly follow those contained in s.26 of the 1976 Act, save that there is no equivalent of the 1976 Act's "outline" provisional grant (which proceeds on the basis of a locality plan and a general description of the applicant's proposals and which requires

---

[46] There could, however, be circumstances in which the manner of modification could give rise to an appeal: for example, where an applicant was given insufficient notice of, or inadequate time to consider, the licensing board's proposal, which would amount to a breach of natural justice (s.131(3)).

[47] As to the status of undertakings, see *Mitchells and Butlers Retail Ltd v Aberdeen City Licensing Board*, 2005 S.L.T. 13; [2004] 30 S.L.L.P. 34. By way of example, some licensing boards have not been content to grant off-sale licences for florist shops, even when offered an undertaking that the licence would only be used for the sale of luxury alcohol products, such as champagne, to those purchasing flowers. It would, in the view of those boards, be difficult to enforce such an undertaking, particularly where the licence had been transferred to another occupant.

to be "affirmed") (1976 Act, s.26(2)); and provisional premises licences have an initial currency of two years, subject to extension, while the under the 1976 Act the provisional grant of a new licence has a currency of one year, subject to renewal. A provisional premises licence may be varied (s.29), a facility which overcomes a weakness in the current system. The provisional grant of a licence made under the 1976 is not a licence "in force"[48] and it is not open to its holder to make application to the licensing board for consent to minor alterations in terms of s.35.

A temporary premises licence may be granted to the holder of a premises licence, whose premises are undergoing, or are to undergo, reconstruction or conversion (s.45, replacing the unsatisfactorily brief provisions of the 1976 Act, s.27).

Sections 56 to 61 set out provisions replacing those contained in ss.33 and 34 of the 1976 Act and permit application to be made for an occasional licence by the holder of a premises licence, the holder or a personal licence or a representative of any voluntary organisation. The new provisions are more much extensive and prescriptive than their antecedents.

Personal licences

The Act makes provision for the grant of personal licences authorising an individual aged 18 or over to supervise or authorise the sale of alcohol (ss.71, 72).[49] Personal licences have a currency of ten years and are renewable.

A licensing board is bound to grant an application for a personal licence provided that:
- the applicant is aged 18 or over and possesses a licensing qualification prescribed by s.91;
- no personal licence previously held by the applicant has been revoked in the preceding five years;
- no notice has been received from the chief constable specifying the applicant's convictions for a "relevant offence or a foreign offence" (s.73).

If conditions (1) and (2) are not satisfied, the application must be refused. Otherwise, if they are satisfied save for condition (3), then the licensing board must hold a hearing to determine whether the application requires to be refused for the purposes "crime prevention objective".

The "fit and proper person" test for licence-holding prescribed by s.17(1)(a) of the 1976 Act has thus been deserted; there is no onus upon an applicant to demonstrate that he has obtained sufficient experience of the licensed trade (although he will require to undertake training: s.87);[50] and the chief constable is not empowered to object to a personal licence application,

---

[48] *Ginera Ltd v City of Glasgow District Licensing Board*, 1982 S.L.T. 136; *Baljaffray Residents' Association v Milngavie and Bearsden District Council Licensing Board*, 1981 S.L.T. (Sh.Ct.) 106.
[49] Nicholson considered that the portability of such a licence would be of assistance to persons such as bar managers moving from one public house to another, possibly in a different part of the country (Report, para.4.1).
[50] A number of licensing boards have promulgated policies in terms of which a minimum amount of experience will be required as a prerequisite for the grant or transfer of a licence, although the *vires* of such an approach is open to doubt.

although he may recommend its refusal having regard to the applicant's conviction(s).

Where the holder of a personal licence is convicted of a "relevant or foreign offence" during its currency or the licensing board becomes aware of a conviction incurred during the application period, it must hold a hearing; and, if it is satisfied that it is necessary to do so for the purposes of the "crime prevention objective", it may (*sic*) revoke, suspend, or endorse[51] the licence (the maximum suspension period is six months).[52]

A nexus between premises licences and personal licences is forged by s.84. Where in the course of a premises licence review hearing (s.38) a finding is made that the holder of a personal licence "acted in a manner inconsistent with any of the licensing objectives", a hearing must be held which may result in the imposition of a sanction mentioned above.

An application for a premises licence must contain prescribed information about the individual who is to be the premises manager (s.20(4)(g)),[53] who must be the holder of a personal licence, and upon whom certain responsibilities fall[54] and who is capable of committing certain offences.[55] Alcohol may not be sold on the premises at any time when:

- there is no premises manager in respect of the premises[56];
- the premises manager does not hold a personal licence;
- the personal licence held by the premises manager is suspended; or
- the licensing qualification held by the premises manager is not the appropriate licensing qualification in relation to the premises (Sch.3, para.4(1)).

Every sale of alcohol made on the premises must by authorised (generally or specifically) by either the premises manager or another personal licence holder (Sch.3, para.5).[57]

Licensed hours

The 1976 Act provides "basic" permitted hours for on-licensed premises and registered clubs (s.53) and "trading hours" for premises which are the subject of an off-sale licence (s.119); only the former are capable of extension, by

---

[51] Three endorsements may lead to the suspension or revocation of the licence: s.86.
[52] Provision is also made for a hearing where the licensing board receives notice of a conviction prior to the determination of a personal licence application: s.75.
[53] Except where application is made for a provisional premises licence: s.45(10). In that case, information in relation to the premises manager is to be provided when application is made to confirm the licence: s.46(3). An individual may not be the premises manager of more than one licensed premises: s.19(2).
[54] The premises manager has a duty to co-operate with licensing standards officers (s.15); and ensure the display of a notice as to the prohibited purchase of alcohol by persons under 18 (s.110).
[55] Section 97(7) (allowing premises to remain open in breach of a closure order); and various offences contained in Part 8 of the Act where the premises manager is a "responsible person": ss.102–122.
[56] Provision is made for the variation of a premises licence so as to substitute another premises manager (ss. 31 and 54). Such a variation is a "minor variation": s.29(6)).
[57] For difficulties which may arise in relation to the accountability of premises managers and other personal licence holders, see notes to s.103 and Sch.3, para.5.

means of an occasional or regular extension (s.64). Nicholson noted that the widespread grant of additional operating hours had effectively eroded the system proposed by Clayson (Nicholson, Report, para.2.1; Clayson, Report, paras 9.45 *et seq*.) but considered that a shift to "very limited permitted hours" with no provision for extensions would meet with "considerable public resistance" as well as being "politically unacceptable" and "commercially disastrous" (Report, paras 2.14, 2.15).

In the result, Nicholson recommended that there should be no hours in the day, or days in the week, when the sale of alcohol was prohibited. Applicants would set out in their operating plan the hours during which they intended to trade. Those hours would be approved or modified by the licensing board having regard to their general policy and the "licensing principles" (Report, paras 5.5 *et seq*.). The Report considered that this approach might not lead to any noticeable difference to the licensing scene as it existed and licensing boards would approach "authorised hours" in a responsible manner (Report, paras 5.6, 5.7). Absolute faith in such an outcome was not forthcoming. Section 64 of the Act provides that the sale of alcohol during a continuous period of 24 hours or more may only be allowed in exceptional circumstances. That safeguard was not, of itself, considered sufficient; and many MSPs expressed fears that the potential relaxation of off-sales hours would produce unacceptable consequences. These anxieties reached their zenith during the Stage 3 debate on the Bill, when licensed hours for off-sale premises were restricted to the period between 10 am and 10 pm. In the result, weekday hours will be reduced by two hours and Sunday hours extended by two and a half hours.[58]

Licensed hours may be extended, either by means of a novel "general" grant made by a licensing board in respect of "a special event of local or national significance" (s.67) or on application by the holder of a premises licence (s.68).

Supervision and compliance

The 1976 Act affords licensing boards limited powers to ensure the satisfactory conduct of licensed premises. A licence may be suspended in terms of s.31 on the ground that the licence holder is no longer a "fit and proper person"; or the use of the premises has caused "undue public nuisance or a threat to public order or safety"; or there has been a breach of conditions attached to the licence by virtue of ss.18A or 18B. However, the ability of the licence holder to trade under appeal negates the effect of the suspension order, possibly for a very extended period. While permitted hours may be restricted by an order made under s.65, the terminal hour may only be reduced following a hearing at a quarterly meeting of the licensing board; and the effect of an order is placed in abeyance where an appeal has been marked. In practice, chief constables have recognised that, tactically, the better approach (in relation to on-licensed premises) is to object to an application for the regular extension of permitted hours: the refusal of such an

---

[58] The current trading hours for off-sale licensed premises are: on Mondays to Saturdays from 8 am to 10 pm; and on Sundays from 12.30 pm to 10 pm. The new hours may be varied by Scottish Ministers: s.65(4).

application is susceptible only to judicial review, a procedure which does not preserve the *status quo*.

Recognising the 1976 Act's deficiencies in relation to premises licences, Nicholson proposed that:

- there should be a broader, more graduated range of sanctions ranging from a formal warning or admonition to the revocation of the licence (Report, para.7.13)[59]; and
- while sanctions involving the closure of premises or a reduction in authorised hours should be capable of taking immediate effect, provision should be made for the interim recall of such a sanction on application to the sheriff.

Adopting the first recommendation, the Act provides that, following a premises licence review hearing, a licensing board may:

- issue a written warning to the licence holder;
- vary the licence;
- suspend the licence for such period as the board may determine; or
- revoke the licence (s.39).

In a critical respect, the Act deviates from the second recommendation. Licensing board decisions continue to have effect despite an appeal (s.132(7)), except that, in terms of s.132(8), where an appeal is taken against the suspension or revocation of a premises licence, the sheriff principal[60] may recall the board's order pending determination of the appeal "if satisfied on the balance of convenience that it is appropriate to do so". There is no provision for the interim recall of a variation (which could amount to a reduction in licensed hours).

Licensing standards officers

The operation of licensed premises will be monitored by council-appointed licensing standards officers ("LSOs"), at least one whom must be a member of a local licensing forum (Sch.2, para.2(3)). These officers will supervise compliance with the conditions of licences; provide a mediation service where disputes have arisen between licence holders or any other persons; and issue notices requiring any breach of conditions to be remedied. They will also be empowered to apply for a premises licence review; but such a review may not be sought in relation to a breach of conditions unless the licence holder has not complied with a notice requiring the breach to be remedied (ss.13, 14, 36(4)). A licensing standards officer may report on an occasional licence application (s.57(3)); and must report on an extended hours application (s.69(3)).

---

[59] Agnew and Baillie notes (at p.42) that the 1976 Act "may not comply with the ECHR because the Act does not give a licensing board sufficient flexibility to allow them to act proportionally in a whole range of circumstances".
[60] The Sheriff Principal may authorise a sheriff to consider and determine an appeal: s.132(4).

LSOs are afforded powers to enter and inspect licensed premises (ss.15, 137), as well as premises which are the subject of a premises licence or occasional licence application (s.137), and may examine vehicles used for the delivery of alcohol (s.119(5)). They may require the production of documents (s.15(3)) and licences (ss.52(4), (5), 93(2)).

Objections and representations

No doubt in the interests of the widest community engagement in the licensing process, "any person" may object to an application for a new premises licence (s.22) or apply for its review (s.36), save where, in the view of the licensing board, the objection or application is "vexatious or frivolous".

While the chief constable is "any person" who may apply for the review of a premises licence, he may only object to a premises licence application on the ground that the applicant or "any connected person" is involved in "serious organised crime" (an expression not defined in the Act) (s.22(2)). Otherwise, he may:

- make a recommendation as to the refusal of a premises licence application where the applicant has been convicted of a relevant or foreign offence (s.21(5));
- not object where the applicant or a connected person is involved in crime which is organised, but not serious;
- object to a premises licence variation application on the "serious organised crime" ground (s.22, as applied by s.29(4));
- recommend the refusal of an application for an occasional licence (s.57(2)) (but may not object);
- not intervene in relation to "general extensions" proposed to be granted by a licensing board in terms of s.67;
- make a recommendation as to the refusal of an application for a personal licence where the applicant has been convicted of a relevant or foreign offence (s.73(4)), but may not object, even where he has reason to believe that he applicant is involved in serious organised crime (or indeed any sort of crime);
- recommend that a personal licence be endorsed, suspended or revoked on a limited ground (s.83(5)).

Objectors are not afforded a right of appeal, save in relation to the grant of an occasional licence and a licensing board's decision following the review of a premises licence.[61]

Offences

Ninety years ago, the Lord Justice-General observed that the doctrine of vicarious responsibility was a necessary adjunct of licensing laws "for reasons which are singularly obvious", so that "a publican may be guilty of an offence even though he is not cognisant of the offence having been

---

[61] See notes to s.131.

committed and has given no authority for its commission to his servants or agents".[62]

Some 60 years later a full bench decision threatened to render nugatory the accountability of licence holders who had delegated the management of their premises. In *Noble v Heatly*[63] a certificate-holder had devolved responsibility to a supervisor, who in turn appointed a manager. The High Court held that the certificate-holder could not be convicted of "knowingly permitting" drunkenness on the premises without any personal knowledge on his part. That decision generated considerable anxiety; and the Secretary of State for Scotland received representations from, among others, the Association of Chief Police Officers (Scotland) seeking the institution of a system of vicarious criminal liability.[64] It appears that the Secretary of State was not seized of the urgency of the matter, on the view that the certificate-holder remained accountable to the licensing court for the proper conduct of his premises; however, when the matter was examined by Clayson, the Committee, by a majority, recommended that a certificate-holder should carry absolute vicarious responsibility for offences committed by his staff (Report, para.10.17 *et seq.*).

In the event, Parliament effectively enacted the minority view by providing a "due diligence" defence in the 1976 Act. Where an offence attracts vicarious responsibility,[65] and the offence is committed by the employee or agent of the licence holder, proceedings may be taken against the licence holder, whether or not the person who actually committed the offence is prosecuted. The licence holder may however prove that the offence occurred without his knowledge or connivance and that he exercised all due diligence to prevent its occurrence (1976 Act, s.67(1), (2)).[66]

This Act abandons the 1976 Act's scheme of vicarious responsibility. A number of offences are committed where a person "allows" or "knowingly allows" something to be done. As explained in the notes to s.103 and Sch.3, para.5, this approach may well give rise to difficulty, standing the decision in *Noble v Heatly*, at least in relation to "knowingly allowing".

A number of offences are modernised re-enactments of those contained in the 1976 Act, for example: the canvassing of licensing board members by applicants (s.8); offences relating to the sale, consumption and taking away of alcohol outwith licensed hours (s.63); the delivery of alcohol by or to a child or young person (s.108); sending a child or young person to obtain alcohol (s.109); and various offences in relation to drunkenness and disorderly conduct (ss.111–116).

Offences in relation to the sale of alcohol to children and young people go several steps beyond the current provisions. Section 102 of this Act provides that a person who sells alcohol to a person under 18 commits an offence, an

---

[62] *Gair v Brewster*, 1916 S.C. (J) 36 at 38; (1916) 1 S.L.T. 388 at 389.
[63] 1967 J.C. 5; 1967 S.L.T. 26.
[64] See Clayson, para.10.11.
[65] 1976 Act, Sch.5, col.3.
[66] Where a licence is held by a non-natural person and a nominee in terms of s.11 of the 1976 Act, any reference to "the holder of a licence includes a reference to both of these persons" (s.11(3)). Thus, the manager of a company licence holder may be criminally accountable for the conduct of a fellow employee. This is an exceptional departure from the general rule that vicarious responsibility does not attach to one servant, even a "superior servant", for the acts or omissions of another: *Shields v Little*, 1954 S.L.T. 146.

enlargement of s.68(1) of the 1976 Act in terms of which it is an offence for the holder of a licence or his employee or agent to sell alcohol to such a person in licensed premises. The offence constituted by s.68(7) attracts a maximum (level 3) fine of £1,000, while s.102(5) provides for a maximum (level 5) fine of £5,000 and/or three months' imprisonment (a similar maximum penalty attached to the offence of "knowingly allowing" the sale of alcohol to a person under 18: s.103).

The Act creates a number of offences which may be characterised as administrative in nature, which appear to have been imported from the Licensing Act 2003, and which may also be considered unnecessary. These are: the failure of a premises licence holder to give timeous notice of a change of name or address or a change in the name or address of the premises manager (s.48); failure timeously to produce a premises licence in certain circumstances (s.49); failure to ensure that the premises licence (or a certified copy) is kept at the premises (s.52); failure to ensure that a summary of the premises licence (or a certified copy) is prominently displayed on the premises (s.52); failure without reasonable excuse to produce a premises licence (or certified copy) to a constable or licensing standards officer (s.52); failure of a personal licence holder to give timeous notice of a change of name or address (s.88); failure to produce personal licence for other updating purposes (s.89); failure of personal licence holder to produce his licence when working on licensed premises (s.93); and failure to display a notice in relation to the purchase of alcohol by or for a person under 18 (s.110).

Human Rights[67]

Section 29(1) of the Scotland Act 1998 (c.46) provides that:

> "(1) An Act of the Scottish Parliament is not law so far as any provision of the Act is outside the legislative competence of the Parliament.
> (2) A provision is outside that competence so far as any of the following paragraphs apply—...
> (d) it is incompatible with any of the Convention rights[68] or with Community law".

In terms of s.57(2):

> "A member of the Scottish Executive has no power to make any subordinate legislation, or to do any other act, so far as the legislation or act is incompatible with any of the Convention rights or with Community law."

Article 6(1) of the ECHR is in the following terms:

---

[67] See, generally, for a more extensive consideration: Agnew and Baillie, pp.40 *et seq.*; "The Human Rights Dimension" (Sir Crispin H. Agnew of Lochnaw, Bt., Q.C.) [2000] 16 S.L.L.P. 20; and, by the same author, "Human Rights Update" [2003] 25 S.L.L.P. 15.

[68] In terms of s.126(1) "the Convention rights" has the same meaning as in the Human Rights Act 1998.

"In the determination of his civil rights and obligations... everyone is entitled to a fair and public hearing within a reasonable time by an independent and impartial tribunal established by law."[69]

A licence is a "possession" for the purposes of art.1 of the 1st Protocol to the ECHR[70], which is in the following terms:

"Every natural or legal person is entitled to the peaceful enjoyment of his possessions. No one shall be deprived of his possessions except in the public interest and subject to the conditions provided for by law and by the general principles of international law.
The preceding provisions shall not, however, in any way impair the right of a State to enforce such laws as it deems necessary to control the use of property in accordance with the general interest or to secure the payment of taxes or other contributions or penalties."

(It appears that *failure to obtain a licence* is not an interference with an applicant's property right.[71] However, an application for the grant of a licence may, in relation to an objector, bring into consideration art.8(1) of the ECHR, which provides that "[e]veryone has the right to respect for his private and family life, his home and his correspondence", as well as art.1 of the 1st Protocol.)[72]

Nicholson considered that licensing boards, as presently constituted, did not satisfy the requirements of art.6; but that shortcoming was not fatal provided that their decisions were subject to review by a judicial body enjoying full jurisdiction.[73] The Report concluded, on the basis of the relevant case law,[74] that it was not necessary to propose a different constitution for the membership of licensing boards or a radically different appeal procedure from that presently in place (Report, Appendix C, para.28).

However, the Committee also had regard to the decision in *County Properties Ltd v The Scottish Ministers*.[75] The Court stressed that, even where any art.6(1) flaw was capable of cure by appeal procedures, the tribunal of first instance was nevertheless bound to conduct its business in a manner which, as far as possible, complied with the requirements of the ECHR. The Report's recommendations (Report, Appendix C, para.29), and the extent to which they have been followed in the Act, are summarised as follows:

---

[69] A licensing board is a body to which art.6 applies: *Tre Trektorer Aktiebolag v Sweden* (1989) 13 E.H.R.R. 309.
[70] *Tre Trektorer Aktiebolag v Sweden* (1989) 13 EHRR 309.
[71] *Catscratch Ltd v City of Glasgow Licensing Board*, 2002 S.L.T. 503 at 507; [2001] 20 S.L.L.P. 12 at 15.
[72] See Nicholson's analysis in Appendix C of the Report, para.9.
[73] *Albert and Le Compte v Belgium* (1983) 5 E.H.R.R. 533.
[74] *Bryan v UK* (1995) 21 E.H.R.R. 342; *Chapman v UK* (2001) 33 E.H.R.R. 399; *R. (Alconbury) v Secretary of State* [2001] 2 All E.R. 929; [2001] 2 W.L.R. 1389; *County Properties Ltd v The Scottish Ministers*, 2001 S.L.T. 1125.
[75] 2001 S.L.T. 1125.

Recommendation	The Act
Retention of certain disqualifications from acting as a licensing board member	Disqualifications retained with modernisations (Sch.1, para.3)
Board members should receive training, including training in judicial behaviour	Training required, content to be prescribed (Sch.1, para.11)
Simplified procedures, designed in part to ensure that all with a legitimate interest may be heard in licensing board proceedings	Wider enfranchisement of objectors and simplified procedure for making objections (s.22); procedures to be followed at hearings yet to be set out in regulations (s.133)
Removal of local authority's entitlement to object to an application for a licence	Not enacted (see below)
Proposals to remove the need for a local authority to apply for a licence in it own name	Local authority may apply for a licence (see below)
Speedier and more effective appeal procedures	Potentially speedier procedures: provision made for majority of appeals to the sheriff principal (s.131); but the sheriff principal may delegate consideration to a sheriff (s.132(4))
Availability of appeal against all decisions except those of a purely procedural nature	Not enacted (see below)

It will be observed that, in three respects, the Act does not follow Nicholson's proposals. Speaking during the passage of the Bill at a Law Society of Scotland Conference in September 2004,[76] Sheriff Principal Nicholson said that, having regard to the provisions of the Scotland Act 1998, an appeal by a thwarted objector to a local authority licence application could prove "disastrous"; and a local authority's entitlement to object to an application was "in clear conflict" with Art.6 of the EHCR.[77]

While public access to the licensing process has been considerably widened by the entitlement of "any person" to object to an application for a premises licence or apply for a review of a licence, objectors' appeal rights are extremely limited: they may only appeal against a decision to grant an occasional licence. An applicant for a premises licence review may appeal in relation to the steps taken at the review hearing but not, it seems, against a decision not to take any step.[78]

E-commerce

As Agnew and Baillie noted (p.39), the sale of alcohol by mail order, fax, on internet sites and from call centres has raised a question as to whether a licence should be obtained for the premises at which the order is accepted or those from which the order is despatched to the customer, bearing in mind that orders accepted in Scotland may be fulfilled from premises located in England or Wales. The Scottish authorities indicate that a licence is required for the premises at which the sale takes place, even if the vendor's stock is

---

[76] The speech is reported at [2004] 29 S.L.L.P. 3.
[77] See *Blusins Ltd v Dundee City Licensing Board*, 2001 S.L.T. 176, case in which a local authority purported to object to an application on the basis of non-payment of rates. The Sheriff observed that it was difficult to see how a licensing board, comprised of councillors, could ever be a fair and impartial tribunal in terms of art.6(1) in the determination of an objection by the local authority. *Cf Alcock v Aberdeenshire Licensing Board (North Division)*, digested at [2005] 30 S.L.L.P. 35, in which the Sheriff held that his "full jurisdiction" overcame a failure to meet the criteria of art.6 where a local authority's head of environmental health had raised a complaint leading to the suspension of a licence.
[78] See notes to s.133.

kept elsewhere.[79] In terms of English law, the sale takes place where the alcohol is appropriated to the customer.[80]

The Act addresses "remote" sales of alcohol, albeit to a limited extent. In terms of s.139, where alcohol is despatched from premises in Scotland the sale is to be treated as having taken place on those premises. As a result, it will be necessary for some operators to alter their licensing arrangements: those holding a off-sale licence for a mail order office, a call centre or premises at which a web server is located will require to obtain a licence for their order fulfilment warehouse.

Transition to the new system

The Scottish Executive has announced that all new licences and the majority of the Act's provisions will take effect on a single appointed day following a period of transition beginning in February 2008 and lasting some 18 months.[81] The following key dates have also been set:

- October 2006: all accompanying regulations and draft statutory guidance will be published for consultation over a three month period.
- February 2007: the regulations and guidance will be laid before the Scottish Parliament.
- June 2007[82] to November 2007: licensing boards will prepare policy statements; licensing standards officers will be appointed and local licensing forums constituted.

It was originally envisaged that the first licensing board policy statements (s.6) would contain a statement as to the extent to which the board considers there to be overprovision of licensed premises or licensed premises of a particular description in any locality (s.7). However, because of the logistical difficulties in involved in assessing the capacity of premises (s.7(3)(a)), Ministers have decided to postpone the commencement of s.7 until the whole Act is brought into force. Boards will, however, be expected to provide a statement of their general approach to overprovision in the first statement.

The Scottish Executive has rejected provision for so-called "grandfather rights" which would allow existing licence holders to enter the new system with their current licensing arrangements undisturbed. Instead, limited concessions will be made:

- Exemption from a possible overprovision ground of refusal, provided there is no change to the size or capacity of premises or the type of operation.

---

[79] *Guild v Freeman* (1898) 25 R. (J) 106; see also *Cameron v Buchan* (1896) 23 R. (J) 46; (1895) 3 S.L.T. 269.
[80] Licensing Act 2003, s.190(2), reflecting what appears to be the common law position in England and Wales: see *Pletts v Beattie* [1896] 1 Q.B. 519; *Mizen v Old Florida Ltd, Egan v Mizen* (1934) 50 T.L.R. 349; *Doak v Bedford* [1964] 2 Q.B. 587.
[81] This extended period is designed to overcome the difficulties encountered in England and Wales where transition to the new system lasted only six months.
[82] Following the May 2007 local authority elections and the election of new licensing boards.

- Exemption from the need to provide planning, building control and food hygiene certificates, provided that the transfer is on a like-for-like basis.
- Where the transfer is on a like-for-like basis, but the licensing board considers that they would nevertheless be minded to refuse the licence on the ground of the "location, character or condition" of the premises, but suitable modifications may be made, the licence will be granted and the licence holder allowed a period of 12 months to make the necessary changes. If these are not carried out timeously the licence would be revoked.

The Licensing (Scotland) Act 2005 (Commencement No. 2 and Transitional Provisions) Order 2006 (SSI 286/2006)[83] brought s.105(1) to (3) of the 2005 Act in to force on 1 June 2006, modifies s.68(2) of the 1976 and s.105(2) of the 2005 Act and provides that *pro tem* the test purchasing of alcohol may only be authorised by the chief constable of Fife Police.[84]

COMMENCEMENT

The Licensing (Scotland) Act 2005 (asp 16) received Royal Assent on December 21, 2005. Other than ss.145 to 148, the Act comes into force on such day as the Scottish Ministers may appoint.

PARLIAMENTARY PROGRESS

The Licensing (Scotland) Bill was introduced to the Scottish Parliament on February 28, 2005. Column references in brackets are to the Official Report.

Stage 1
Local Government and Transport Committee

7th Report 2005, June 13, 2005 (SP Paper 378); 11th meeting, March 22, 2005 (cols 2186-2263); 12th meeting, April 12, 2005 (cols 2263-2310); 13th meeting, April 19, 2005 (cols 2346-2382); 14th meeting, April 26, 2005 (cols 2416-2446); 15th meeting, May 3, 2005 (cols 2450-2484); 17th meeting, May 17, 2005 (cols 2558-2610).

Subordinate Legislation Committee

16th meeting, May 17, 2005 (cols 1039-1047); 17th meeting, May 24, 2005 (cols 1056-1059).

Stage 2
Local Government and Transport Committee

---

[83] The Order revokes the Licensing (Scotland) Act 2005 (Commencement No. 1 and Transitional Provisions) Order 2006 (SSI 239/2006) which, by oversight, failed to preserve the ability of a person aged 16 or over to purchase beer, wine, made-wine, porter, cider or perry for consumption with a meal in the circumstances set out in s.68(4) of the 1976 Act.
[84] See notes to s.105.

24th meeting, September 20, 2005 (cols 2826-2872); 25th meeting, September 27, 2005 (cols2884-2924); 26th meeting, October 3, 2005 (cols 2928-2964).

Consideration by Parliament

Stage 1 debate and Parliamentary vote, June 22, 2005 (cols 18162-18210, 18214-18216); Stage 3 debate and Parliamentary vote, November 16, 2005 (cols 20675-20768, 20772-20774).

LICENSING (SCOTLAND) ACT 2005

(2005 asp 16)

CONTENTS

PART 1
CORE PROVISIONS

SECTION
1 Prohibition of unlicensed sale of alcohol
2 Meaning of "alcohol"
3 Certain supplies of alcohol to be treated as sales
4 The licensing objectives

PART 2
LICENSING BODIES AND OFFICERS

Licensing Boards

5 Licensing Boards
6 Statements of licensing policy
7 Duty to assess overprovision
8 Applicants attempting to influence Board members
9 Licensing Board's duty to keep a public register

Local Licensing Forums

10 Local Licensing Forums
11 General functions of Local Licensing Forums
12 Licensing Boards' duties in relation to Local Licensing Forums

Licensing Standards Officers

13 Licensing Standards Officers
14 General functions of Licensing Standards Officers
15 Powers of entry and inspection
16 Training of Licensing Standards Officers

PART 3
PREMISES LICENCES

Introductory

17 Premises licence
18 Meaning of "appropriate Licensing Board"
19 Premises manager

Premises licence applications

20 Application for premises licence
21 Notification of application
22 Objections and representations
23 Determination of premises licence application
24 Applicant's duty to notify Licensing Board of convictions
25 Further application after refusal of premises licence application
26 Issue of licence and summary

Conditions of premises licence

27 Conditions of premises licence

Duration of premises licence

28 Period of effect of premises licence

Variation of premises licence

29 Application to vary premises licence
30 Determination of application for variation
31 Variation to substitute new premises manager
32 Further application after refusal of application for variation

Transfer of premises licence

33 Transfer on application of licence holder
34 Transfer on application of person other than licence holder
35 Variation on transfer

Review of premises licence

36 Application for review of premises licence
37 Review of premises licence on Licensing Board's initiative
38 Review hearing
39 Licensing Board's powers on review
40 Review of Licensing Board's decision to vary or suspend licence

Conviction of licence holder etc. for relevant or foreign offence

41 Duty to notify court of premises licence
42 Court's duty to notify Licensing Board of convictions
43 Licence holder's duty to notify Licensing Board of convictions
44 Procedure where Licensing Board receives notice of conviction

Premises under construction or conversion

45 Provisional premises licence
46 Confirmation of provisional premises licence
47 Temporary premises licence

Updating of licence

48 Notification of change of name or address
49 Licensing Board's duty to update premises licence

Miscellaneous

50 Certificates as to planning, building standards and food hygiene
51 Notification of determinations
52 Duty to keep, display and produce premises licence
53 Theft, loss etc. of premises licence or summary
54 Dismissal, resignation, death etc. of premises manager
55 Certified copies

PART 4
OCCASIONAL LICENCES

56 Occasional licence
57 Notification of application to chief constable and Licensing Standards Officer
58 Objections and representations
59 Determination of application

60 Conditions of occasional licence
61 Notification of determinations

PART 5
LICENSED HOURS

General

62 Licensed hours
63 Prohibition of sale, consumption and taking away of alcohol outwith licensed hours
64 24 hour licences to be granted only in exceptional circumstances
65 Licensed hours: off-sales
66 Effect of start and end of British Summer Time

Occasional extensions

67 Power for Licensing Board to grant general extensions of licensed hours
68 Extended hours applications
69 Notification of extended hours application
70 Determination of extended hours application

PART 6
PERSONAL LICENCES

Introductory

71 Personal licence

Grant and renewal of personal licence

72 Application for personal licence
73 Notification of application to chief constable
74 Determination of personal licence application
75 Applicant's duty to notify Licensing Board of convictions
76 Issue of licence
77 Period of effect of personal licence
78 Renewal of personal licence
79 Notification of determinations

Conviction of licence holder for relevant or foreign offence

80 Duty to notify court of personal licence
81 Court's duty to notify Licensing Board of convictions
82 Licence holder's duty to notify Licensing Board of convictions
83 Procedure where Licensing Board receives notice of conviction

Conduct inconsistent with licensing objectives

84 Conduct inconsistent with the licensing objectives

Endorsements

85 Expiry of endorsements
86 Suspension of licence after multiple endorsements

Licence holder's duty to undertake training

87 Licence holder's duty to undertake training

Update of licence

88 Notification of change of name or address
89 Licensing Board's duty to update licence

Miscellaneous

90 Power to specify which Licensing Board is to exercise functions under this Part
91 Power to prescribe licensing qualifications
92 Theft, loss etc. of personal licence
93 Licence holder's duty to produce licence

PART 7
CONTROL OF ORDER

Exclusion of violent offenders

94 Exclusion orders
95 Breach of exclusion order
96 Exclusion orders: supplementary provision

Closure of premises

97 Closure orders
98 Termination of closure orders
99 Extension of emergency closure order
100 Regulations as to closure orders
101 Interpretation of sections 97 to 100

PART 8
OFFENCES

Offences relating to children and young people

102 Sale of alcohol to a child or young person
103 Allowing the sale of alcohol to a child or young person
104 Sale of liqueur confectionery to a child
105 Purchase of alcohol by or for a child or young person
106 Consumption of alcohol by a child or young person
107 Unsupervised sale of alcohol by a child or young person
108 Delivery of alcohol by or to a child or young person
109 Sending a child or young person to obtain alcohol
110 Duty to display notice

Drunkenness and disorderly conduct

111 Drunk persons entering or in premises on which alcohol is sold
112 Obtaining of alcohol by or for a drunk person
113 Sale of alcohol to a drunk person
114 Premises manager, staff etc. not to be drunk
115 Disorderly conduct
116 Refusal to leave premises

Miscellaneous offences

117 Offences relating to sale of alcohol to trade
118 Prohibition of unauthorised sale of alcohol on moving vehicles
119 Delivery of alcohol from vehicles etc.
120 Prohibition of late-night deliveries of alcohol
121 Keeping of smuggled goods

Interpretation of Part

122 Interpretation of Part 8

PART 9
MISCELLANEOUS AND GENERAL

Excluded and exempt premises

123 Excluded premises
124 Exempt premises

Special provision for certain clubs

125 Special provisions for certain clubs

Vessels, vehicles and moveable structures

126 Vessels, vehicles and moveable structures
127 Power to prohibit sale of alcohol on trains
128 Power to prohibit sale of alcohol on ferries

Relevant and foreign offences

129 Relevant offences and foreign offences
130 Effect of appeal against conviction for relevant or foreign offence

Appeals

131 Appeals
132 Appeals: supplementary provision

Procedures, forms etc.

133 Hearings
134 Form etc. of applications, proposals, and notices
135 Power to relieve failure to comply with rules and other requirements
136 Fees

Miscellaneous

137 Inspection of premises before grant of licence etc.
138 Police powers of entry
139 Remote sales of alcohol
140 Presumption as to liquid contents of containers
141 Offences by bodies corporate etc.

General

142 Guidance
143 Crown application
144 Modification of enactments
145 Ancillary provision
146 Orders and regulations
147 Interpretation
148 Index of defined expressions
149 Repeals
150 Short title and commencement

Schedule 1 — Licensing boards
Schedule 2 — Local licensing forums

Schedule 3 — Premises licences: mandatory conditions
Schedule 4 — Occasional licences: mandatory conditions
Schedule 5 — Appeals

Schedule 6 — Modification of enactments
Schedule 7 — Repeals

An Act of the Scottish Parliament to make provision for regulating the sale of alcohol, and for regulating licensed premises and other premises on which alcohol is sold; and for connected purposes. The Bill for this Act of the Scottish Parliament was passed by the Parliament on 16th November 2005 and received Royal Assent on 21st December 2005

PART 1

CORE PROVISIONS

1. Prohibition of unlicensed sale of alcohol

(1) Alcohol is not to be sold on any premises except under and in accordance with-
   (a) a premises licence, or
   (b) an occasional licence,
granted under this Act in respect of the premises.
(2) Subsection (1) does not apply to the selling of alcohol-
   (a) on exempt premises, or
   (b) to trade.
(3) A person who-
   (a) sells alcohol, or
   (b) knowingly allows alcohol to be sold,
in breach of subsection (1) commits an offence.
(4) A person guilty of an offence under subsection (3) is liable on summary conviction to-
   (a) a fine not exceeding £20,000,
   (b) imprisonment for a term not exceeding 6 months, or
   (c) both.

DEFINITIONS
"alcohol": see s.2 of this Act
"premises": see s.147(1) of this Act
"premises licence": see s.17 of this Act
"occasional licence": see s.56(1) of this Act
"exempt premises": see s.124 of this Act
"selling to trade": see s.147(2) of this Act
"sells": see s.147(1) of this Act

GENERAL NOTE
This section effectively recreates in an expanded form the offence of trafficking found in s.90 (and defined in s.139(1) of) the 1976 Act.

Subsection (1)
See s.3 for circumstances in which the supply of alcohol will be deemed to be a sale.

Under the scheme of the 1976 Act:

- the offence of "trafficking" may only be committed "in any premises or place" (s.90(a));
- vehicles are incapable of being licensed;
- a licence is not required for the trafficking in alcohol in a passenger vessel while it is in the course of being navigated (1976 Act, s.138(1)(c)), although licences have been granted for moored craft (*cf Gate v Bath Justices* (1983) 147 J.P. 289).

In this Act, "premises" means "any place and includes a vehicle, vessel or moveable structure" (s.147(1)); and a licence is required for the sale of alcohol:

- on moving vehicles (ss.118, 126);
- on vessels (s.126), unless engaged on an international journey or a journey forming part of a ferry service (s.124(1)(d)).

Subsections (2), (3)

It is an offence to sell alcohol or knowingly allow alcohol to be sold otherwise than from licensed premises; exempt premises; or premises which are used exclusively for the purpose of the selling of goods (whether solely alcohol or not) to trade: see s.117(1).

The concept of "selling to trade" replaces the concept of "wholesale" sales contained in the 1976 Act (with "wholesale" being defined by reference to the quantity sold in any one transaction). The 1976 Act exempts wholesalers from its ambit, provided that sales take place:

- "from premises used exclusively for wholesale trading (whether solely of alcoholic liquor or not)"; or
- "from licensed premises... during the hours in respect of which it is lawful to sell alcohol by retail from or in these premises". (See 1976 Act, ss.90A(1), 138(2)(b)).

Since the quantity of alcohol sold is now irrelevant, having regard to the definition of "selling to trade" (s.147(2)):

- the sale of alcohol in any quantity to members of the public who are not traders will require to be authorised by a premises licence (or an occasional licence); and
- the sale of alcohol in any quantity to trade customers from premises used *only* for trade purchases (*whether or not these are alcohol purchases*) will not require to be licensed.

It appears that, by drafting oversight rather than design, a premises licence will be required for the bulk sale of alcohol to a members' club. Currently, these sales will normally take place from unlicensed distribution depots. Under the Act, the supply of alcohol in a members' club will be treated as a "sale" (see s.3(2)); but on no view are members' clubs engaged in any "trade". In terms of the 2003 Act, the sale of alcohol by retail is a "licensable activity" (s.1(1)(a)); but the sale of alcohol is not a "sale by retail" where the sale is to "a club, which holds a club premises certificate, for the purposes of that club" (s.192(2)(b)). There is no parallel provision in the Act.

For a consideration of "knowingly allows", see notes to s.103 and Sch.3, para.5.

Subsection (4)

Three other offences are potentially visited with a £20,000 fine: breach of a closure order (s.97(8)); the unauthorised sale of alcohol on moving vehicles (s.118(2)); the breach of order prohibiting sale of alcohol on trains (s.127(5)); the breach of order prohibiting sale of alcohol on ferries (s.128(6)); but, inconsistently, in these other cases the maximum possible prison sentence is three months.

2. Meaning of "alcohol"

(1) In this Act, "alcohol"-
  (a) means spirits, wine, beer, cider or any other fermented, distilled or spirituous liquor, but
  (b) does not include-
   (i) alcohol which is of a strength of 0.5% or less at the time of its sale,
   (ii) perfume,
   (iii) any flavouring essence recognised by the Commissioners of Customs and Excise as not being intended for consumption as or with dutiable alcoholic liquor,
   (iv) the aromatic flavouring essence commonly known as angostura bitters,
   (v) alcohol which is, or is included in, a medicinal product,
   (vi) denatured alcohol,
   (vii) methyl alcohol,
   (viii) naphtha, or
   (ix) alcohol contained in liqueur confectionery.
(2) In this section-
  "beer", "cider", "denatured alcohol", "dutiable alcoholic liquor" and "wine" have the same meanings as in the Alcoholic Liquor Duties Act 1979 (c.4), and
  "medicinal product" has the same meaning as in section 130 of the Medicines Act 1968 (c.67).

DEFINITIONS
"beer", "cider", "denatured alcohol", "dutiable alcoholic liquor", "wine": see subs.(2)
"strength": see s.147(1) of this Act
"medicinal product": see subs.(2)
"liqueur confectionery": see s.147(1) of this Act

GENERAL NOTE
This section modernises the definition of "alcoholic liquor" contained in s.139(1) of the 1976 Act and contains additional exemptions.

Subsection (1)
The sale of liqueur confectionery to a child is an offence: see s.104.

Subsection (2)
The definition of "denatured alcohol" contained in s.4 of the Alcoholic Liquor Duties Act 1979 is amplified in s.5 of the Finance Act 1985.

3. Certain supplies of alcohol to be treated as sales

(1) A supply of alcohol which is not otherwise a sale of the alcohol is, in the circumstances described in subsection (2) or (3), to be treated for the purposes of this Act as if it were a sale of the alcohol.
(2) The first set of circumstances is where the supply is by or on behalf of a club to, or to the order of, a member of the club.
(3) The second set of circumstances is where the supply is made to, or to the order of, a person pursuant to a right acquired by the person under a contract.

DEFINITIONS
"sale": see s.147(1) of this Act
"alcohol": see s.2 of this Act

GENERAL NOTE

This "catch all" provision is intended to ensure that certain transactions, which might not otherwise be regarded as "sales", are treated as sales of alcohol for the purposes of the Act.

Subsection (2)

The Act brings members' clubs fully within the jurisdiction of licensing boards for the first time (subject to certain dispensations: see s.125). Presently, in terms of the 1976 Act, the supply of alcohol in a member's club is authorised by a certificate of registration granted by the sheriff. In a registered club alcohol is not "sold": see *Crossgates British Legion Club v Davidson*, 1954 S.L.T. 124. This subsection ensures that the supply of alcohol is treated as a "sale".

Subsection (3)

At common law, a number of English decisions indicate that a "sale" will be considered to have taken place although it is impossible to ascribe any part of a purchase price for the "free" article: see *Scott & Co v Solomon* [1905] 1 K.B. 577; *Taylor v Smetten* (1883) 11 QBD 207 *Doak v Bedford*, [1964] 2 Q.B. 587.

The effect of this provision is to treat as "sales" commercial transactions involving the supply of alcohol where the price of the alcohol may not be separately identified. For example, a limousine hire company offering the use of a vehicle and chauffeur with "free bubbly" as part of a package price will require to obtain a licence for the premises from which the alcohol is supplied. (See further notes to s.118, which prohibits the unauthorised sale of alcohol in moving vehicles.)

In *Macdonald v Skinner*, 1979 J.C. 29; 1978 S.L.T. (Notes) 52, a hotelier who had dispensed free drinks to his customers following the loss of his licence was convicted of trafficking. There was no evidence that the charges for other hotel services had been inflated to include a covert payment for the alcohol. On appeal, the High Court was not prepared to find that the hotelier's conduct amounted to "dealing in" alcohol by retail. Applying the facts of that case to the provisions of this subsection, it appears that no offence would be committed if the view were to be taken on the view that the beneficiaries of the hotelier's largesse were not supplied with alcohol pursuant to a right acquired under a contract.

4. The licensing objectives

(1) For the purposes of this Act, the licensing objectives are-
   (a) preventing crime and disorder,
   (b) securing public safety,
   (c) preventing public nuisance,
   (d) protecting and improving public health, and
   (e) protecting children from harm.
(2) In this Act, references to the "crime prevention objective" are references to the licensing objective mentioned in subsection (1)(a).

DEFINITION
"child": see s.147(1) of this Act

GENERAL NOTE

The "licensing objectives" are, in a sense, the engine which drives this Act. They are not ranked in hierarchical order.

In *Argyll Arms (McManus) Ltd v Lorn, Mid-Argyll, Kintyre and Islay Divisional Licensing Board*, 1988 S.L.T. 290, Lord Clyde observed (at p.292) that it was "at least difficult to find a clear pattern or consistent philosophy" in the 1976 Act. Nicholson recommended that certain guiding principles should be enshrined in statute to guide licensing boards in the exercise of their functions at all times (Report, para.2.23).

Nicholson also noted that the Licensing Bill progressing through the Westminster Parliament at the time of the Committee's work proposed similar objectives, but without any reference to public health. The promotion of public health was, in the Committee's view, as important as any other.

PART 2

LICENSING BODIES AND OFFICERS

Licensing Boards

5. Licensing Boards

(1) There is to continue to be a Licensing Board for-
   (a) the area of each council whose area is not, at the time this section comes into force, divided into licensing divisions under section 46(1) of the Local Government etc. (Scotland) Act 1994 (c.39) ("the 1994 Act"), and
   (b) each licensing division of such an area which is so divided at that time.
(2) A council whose area is not so divided at that time may subsequently make a determination that their area is to be divided into divisions for the purposes of this Act.
(3) Where a council makes such a determination-
   (a) there is to be a separate Licensing Board for each of the divisions,
   (b) the Licensing Board for the council's area is dissolved on the date on which those separate Licensing Boards are elected in accordance with schedule 1, and
   (c) anything done by the Licensing Board for the council's area before the Board is dissolved is, to the extent that it has effect at that time, to have effect after that time as if done by such of the separate Licensing Boards as the council may determine.
(4) A council which has made a determination (whether under subsection (2) or section 46(1) of the 1994 Act) that their area is to be divided into divisions may revoke the determination.
(5) Where a council revokes such a determination-
   (a) there is to be a single Licensing Board for the whole of the council's area,
   (b) each of the Licensing Boards for the divisions is dissolved on the date on which the single Licensing Board is elected in accordance with schedule 1, and
   (c) anything done by the Licensing Boards for the divisions before they are dissolved is, to the extent that it has effect at that time, to have effect after that time as if done by the single Licensing Board.
(6) Subsection (7) applies where a council-
   (a) makes a determination under subsection (2), or
   (b) revokes such a determination or a determination made under section 46(1) of the 1994 Act.
(7) The council must, no later than 7 days after the making of the determination or the revocation-
   (a) notify the Scottish Ministers of the determination or revocation, and

(b) publicise it in such manner as the council sees fit.
(8) Schedule 1 makes further provision about the constitution of Licensing Boards, their procedure and other administrative matters relating to them.

DEFINITIONS
"area": see s.147(1) of this Act
"council": see s.2 of this Act

GENERAL NOTE
The Act continues to entrust the administration of the licensing system to licensing boards, which are a creation of the 1976 Act. There will continue to be a licensing board, or divisional licensing boards, for each council area. Boards which are not presently divisionalised may become divided where the council makes a determination in accordance with the procedures set out in this section; such a determination may also be revoked.

6. Statements of licensing policy

(1) Every Licensing Board must, before the beginning of each 3 year period, publish a statement of their policy with respect to the exercise of their functions under this Act during that period (referred to in this Act as a "licensing policy statement").
(2) A Licensing Board may, during a 3 year period, publish a supplementary statement of their policy with respect to the exercise of their functions during the remainder of that period (referred to in this Act as a "supplementary licensing policy statement").
(3) In preparing a licensing policy statement or a supplementary licensing policy statement, a Licensing Board must-
   (a) ensure that the policy stated in the statement seeks to promote the licensing objectives, and
   (b) consult-
      (i) the Local Licensing Forum for the Board's area,
      (ii) if the membership of the Forum is not representative of the interests of all of the persons specified in paragraph 2(6) of schedule 2, such person or persons as appear to the Board to be representative of those interests of which the membership is not representative, and
      (iii) such other persons as the Board thinks appropriate.
(4) In exercising their functions under this Act during each 3 year period, a Licensing Board must have regard to the licensing policy statement, and any supplementary licensing policy statement, published by the Board in relation to that period.
(5) At the request of a Licensing Board-
   (a) the appropriate chief constable, or
   (b) the relevant council,
must provide to the Board such statistical or other information as the Board may reasonably require for the purpose of preparing a licensing policy statement or supplementary licensing policy statement.
(6) On publishing a licensing policy statement or a supplementary licensing policy statement, a Licensing Board must-
   (a) make copies of the statement available for public inspection free of charge, and
   (b) publicise-

(i) the fact that the statement has been published, and
(ii) the arrangements for making copies available for public inspection in pursuance of paragraph (a).
(7) In this section, "3 year period" means-
(a) the period of 3 years beginning with such day as the Scottish Ministers may by order appoint, and
(b) each subsequent period of 3 years.

DEFINITIONS
"licensing policy statement": see subs.(1)
"supplementary licensing policy statement": see subs.(2)
"licensing objectives": see s.4(1) of this Act
"appropriate chief constable": see s.147(1) of this Act
"relevant council": see s.147(1) of this Act
"3 year period": see subs.(7)

GENERAL NOTE
As Nicholson observed, a number of licensing boards from time to time prepare and issue statements setting out the policy which they are likely to follow in relation to, for example, the fitness of licence holders and the grant of extended permitted hours. Such an approach would be "highly beneficial" in the context of the new licensing system (Report, paras.6.38, 6.39).

The policy statement must promote the licensing objectives and be prefaced by consultation with *inter alia* the Local Licensing Forum. The determination of the policy may not be delegated: see Sch.1, para.10(2)(a).

The ability to issue a supplementary policy statement within the three year period allows boards to address emerging issues which had not been anticipated when the policy was formulated.

According to the Policy Memorandum (para.46), the Scottish Executive intends to issue guidance on the areas which the policy statement must address.

A policy which was *ultra vires* of the board would, of course, be open to review by the court: see, for example, *Mitchells & Butlers Retail Ltd v Aberdeen City Licensing Board*, 2005 S.L.T. 13; [2005] 30 SLLP 24.

7. Duty to assess overprovision

(1) Each licensing policy statement published by a Licensing Board must, in particular, include a statement as to the extent to which the Board considers there to be overprovision of-
(a) licensed premises, or
(b) licensed premises of a particular description,
in any locality within the Board's area.
(2) It is for the Licensing Board to determine the "localities" within the Board's area for the purposes of this Act.
(3) In considering whether there is overprovision for the purposes of subsection (1) in any locality, the Board must-
(a) have regard to the number and capacity of licensed premises in the locality, and
(b) consult the persons specified in subsection (4).
(4) Those persons are-
(a) the appropriate chief constable,
(b) such persons as appear to the Board to be representative of the interests of-
(i) holders of premises licences in respect of premises within the locality,
(ii) persons resident in the locality, and

(c) such other persons as the Board thinks fit.

(5) In this section, references to "licensed premises" do not include references to any premises in respect of which an occasional licence has effect.

DEFINITIONS
"licensed premises": see s.147(1) of this Act, subject to subs.(5) of this section
"locality": see subs.(2)
"area": see s.147(1) of this Act
"capacity": see s.147(1) of this Act
"appropriate chief constable": see s.147(1) of this Act
"premises licence": see s.17 of this Act

GENERAL NOTE
The duty imposed upon licensing boards to make this pro-active assessment of overprovision is one of the central pillars of the Scottish Executive's approach to the new licensing regime.

It appears to be predicated on the belief that, in the past, licensing boards have been too ready to grant licences, particularly off-sale licences, especially where there have been no objections.

Quoted in an Executive press release (February 2003), Cathy Jamieson, the minister originally responsible for the Bill, said that: "There are three times as many off-licences now than there were 50 years ago - yet our population has hardly changed. On or two off-licences may be a useful asset for a community. Too many can be a scourge." (Between 1945 and 2004 off-sale licences in force rose from 2,188 to 6,103, although in recent years the number has been in decline). The Policy Memorandum suggests (para.23) that "overprovision is the root of problems being experienced by many communities where there has been no coherent overall policy in place"; and that is "why the [Act] requires Licensing Boards to conduct new overprovision assessments as part of their policy statements".

There would appear to be no obligation to divide a board's area into separate localities, although the board would require to examine the whole area without a view to identifying localities where an assessment was warranted.

A determination as to whether there is any overprovision in a locality may not be delegated: see Sch.1, para.10(2)(a).

The approach to the overprovision assessment will be the subject of ministerial guidance, setting out a national policy, to be issued in terms of s.145 of the Act.

Subsection (1)
A licensing board may decide that a locality has reached a state of overprovision, or make a determination as to the extent to which overprovision exists. The option of basing the assessment not simply on licensed premises but licensed premises "of a particular description" will allow boards to take into account distinct styles of operation and their different impact on communities.

Subsection (2)
Licensing boards currently enjoy a wide discretion in the selection of localities for the purpose of s.17(1)(d) of the 1976 Act, even where the selection might well appear arbitrary: *Lazerdale v City of Glasgow District Licensing Board* [1996] 4 SLLP 6, approved by the House of Lords in *Caledonian Nightlcubs Ltd v City of Glasgow Licensing Board*, 1996 S.L.T. 451; [1996] 4 SLLP 11. That discretion looks set to continue. The Scottish Executive believes that the determination of a locality should be as flexible as possible "to reflect the very different pressures which may apply in different geographical areas throughout the country" (Policy Memorandum, para.48). A "locality" could be "a street, several streets or a council ward" (Policy Memorandum, para.47).

Subsection (3) (a)
The consideration of capacities is novel. For the purpose of s.17(1)(d) of the 1976 Act a board need only select a locality; identify the number and type of licensed premises in that locality and the authority for the sale of alcohol conferred by each type of licence; and then, using its local knowledge and experience, come to a decision as to whether the grant of a further licence would result in overprovision (*Chung v Wigtown District Licensing Board*, 1993 S.L.T. 1118).

Nicholson considered that this "largely arithmetical exercise" was "imprecise and unworkable" (Report, para.6.34). Levels of disturbance and public nuisance caused by the density of licensed premises were likely to be exacerbated where premises were of a size which enables "many hundreds of patrons to be inside a single pub or club at the same time", with the result that "several thousand patrons may emerge onto the streets at about the same time". Account should be taken not only of the number of licensed premises in a particular area "but also of their type, size and capacity" (Report, para.6.35).

In his written evidence to the Local Government and Transport Committee, Sheriff Principal Nicholson suggested that the reference to "number and capacity" in this subsection (and elsewhere in the Bill) should be replaced by the "type, number, size and capacity" formulation as "the use of all of these words would enable a board to focus on all of the characteristics which might be relevant to an assessment of overprovision".

The duty to consult contained in subs.(3)(b) is subject to the over-arching policy consultation provided for in s.6(3)(b).

Subsection (4)

Transitional regulations will no doubt provide that consultation prior to the publication of the first policy statement will take place with holders of licences granted under the 1976 Act.

8. Applicants attempting to influence Board members

(1) If a person making an application under this Act to a Licensing Board attempts, at any time before the application is determined by the Board, to influence a member of the Board to support the application, the person commits an offence.

(2) If, in relation to any application made to, but not yet determined by, a Licensing Board under this Act, proceedings for an offence under subsection (1) are brought against the applicant-
   (a) the Board must not determine the application until after the proceedings are concluded, and
   (b) if the applicant is convicted of the offence, the Board may refuse to consider the application.

(3) A person guilty of an offence under subsection (1) is liable on summary conviction to a fine not exceeding level 3 on the standard scale.

DEFINITION
"applicant": see s.147(1) of this Act

GENERAL NOTE

In terms of s.19 of the 1976 Act it is an offence for certain types of applicant to attempt to influence a licensing board member to support an application before its consideration by the board.

Nicholson recommended the retention of the offence; but considered it "somewhat strange" that it applied only to applicants and no to objectors. It recommended that it should also be an offence for an objector to attempt to improperly influence the decision of a board member (Report, para.3.13).

In the result, the Executive was swayed by respondents to the White Paper consultation who considered that "it would be difficult to ban constituents from talking to their own councillors" (Policy Memorandum, para.64). It was accordingly decided not to make any special provision in relation to objectors "since the Code of Conduct established by the Ethical Standards in Public Life etc (Scotland) Act 2000 applies to members of licensing boards as it does to all councillors in the normal way" (*ibid.* para.42).

Leaving aside the operation of the Code of Conduct, it requires to be kept in view that circumstances giving rise to a reasonable suspicion of bias on the part of a board member will result in the board's decision being reversed by the court, as, for example, where a board member made a private visit to an objector's premises and, upon leaving, gave him a "friendly wave": *Mahmood v West Dunbartonshire Licensing Board* 1998 SCLR 843.

The canvassing of board members by another member may result in a decision being set aside: *Macdougall v Millar*, (1900) 8 S.L.T. 284; *cf Ahmed v Stirling Licensing Board*, 1980 S.L.T. (Sh Ct) 51.

Subsection (2)
The provisions reflect those contained in s.19(2), (3) of the 1976 Act, save that in terms of s.19(2) a board "may adjourn" consideration of an application where there are pending proceedings, while subs.2(a) provides that a board must not determine the application until the proceedings are concluded.

9. Licensing Board's duty to keep a public register

(1) Each Licensing Board must keep a register (referred to in this Act as a "licensing register") containing information relating to-
 (a) premises licences, personal licences and occasional licences issued by the Board,
 (b) the Board's decisions in relation to applications made to the Board under this Act, and
 (c) other decisions of the Board relating to the licences mentioned in paragraph (a).
(2) The Scottish Ministers may by regulations make provision as to-
 (a) matters, in addition to those specified in paragraphs (a) to (c) of subsection (1), in relation to which licensing registers are to contain information,
 (b) the information which such registers are to contain, and
 (c) the form and manner in which the registers are to be kept.
(3) A Licensing Board must make the licensing register kept by the Board available for public inspection at all reasonable times.

DEFINITIONS
"premises licence": see s.17 of this Act
"personal licence": see s.71 of this Act
"occasional licence": see s.56(1) of this Act

GENERAL NOTE
Licensing boards are required to maintain a licensing register containing the information set out in subss.(1)(a)-(c). Subsection 2 provides that Scottish Ministers may by regulations make supplementary provisions.

This section replaces the ecletic provisions of s.20 of the 1976 Act which simply requires boards to keep a register of applications for licences and "at the end of each day's meeting of the board enter in the register the decisions taken on the applications" (together with an obligation to make the register available for public inspection).

Local Licensing Forums

10. Local Licensing Forums

(1) Each council must establish a Local Licensing Forum for their area.
(2) However, where the area of a council is divided into licensing divisions, the council may, instead of establishing a Local Licensing

Forum for their area, establish separate such Forums for each division.
(3) Each Licensing Board must hold, at least once in each calendar year, a joint meeting with the Local Licensing Forum for the Board's area.
(4) Schedule 2 makes further provision about Local Licensing Forums, including provision about their membership and procedural and other administrative matters in relation to them.

DEFINITIONS
"area": see s.147(1) of this Act
"council": see s.147(1) of this Act

GENERAL NOTE
Nicholson noted that a number of licensing boards had already created local licensing forums which were seen as operating successfully and effectively "as a satisfactory medium for bringing to the attention of licensing boards facts and concerns which might otherwise pass unnoticed" (Report, para.3.17). This section enacts the Nicholson recommendation that such arrangements should be placed on a statutory footing, "ensuring that any board policies are well-informed and are based on an appreciation of the concerns of the wider community" (Report, para.3.18).

Subsection (2)
For divisionalisation procedures see s.5.

Subsection (4)
See notes to Sch.2.

11. General functions of Local Licensing Forums

(1) Each Local Licensing Forum has the following general functions-
  (a) keeping under review-
    (i) the operation of this Act in the Forum's area, and,
    (ii) in particular, the exercise by the relevant Licensing Board or Boards of their functions, and
  (b) giving such advice and making such recommendations to that or any of those Boards in relation to those matters as the Forum considers appropriate.
(2) Subsection (1) does not enable a Local Licensing Forum to-
  (a) review, or
  (b) give advice, or make recommendations, in relation to,
the exercise by a Licensing Board of their functions in relation to a particular case.
(3) In this section, section 12 and schedule 2, "relevant Licensing Board", in relation to a Local Licensing Forum, means-
  (a) the Licensing Board for the Forum's area, or
  (b) in the case of a Local Licensing Forum for a council area which is divided into licensing divisions, each of the Licensing Boards for those divisions.

DEFINITIONS
"area": see s.147(1) of this Act
"relevant licensing board": see subs.(3)

GENERAL NOTE
This provision effectively enacts the Nicholson recommendation that the function of forums should be to keep the licensing system in the forum's area under regular review and to advise the licensing board in relation to matters of concern, other than current licensing applications (Report, para.3.18). The White Paper (p.11) suggested the forums would "allow active participation in local decision making" and "feed in the grass roots perspective".

Subsection (2)
Licensing forums are disabled from reviewing, giving advice or making recommendations in relation to any particular case. Nicholson considered that it would not be appropriate for a forum "to offer views in relation to particular applications which are currently being considered by a board" (Report, para.3.18).

12. Licensing Boards' duties in relation to Local Licensing Forums

(1) A Licensing Board must-
  (a) in exercising any function, have regard to any advice given, or recommendation made, to them in relation to the function by a Local Licensing Forum, and
  (b) where the Board decides not to follow the advice or recommendation, give the Forum reasons for the decision.
(2) At the request of a Local Licensing Forum, a relevant Licensing Board must provide to the Forum copies of such relevant statistical information as the Forum may reasonably require for the purposes of the Forum's general functions.
(3) In this section, "relevant statistical information" means, in relation to a Licensing Board, such statistical information as the Board may have obtained under section 6(5).

DEFINITIONS
"relevant licensing board": see s.11(3) of this Act
"relevant statistical information": see s.6(5) of this Act

GENERAL NOTE
A licensing board must exercise its functions having regard to advice given, or recommendations made, by the local licensing forum. Where the board decides to depart from the advice or recommendation, it is under an obligation to provide the forum with reasons for its decision. The forum is entitled to receive from the board certain types of statistical information reasonably required for the forum's functions.

The local licensing forum requires to be consulted by the board in relation to the preparation of policy statements: see s.6(5).

Subsection (2)
In terms of s.6(5) a licensing board is entitled to be provided by the chief constable or council with statistical or other information reasonably required for the purpose of the preparation of policy statements. This subsection provides for the transmission of this information to the forum. Nicholson considered that forums ought to be provided on a regular basis with relevant local data and statistics from the public and public health departments (Report, para.31.8).

13. Licensing Standards Officers

(1) Each council must appoint for their area one or more officers to be known as Licensing Standards Officers.
(2) A person may hold more than one appointment under subsection (1) (so as to be a Licensing Standards Officer for more than one council area).
(3) A Licensing Standards Officer is to exercise, in relation to the (or each) council area for which the Officer is appointed, the functions conferred on a Licensing Standards Officer by virtue of this Act.
(4) The number of Licensing Standards Officers for any council area is to be such as the council may determine.
(5) The Scottish Ministers may by regulations prescribe qualifications and experience required for appointment as a Licensing Standards Officer.
(6) Where the Scottish Ministers have made regulations under subsection (5), a council must not appoint an individual to be a Licensing Standards Officer unless the individual possesses the qualifications and experience prescribed in the regulations in relation to that appointment.
(7) Otherwise, the terms and conditions of appointment of a Licensing Standards Officer appointed by a council under this section are to be such as the council may determine.

DEFINITIONS
"council": see s.147(1) of this Act
"area": see s.147(1) of this Act

GENERAL NOTE
Nicholson considered that licensing boards should employ licensing standards officers (LSOs) whose functions would be to supervise and monitor the operation of the licensing system in a licensing board's area (Report, para.7.5).
The role of LSOs is further considered in the notes to s.14.
Schedule 2, para.2(1) provides that at least one of the members of the local licensing forum must be an LSO.

Subsection (1)
Nicholson proposed that LSOs should be employed by licensing boards (Report, para.7.5). However, the Act provides that their appointment will be in the hands of the council, adopting the Daniels recommendation that they should operate at arm's length from licensing boards (Report, para.4.47).

Subsection (2)
Councils may share the use of LSOs across their area boundaries.

Subsection (4)
Councils must appoint at least one LSO, but otherwise enjoy complete discretion in deciding the appropriate number for their area. Nicholson considered that, although the geographical spread would be a factor, it was likely that each area would require to be supervised by three or four LSOs (Report, para.7.4). The costs associated with the employment of LSOs will be met through licensing fees.

14. General functions of Licensing Standards Officers

(1) A Licensing Standards Officer for a council area has the following general functions-
   (a) providing to interested persons information and guidance concerning the operation of this Act in the area,
   (b) supervising the compliance by the holders of-
      (i) premises licences, or
      (ii) occasional licences,
   in respect of premises in the area with the conditions of their licences and other requirements of this Act,
   (c) providing mediation services for the purpose of avoiding or resolving disputes or disagreements between-
      (i) the holders of the licences referred to in paragraph (b), and
      (ii) any other persons,
   concerning any matter relating to compliance as referred to in that paragraph.
(2) The function under subsection (1)(b) includes, in particular, power-
   (a) where a Licensing Standards Officer believes that any condition to which a premises licence or occasional licence is subject has been or is being breached-
      (i) to issue a notice to the holder of the licence requiring such action to be taken to remedy the breach as may be specified in the notice, and
      (ii) if, in the case of a premises licence, such a notice is not complied with to the satisfaction of the Officer, to make a premises licence review application in respect of the licence,
   (b) in relation to a premises licence, to make an application under that section for review of the licence on any other competent ground for review.

DEFINITIONS
"council": see s.147(1) of this Act
"area": see s.147(1) of this Act
"premises licence": see s.17 of this Act
"occasional licence": see s.56(1) of this Act
"premises licence review application": see s.36(2) of this Act

GENERAL NOTE
Daniels supported Nicholson's recommendation that LSOs should monitor compliance with licence conditions (as to which see s.27) but also suggested that LSOs should have "an educational and mediation role in addition to their monitoring role" (Daniels, para.4.50).

Subsection (1)
No assistance is offered as to the types of "interested persons" to whom information and guidance is to be provided in terms of subs.(1)(a). In addition to the compliance monitoring function, the Policy Memorandum (para.109) refers to a "guidance" role in terms of which LSOs would "act as a source of advice and guidance for licensees and for the community"; and a "mediation" role, allowing LSOs to "mediate between communities and the trade or between any two parties where there is a need to resolve a local problem and develop a local solution". This approach may avoid the necessity for a party to pursue a formal complaint.

The mediation role is restricted to compliance matters which may arise in relation to licence conditions (subs.1(b)).

It remains to be seen whether LSOs will have a role to play in the enforcement of the prohibition on smoking in public places introduced by the Smoking, Health and Social Care (Scotland)

Act 2005 (asp 13), which came into force on March 26, 2006. The Policy Memorandum suggests that the compliance function "could also include monitoring the implementation of the ban on smoking in licensed premises" (para.109). Compliance with the smoking ban is not, of course, is not a requirement of the Act for the purpose of subs.(1)(b); but a premises licence review application (s.36) may be made on a ground relevant to the licensing objectives set out in s.4, and those objectives include "protecting and improving public health" and "protecting children from harm".

Subsection (2)
An LSO is empowered to apply for a premises licence review (s.36) in the event of failure to comply with a notice requiring breach of a licence condition to be remedied. In relation to a premises licence, an LSO may also apply for a review on any other competent ground: see notes to s.36. (The reference in subs.(2)(b) to "that section" is presumably intended to be a reference to s.36.)

15. Powers of entry and inspection

(1) A Licensing Standards Officer for a council area may, for the purpose of determining whether the activities being carried on in any licensed premises in the area are being carried on in accordance with-
   (a) the premises licence or, as the case may be, occasional licence in respect of the premises, and
   (b) any other requirements of this Act,
exercise the powers specified in subsection (2).
(2) The powers referred to subsection (1) are-
   (a) power to enter the premises at any time for the purpose of exercising the power specified in paragraph (b), and
   (b) power to carry out such inspection of the premises and of any substances, articles or documents found there as the Officer thinks necessary.
(3) Where a Licensing Standards Officer exercises either of those powers in relation to any licensed premises, the persons specified in subsection (4) must-
   (a) give the Officer such assistance,
   (b) provide the Officer with such information, and
   (c) produce to the Officer such documents,
as the Officer may reasonably require.
(4) The persons referred to in subsection (3) are-
   (a) the holder of the premises licence or, as the case may be, occasional licence in respect of the premises,
   (b) in the case of licensed premises in respect of which a premises licence has effect, the premises manager, and
   (c) in any case, any person working on the premises at the time the Officer is exercising the power.
(5) A person who-
   (a) intentionally obstructs a Licensing Standards Officer in the exercise of any power under subsection (2), or
   (b) refuses or fails, without reasonable excuse, to comply with a requirement made under subsection (3),
commits an offence.
(6) A person guilty of an offence under subsection (5) is liable on summary conviction to a fine not exceeding level 3 on the standard scale.

DEFINITIONS
"council": see s.147(1) of this Act
"area": see s.147(1) of this Act
"licensed premises": see s.147(1) of this Act
"premises licence": see s.17 of this Act
"occasional licence": see s.56(1) of this Act
"premises manager": see s.19(1) of this Act

GENERAL NOTE
Nicholson recommended that LSOs should have a statutory right of entry to all licensed premises (Report, para.7.5). The provisions of this section go further, although the powers afforded to them were trimmed during the Bill's Parliamentary progress. It was originally proposed that LSOs should have power to enter unlicensed premises if alcohol was being sold there or the officer had reasonable grounds for so believing; and that the power of entry would be available for the purpose of determining whether the activities in the premises were being carried on in accordance with the licensing objectives.

In their written evidence to the Local Government and Transport Committee, the Association of Chief Police Officers (Scotland) expressed concern that LSOs would be empowered to enter domestic dwellinghouses without a warrant and suggested that the inspection of unlicensed premises was a role for which the police were better trained and equipped. The National Licensing Forum suggested that the reference to the licensing objectives would allow LSOs to access documents and other articles which were not relevant to the conduct of the premises. The Bill was adjusted accordingly.

Subsections (1), (2)
LSOs are empowered to enter licensed premises at any time, without any further authority, for the purpose of determining whether the activities being carried on in licensed premises are being carried on in accordance with the premises licence or an occasional licence (as the case may be) and any other of the Act's requirements. They need not have any reason to believe that the premises are being operated unlawfully. As they think necessary, they may inspect the premises and any substances, articles or documents found there.

Subsections (3), (4)
These subsections require licence holders and those managing and employed in licensed premises to facilitate the exercise of the LSOs' powers by providing information and assistance and producing documents as may reasonably be required. The power to inspect documents does not extend to their removal from the premises.

Subsection (5)
A person (who need not be a person referred to in subs.(4)) who intentionally obstructs an LSO in the exercise of the powers conferred by subs.(2) or who refuses or fails, without reasonably excuse, to comply with a requirement made under subs.(3) commits an offence.

16. Training of Licensing Standards Officers

(1) A Licensing Standards Officer must comply with such requirements as to the training of Licensing Standards Officers as may be prescribed.
(2) If a Licensing Standards Officer fails to comply with subsection (1), the (or each) council which appointed the Officer must terminate the Officer's appointment.
(3) Regulations under subsection (1) prescribing training requirements may, in particular-
  (a) provide for accreditation by the Scottish Ministers of-
    (i) courses of training, and
    (ii) persons providing such courses,

for the purposes of the regulations,
- (b) prescribe different requirements in relation to different descriptions of Licensing Standards Officers, and
- (c) require that any person providing training or any particular description of training in accordance with the regulations holds such qualification as may be prescribed in the regulations.

DEFINITION
"prescribed": see s.147(1) of this Act

GENERAL NOTE
This section provides for the training of LSOs, the detail of which will be prescribed by regulations. Daniels considered that consideration should be given to making diversity and racial awareness training an essential component of the regime as this "should help to build bridges which would ensure successful communication leading to better engagement and a mutually beneficial relationship between the [LSOs] and the many licence holders of ethnic origin" (Report, para.4.50).

PART 3

PREMISES LICENCES

Introductory

17. Premises licence

In this Act, "premises licence", in relation to any premises, means a licence issued by a Licensing Board under section 26(1) or 47(2) authorising the sale of alcohol on the premises.

GENERAL NOTE
The new, single premises licence replaces the seven fixed licence categories available under the 1976 Act.
In addition to what might shortly be termed a "permanent licence", a licensing board may also in appropriate circumstances grant a temporary premises licence in terms of s.47.

18. Meaning of "appropriate Licensing Board"

(1) In this Part, "the appropriate Licensing Board" means, in relation to any premises or premises licence issued in respect of any premises-
  (a) the Licensing Board in whose area the premises are situated, or
  (b) where the premises are situated in the area of more than one Licensing Board-
    (i) the Board in whose area the greater or greatest part of the premises is situated, or
    (ii) if neither or none of those Boards falls within sub-paragraph (i), such of the Boards as is nominated in accordance with subsection (2).
(2) In a case falling within subsection (1)(b)(ii), the applicant for a premises licence in respect of the premises must nominate one of the Licensing Boards to be the Licensing Board for the purposes of the application of this Part in relation to the premises.

DEFINITIONS
"appropriate Licensing Board": see subs.(1)
"premises": see s.147(1) of this Act
"premises licence": see s.17 of this Act
"applicant": see s.147(1) of this Act

GENERAL NOTE
There have been unusual situations in which premises have straddled two licensing board areas, leading to uncertainty as to the identity of the licensing board to whom application should be made for a licence. In at least one case, premises have been licensed by two boards. In terms of this helpful provision, where premises are situated within more than one board area jurisdiction will lie with the board in whose area the greater or greatest part of the premises are situated; or in other (no doubt very rare) cases the board nominated by an applicant for a premises licence. (There is no parallel provision in relation to occasional licences which may be granted by virtue of s.56.)

19. Premises manager

(1) In this Act, "premises manager", in relation to any licensed premises in respect of which a premises licence has effect, means the individual for the time being specified as such in the premises licence.

(2) An individual may not, at any one time, be the premises manager of more than one licensed premises; and, accordingly, if an individual who is the premises manager of licensed premises is subsequently specified in the premises licence of other licensed premises as the premises manager of those other premises, the subsequent specification is of no effect.

DEFINITIONS
"premises manager": see subs.(1)
"premises": see s.147(1) of this Act

GENERAL NOTE
Each licensed premises will have a premises manager who will be specified in the premises licence.

Subsection (2)
An individual may only be the premises manager of one set of premises. If an individual is subsequently specified in the premises licence for other premises the subsequent specification is of no effect, so that alcohol may not be sold on those premises.

Premises licence applications

20. Application for premises licence

(1) Any person, other than an individual under the age of 18, may apply to the appropriate Licensing Board for a premises licence in respect of any premises.

(2) An application under subsection (1) must-
 (a) contain a description of the subject premises, and
 (b) be accompanied by-
  (i) an operating plan for the subject premises,

(ii) a plan (referred to in this Act as a "layout plan"), in the prescribed form, of the subject premises, and

(iii) the certificates required by section 50(1).

(3) An application under subsection (1) which complies with subsection (2) is referred to in this Act as a "premises licence application".

(4) An "operating plan" in relation to any premises is a document in the prescribed form containing-

(a) a description of the activities to be carried on in the premises,

(b) a statement of the times during which it is proposed that alcohol be sold on the premises,

(c) a statement as to whether the alcohol is to be sold for consumption on the premises, off the premises or both,

(d) a statement of the times at which any other activities in addition to the sale of alcohol are to be carried on in the premises,

(e) where alcohol is to be sold for consumption on the premises, a statement as to whether children or young persons are to be allowed entry to the premises and, if they are to be allowed entry, a statement of the terms on which they are allowed entry including, in particular-

(i) the ages of children or young persons to be allowed entry,

(ii) the times at which they are to be allowed entry, and

(iii) the parts of the premises to which they are to be allowed entry,

(f) information as to the proposed capacity of the premises,

(g) prescribed information about the individual who is to be the premises manager, and

(h) such other information in relation to the premises and the activities to be carried on there as may be prescribed.

(5) Where alcohol is to be sold both for consumption on and for consumption off any premises, the operating plan for the premises may, under subsection (4)(b), state different times for-

(a) the sale of alcohol for consumption on the premises, and

(b) the sale of alcohol for consumption off the premises.

DEFINITIONS

"appropriate Licensing Board": see s.18 of this Act
"premises licence": see s.17 of this Act
"premises": see s.147(1) of this Act
"layout plan": see subs.(2)
"premises licence application": see subs.(3)
"operating plan": see subs.(4)
"alcohol": see s.2 of this Act
"child": see s.147(1) of this Act
"young person": see s.147(1) of this Act
"capacity": see s.147(1) of this Act
"prescribed": see s.147(1) of this Act
"premises manager": see s.19 of this Act

GENERAL NOTE

The creation of the premises licence and the approach to the premises licence application bring about a fundamental change in Scottish licensing law. At present, there are seven fixed licence categories, each of which confers a particular authority to sell or supply alcoholic liquor (1976 Act, Sch.1). A public house licence, for example, simply allows the sale or supply of alcohol for consumption off the premises. The definition of "public house" in s.139(1) of the 1976 Act demonstrates the Act's antiquity: it includes "an inn, ale-house, victualling house or other premises in which alcoholic liquor is sold for consumption either on or off the premises".

Unsurprisingly, many modern licensed developments have struggled to accommodate themselves with one of the current categories. Many premises which are not public houses in the conventional sense can only be operated under a public house licence. For example, a delicatessen offering a range of luxury grocery products and small selection of wines and spirits and containing a caf area could not operate under an off-sale licence, which would prevent the sale of alcohol for consumption on the premises. Public house licences have been obtained for large department stores with restaurants and off-sale departments. So-called "hybrid" premises with bar and entertainment facilities have on occasions laboured to obtain entertainment licences since entertainment may not be provided continuously throughout the whole hours of operation.

These problems with disappear with the Act's reforms. Licensing boards will have a clearer view - through the operating plan (subs.4) - of the manner in which the premises will be operated. They need no longer be invited to accept undertakings as to the proposed style of operation since alcohol may only be sold in accordance with the operating plan: Sch.3, para.2(1).

The Policy Memorandum (para.77) recognises that "a licensing board and the local community should know with some certainty the kind of operation which would be permitted in terms of the licence, and that an operation of that kind should be adhered to by the licence holder thereafter".

A premises licence may not be granted in respect of certain types of premises, referred to in the Act as "excluded premises" (see s.123). There is, however, no impediment to the grant of a licence in respect of local authority premises. Section 124 of the 1976 Act removed such a prohibition. Nicholson considered that, since members of a licensing board would be councillors of the very authority seeking a licence, local authority applications were "plainly incompatible with the requirements of art.6 of the [European Convention on Human Rights ("ECHR")]" (Report, para.6.2). It recommended that it should not be lawful for a local authority to hold a premises licence in its own name. All local authorities presently holding liquor licences in respect of premises owned or leased by them should, in future, make other arrangements. For example, catering facilities on local authority premises could be franchised or leased.

Although Nicholson's enquiries revealed that the number of licences held by councils was very small, the proposal was greeted unenthusiastically by local authorities in the consultation process following publication of the Nicholson Report. Around two-thirds of respondents rejected the suggested prohibition, "some vehemently" according to the analysis of response prepared for the Scottish Executive.

The White Paper recorded this "depth of feeling". Following the Executive's own consideration of the ECHR issues involved, it considered that local authorities may continue to hold licences in their own name (and could also continue to object to applications: see notes to s.22). This was important "so that local authorities are not limited from providing services to enhance their communities" (White Paper, p.10). Speaking at a Law Society of Scotland conference in September 2004, Sheriff Principal Nicholson warned that the Executive's decision to take a different view on ECHR compliance could spell "disaster" for the Act. It was, he said, "unfortunate" that such a "radical departure" had not been properly explained. He also drew attention to the provisions of the Scotland Act 1998 (c.46), in terms of which an Act of the Scottish Parliament is not law so far as any provision is outwith its legislative competence; and a provision is outwith that competence if "it is incompatible with any of the Convention rights or with Community law...". (See further "Human rights breach could spell 'disaster' for reform" [2004] 29 SLLP 3.)

Except in certain circumstances, a premises licence will have an indefinite duration (see s.28). Currently, licences require to be renewed every three years and application made at least annually for a regular extension of the permitted hours.

Provision is separately made for a provisional premises licence: see s.45.

Subsection (1)

No one under the age of 18 may apply for a premises licence. Presently, there is no minimum age of licence-holding. In practice, it is rare for applications to be made by persons younger than, say, 21. A number of licensing boards operate a "fitness to hold a licence" policy which desiderate minimum levels of experience in the licensed trade which could not be attained by a person aged 18, having regard to the 1976 Act's employment restrictions.

Subsection (2)

Applications for the grant of a new licence (except an off-sale licence) or for the provisional grant of a new licence must, in terms of the 1976 Act, be accompanied by a plan of the premises.

There must also be produced (except in off-sale applications) certificates of suitability in relation to planning, building control and food hygiene (1976 Act, s.23).

Under the new regime, an operating plan will be required. The required content of layout plans (which presently varies from area to area) will be prescribed for the first time. All applicants will be required to produce certificates in relation to planning, building standards and (if food is supplied on the premises) food hygiene (s.50(1)).

Subsection (4)

This subsection provides the content of the operating plan which will give the licensing board a very clear view of the applicant's proposals and the scale of the venture.

In relation to licensing hours, subs.(4)(b) reflects the end of statutorily permitted hours, with the intended trading times being put forward by the applicant. The choice of these hours will require careful consideration, having regard to the "duty to trade" (see notes to s.63).

In terms of the 1976 Act, on-licensed premises enjoy "basic" permitted hours supplemented by regular or occasional extensions; off-sale premises have fixed "trading hours" which are not capable of extension. There are no "opening" or "closing" times for licensed premises, save that alcohol may only be sold, supplied or consumed in on-licensed premises during the permitted hours (subject to certain exceptions) (*ibid.* s.54); and off-sale licensed premises are not to be open for the sale of alcoholic liquor outwith trading hours (s.119).

Certain activities taking place outwith these hours may, however, require to be licensed under the Civic Government (Scotland) Act 1982: the provision of public entertainment or the provision of meals or refreshments (1982 Act, ss.41, 42, which are amended by this Act, Sch.6, para.6).

Although it may not be immediately apparent, this Act effectively establishes opening and closing times. By virtue of subs.4(d) an applicant for a premises licence is required to provide in the operating plan not only the times during which alcohol will be sold for consumption on or off the premises but also "a statement of the times at which any other activities in addition to the sale of alcohol" are to be carried on. While para.2 of Sch.3 provides that alcohol may only be sold in accordance with the operating plan, para.3 imposes a similar constraint in relation to "any other activity". Accordingly, if during the currency of a premises licence the operator decided, for example, that it would be advantageous to open during the morning for the provision of breakfasts and non-alcoholic refreshments it would be necessary to apply to the licensing board for a variation of the licence. Such a variation would not be a "minor variation" (see s.29(5)(b), (6)).

The system of children's certificates is swept away. The applicant will declare in the operating plan whether children or young persons are to be allowed entry and provide: the ages of children or young persons proposed to be admitted; the times at which they will be allowed entry; and the parts of the premises to which entry will be permitted.

According to the Policy Memorandum (para.138), those making provision for on-sales will require to "think actively and seriously about whether their premises are suitable for children" before proposing to allow entry and give consideration as to "whether children would be accompanied or unaccompanied, suitable hours for access and in which areas to allow access".

Under the 1976 Act, there are surprisingly few restrictions. Broadly speaking, children of all ages may be admitted to all parts of premises which are the subject of a public house, off-sale, hotel, restricted hotel, restaurant or entertainment licence, save that (subject to certain exceptions) children under the age of 14 may not be present in a bar except where a children's certificate is in force. Children may only be admitted to premises which are the subject of a refreshment licence provided that they are accompanied by a person aged 18 or over; and may not remain on the premises after 8 pm. The provisions of subs.(4)(e) stand at variance with the Nicholson approach, in terms of which an operator would opt-out of allowing children's access, rather than opt-in, with "a statutory presumption in favour of allowing children and young persons into all parts of licensed premises" (Report, para.13.7). The presumption would, however, be subject to restrictions proposed in the operating plan which could be authorised, with or without modification, by the licensing board.

Implementation of the Nicholson recommendations was seen as too bold a step by the Scottish Executive. While at pains to labour their intention "to make licensed premises more child-friendly in Scotland", the Executive considered that the country was not "ready for café-society". Many licensed premises were "completely unsuitable for children". There were also "very strong reservations about bringing forward a system which has as its basic premise the idea that all licensed premises are suitable for children" (Policy Memorandum, para.141). That proposition does less than justice to the rationale behind the Nicholson proposals. The recommended statutory presumption in favour of children's access was qualified by the recognition that "Plainly, of course, there will be some licensed premises of a kind where it would not be appropriate for entry to be permitted" (Report, para 13.7). The requirements of subs.(4)(e) only apply where alcohol is to be sold for consumption on the premises. For off-sales, it appears that "operation of a "no proof, no sale "system would be sufficient to allow access by children" (Policy Memorandum, para.138).

Possible problems with the Act's approach to children's access are considered in the notes to s.23.

21. Notification of application

(1) Where a Licensing Board receives a premises licence application, the Board must give notice of the application to-
   (a) each person having a notifiable interest in neighbouring land,
   (b) any community council within whose area the premises are situated,
   (c) the council within whose area the premises are situated (except where the council is the applicant),
   (d) the appropriate chief constable, and
   (e) the enforcing authority within the meaning of section 61 of the Fire (Scotland) Act 2005 (asp 5) in respect of the premises.
(2) A notice under subsection (1) must be accompanied by a copy of the application.
(3) The appropriate chief constable must, within 21 days of the date of receipt of a notice under subsection (1)(d), respond to the notice by giving the Licensing Board-
   (a) one or other of the notices mentioned in subsection (4), and
   (b) a report detailing-
      (i) all cases of antisocial behaviour identified within the relevant period by constables as having taken place on, or in the vicinity of, the premises, and
      (ii) all complaints or other representations made within the relevant period to constables concerning antisocial behaviour on, or in the vicinity of, the premises.
(4) Those notices are-
   (a) a notice stating that neither-
      (i) the applicant, nor
      (ii) in the cases where the applicant is neither an individual nor a council, or where the application is in respect of premises which are to be used wholly or mainly for the purposes of a club, any connected person,
   has been convicted of any relevant offence or foreign offence, or
   (b) a notice specifying any convictions of-
      (i) the applicant, or
      (ii) in any of the cases mentioned in paragraph (a)(ii), any connected person,
   for a relevant offence or a foreign offence.
(5) Where the appropriate chief constable-
   (a) proposes to give a notice under subsection (4)(b), and
   (b) considers that, having regard to any conviction to be specified in the notice, it is necessary for the purposes of the crime prevention objective that the application be refused,

the chief constable may include in the notice a recommendation to that effect.

(6) In this section-

"antisocial behaviour" has the same meaning as in section 143 of the Antisocial Behaviour etc. (Scotland) Act 2004 (asp 8),

"neighbouring land" and, in relation to that expression, "notifiable interest" have such meanings as may be prescribed for the purposes of this section, and

"relevant period" means the period of one year ending with the date on which the appropriate chief constable receives notice under subsection (1)(d).

DEFINITIONS
"premises licence application": see s.20(3) of this Act
"notifiable interest": see subs.(6)
"neighbouring land": see subs.(6)
"community council": see s.147(1) of this Act
"council": see s.147(1) of this Act
"applicant": see s.147(1) of this Act
"area": see s.147(1) of this Act
"appropriate chief constable": see s.147(1) of this Act
"antisocial behaviour": see subs.(6)
"relevant period": see subs.(6)
"applicant": see s.147(1) of this Act
"connected person": see s.147(3) of this Act
"relevant offence": see s.129(1) of this Act
"foreign offence": see s.129(2) of this Act
"crime prevention objective": see s.4(2) of this Act

GENERAL NOTE

This section places licensing boards under an obligation to notify the persons specified in subs.(1) of the premises licences applications which they have received and to provide those persons with a copy of the application. There is no parallel provision in the 1976 Act, although licensing boards will, in practice, send copies of all new licence applications to the chief constable and local authority departments such as building control and environmental health. Some licensing boards provide community councils with a list of applications due to come before them.

Section 134(1) provides that Scottish Ministers may by regulations prescribe requirements as to the publicising of any application under the Act.

The chief constable is obliged to notify the board of certain types of convictions attaching to applicants and to provide the board with antisocial behaviour reports. The latter requirement appears to have been introduced following concerns expressed by certain MSPs at Stage 2 of the Bill's consideration. Paul Martin MSP contended for a "recognised and consistent" format of reporting to ensure that the reporting of antisocial behaviour was not left to the discretion of the chief constable. He said that community representatives were concerned that "significant antisocial behaviour was not being reported to licensing boards". (See Official Report, cols 2218, 2419 et seq., 2242 et seq.)

Subsection (3)

Within 21 days of receiving notification of a premises licence application the chief constable must respond with a notice stating that neither the applicant nor, in certain cases, any "connected person", has been convicted of any relevant or foreign offence. See notes to subs.(4).

The same time limit applies to the provision of antisocial behaviour reports relating to the period of one year ending with the date on which the chief constable received notice of the premises licence application (see subs.(6)). The Bill's original provisions would have required these reports to be produced on an open-ended basis without the one-year cap. The burden which such a requirement would have placed on police forces was recognised at Stage 3. The manner in which licensing boards will respond to the antisocial behaviour reports remains to be seen; but it may be considered that the amorphous terms of subs.(3)(b)(i), (ii) may result in them receiving information which may be of limited use. Certainly, in an application under the 1976 Act, it was held that the chief constable's supply of statistics relating to crimes of disorder in a locality (simply supplied in accordance with the practice of the Board concerned) could not be relied upon to justify the refusal of a new licence where these had not been causally related to the operation of licensed premises: *Pagliocca v Glasgow District Licensing Board*, 1995 S.L.T. 180.

During the Stage 3 debate, responding to a request for an assurance that the standard of reporting would be consistent and a fear that licensed premises might wrongly be associated with antisocial behaviour, George Lyon, Minister in charge of the Bill, said he expected the police "to put forward a consistent report to licensing boards where antisocial behaviour is identified as being associated with individual premises" (Official Report, col.20682).

Subsection (4)

The types of relevant offences have yet to be prescribed in terms of s.129(1). The list is likely to be wide-ranging. For the purposes of the 2003 Act, it includes offences under that Act; offences involving violence; sexual offences; and offences under firearms, road traffic, misuse of drugs, gaming and customs and excise legislation. In terms of s.129(2), "foreign offence" is simply defined as "any offence (a) under the law of any place other than Scotland, and (b) which is similar in nature to any relevant offence".

A conviction for a relevant or foreign offence is to be disregarded if it is spent for the purposes of the Rehabilitation of Offenders Act 1974 (c.53) (see s.129.(4)). Licensing boards may presently take into account spent convictions where they are satisfied that justice cannot otherwise be done: see Cummins, pp.80 *et seq.*

The inclusion of "connected persons" addresses the present difficulty in "lifting the veil" where application is made by a person other than an individual natural person. While the 1976 Act (s.17(1)(a)) provides that an application for a new licence, the renewal of a licence or the permanent transfer of a licence must be refused if the board finds that the applicant or the person for whose benefit the application will manage the premises is not a fit and proper person, the assessment of those who might shortly be termed "corporate" applicants has proved problematic: see Cummins, pp.83 and 84.

Subsection (5)

Where the chief constable proposes to give the licensing board notice of a relevant or foreign offence and considers that the crime prevention objective (the prevention of crime and disorder) requires the application to be refused, he may include a recommendation to that effect in the notice.

For the chief constable's limited right to object to an applications, see s.22(2).

Subsection (6)

The Scottish Executive's memorandum to the Subordinate Legislation Committee indicates that they are considering a range of 50 metres for the purpose of "notifiable interest".

22. Objections and representations

(1) Where a premises licence application is made to a Licensing Board, any person may, by notice to the Licensing Board-
  (a) object to the application on any ground relevant to one of the grounds for refusal specified in section 23(5), or
  (b) make representations to the Board concerning the application, including, in particular, representations-
    (i) in support of the application,
    (ii) as to modifications which the person considers should be made to the operating plan accompanying the application, or
    (iii) as to conditions which the person considers should be imposed.
(2) The appropriate chief constable may, under subsection (1)(a), object to a premises licence application only on the ground that-

(a) the chief constable has reason to believe that-
  (i) the applicant, or
  (ii) in the cases where the applicant is neither an individual nor a council or where the application is in respect of premises which are to be used wholly or mainly for the purposes of a club, any connected person,
is involved in serious organised crime, and
(b) by reason of that involvement, the chief constable considers that it is necessary for the purposes of the crime prevention objective that the application be refused.

(3) Where a Licensing Board receives a notice of objection or representation under subsection (1) relating to any premises licence application made to the Board, the Board must-
   (a) give a copy of the notice to the applicant in such manner and by such time as may be prescribed, and
   (b) have regard to the objection or representation in determining the application,
unless the Board rejects the notice under subsection (4).

(4) A Licensing Board may reject a notice of objection or representation received by the Board under subsection (1) if the Board considers the objection or representation is frivolous or vexatious.

(5) Where a Licensing Board rejects a notice of objection or representation under subsection (4), the Board may recover from the person who gave the notice any expenses incurred by the Board in considering the notice.

(6) In any proceedings by a Licensing Board for the recovery of expenses under subsection (5), a copy of any minute of proceedings of the Licensing Board-
   (a) recording the Board's rejection of the notice and the grounds for the rejection, and
   (b) certified by the clerk of the Board to be a true copy,
is sufficient evidence of the rejection and of the establishment of the ground for rejection.

DEFINITIONS
"premises licence application": see s.20(3) of this Act
"operating plan": see s.20(4) of this Act
"council": see s.147(1) of this Act
"connected person": see s.147(3) of this Act
"appropriate chief constable": see s.147(1) of this Act
"applicant": see s.147(1) of this Act
"crime prevention objective": see s.4(2) of this Act

GENERAL NOTE
This section makes sweeping changes to the categories of persons who may object to an application in the interests of wider community involvement, limits the role of the chief constable, abandons the "fit and proper test" currently used to assess the suitability of applicants and relieves objectors from the necessity to intimate their objection to the applicant.

Subsection (1)
Any person may object to a premises licence application on one of the grounds for refusal provided in s.23(5). Such a person may also make representations to the board in support of the application (pursuant to a Daniels recommendation (Report, para.3.11); and propose (a) operating plan modifications (see s.23(7)); or (b) conditions which it is considered should be attached to the licence (see s.27).

Those who may object to licensing applications under the 1976 Act are: (a) any person owning or occupying property situated in the neighbourhood of the premises to which the application relates or any organisation which in the opinion of the board represents such persons; (b) a community council for the area in which the premises are situated; (c) any organised church which, in the opinion of the licensing board, represents a significant body of opinion among persons residing in the neighbourhood of the premises; (d) the chief constable; (f) the fire authority for the area; and (g) the local authority for the area (1976 Act, s.16(1)).

Nicholson agreed with consultees that the foregoing list was unsatisfactory in several respects (Report, para.6.14 *et seq*). In particular, it considered that the artificial restriction imposed by the words "occupying property" should be eliminated and that residence (along with ownership) should become the main qualifications for an entitlement to object to applications, provided that the objector's property was situated "in or near the neighbourhood" of the application premises.

On the Nicholson model, the chief constable, the fire authority and local authority officials would be empowered to submit observations or representations in relation to any application.

Daniels considered that the reforms proposed by Nicholson, which offering an improvement, did not go far enough. In the interests of wider community involvement (an objective which the Act as a whole now seeks to pursue), it should be possible for any person or organisation to object or make representations provided that they could demonstrate a "real and material interest" (Report, para.3.9).

In the event, neither approach found favour with the Scottish Executive, who decided that community involvement should be even further expanded. Subsection (1) provides that "any person" may object to an application or make representations.

No doubt recognising that such an expansion could easily open the floodgates to objections from those who no real interest in applications, a so-called "choke mechanism" has been provided by subs.(4): a licensing board may reject a notice of objection or representation if it considers that the objection or representation is "frivolous or vexatious". In his oral evidence to the Local Government and Transport Committee, the Scottish Executive's solicitor said that there were "difficult drafting questions" arising from the "real and material interest" test which had been proposed by Daniels. He said: "We thought letting everybody make objections, but filtering them if there were problems, the more pragmatic approach and the one more likely to achieve the effect we are after" (Official Report, col.2216).

But this safeguard has not impressed those who consider that the enfranchisement of "any person" is a step too far. In his oral evidence to the Committee, Sheriff Principal Nicholson said that "allowing someone who on any sensible view has no proper interest in the subject matter in question to [object] once, but to stop them the second or third time on the ground that they would be at that point being either vexatious or frivolous, is not a good recommendation for legislation" (Official Report, col.2222).

During the Stage 3 debate on the Bill, Bruce Crawford MSP told the chamber that only one source had supported the Scottish Executive's position, while seven sources considered that the objection provision had been drawn too widely (Official Report, col.20683). His amendment, which would have provided for objections from an "interested person", was defeated.

The expression "any person" includes a local authority; but not, according to the Scottish Executive, the chief constable (as to whose position see notes to subs.(2)). Unsurprisingly, given its position on licenceholding by local authorities (see notes to s.20), Nicholson recommended that they should no longer enjoy a right of objection: "In any case where an objection is taken by a local authority... the consequence, of course, is that members of the licensing board, who are also local councillors in that authority, are being asked to give an independent and impartial decision where one of the parties, as it were, is the very authority of which they are all members". It was accordingly "impossible to say that such a situation satisfies the objective test required by art.6 of the [ECHR] and as explained in the case of *Findlay* [*sc Findlay v United Kingdom* (1997) 24 EHRR 221, para.73]". The Scottish Executive rejected this advice, although its reasons for so doing have not been explained. For a consideration of the ECHR difficulties which arose under the 1976 Act when a licensing board considered a local authority objection, see *Blusins v City of Dundee Licensing Board*, 2001 S.L.T. (Sh Ct) 176.

Subsection (2)

The chief constable may only object to an application on the ground that he has reason to believe the applicant or a connected person is involved in "serious organised crime"; and, by reason of that involvement, the application ought to be refused for the purpose of the crime prevention objective.

This narrowness of this provision diminishes the chief constable's role in the licensing process. Under the 1976 Act, he has power to object on any competent ground, including the ground that an applicant for a new licence or for the renewal or permanent transfer of a licence is not a "fit and proper person" (1976 Act, ss.16(1), 17(1)(a)); and he may also submit observations in relation to an application whether or not they are relevant to a ground for refusal (s.16A).

Giving oral evidence to the Local Government and Transport Committee during the initial stages of the Bill's scrutiny, the head of the Scottish Executive's Bill team said that the "fit and proper person" test "can be considered quite vague and subjective" and can be "overused" (Official Report, col.2219). At the same Committee session, Sheriff Principal Nicholson emphasised that his Committee's approach, which differentiated between a list of statutory objectors (those not normally involved in the licensing process) and officials such as the chief constable (who would be entitled to submit observations or representations regarding an application), "had nothing to do with the removal of the old fit-and-proper-person test" (Official Report, col.2222). Nicholson considered that the need for the "fit and proper person" ground for refusal would disappear if effect was given to the recommendations for separate premises and personal licences: in that event, "fit and proper" considerations would only arise in respect of applicants for personal licences (as to which see ss.71 *et seq*) (Report, para.6.31).

Sheriff Principal Nicholson also expressed the view that, as a matter of statutory interpretation, the chief constable could be considered to be "any person" for the purpose of s.22(1) and regretted the truncation of his role:

> "I would have thought that the chief constable might have a perfectly proper, legitimate and important interest in a wider range of matters [other than an applicant's convictions] and that he should be capable of making his views on them known to a licensing board. As a result, I am a little alarmed if a chief constable's role is to be constricted in such a way. If, as it appears, the Executive considers that this matter has no European Convention on Human Rights implications, a chief constable should simply be treated as an objector." (Official Report, col.2223.)

Following these concerns and representations made by the Association of Chief Police Officers (Scotland), the Scottish Executive recognised that there may be instances where the police can provide useful intelligence on the involvement of an applicant, or someone connected with the applicant, in organised criminal activity; and it was appropriate to allow the chief constable to object to a premises licence application where he had reason to believe that the applicant, or a connected person, is involved in serious organised crime (Official Report, col.2861). The Act does not provide any definition of the expression "serious organised crime" but it is no doubt apt to include activities such as drug trafficking, involvement in prostitution and money laundering. In the result, the chief constable may be disabled from objecting even where he suspects that the applicant is involved in organised crime which does not meet the standard of "serious organised crime".

The chief constable's entitlement to object is in addition to his power to "recommend" the refusal of an application in pursuit of the crime prevention objective where the applicant, or a connected person, has incurred convictions (see s.21(5)). The expression "any person" in s.36 appears to include the chief constable, so that he would be entitled to seek the review of a premises licence (see notes to that section).

Subsection (3)

The licensing board is required to provide an applicant with a copy of a notice of objection or representation in such manner and by such time as may be prescribed; and have regard to the objection or representation in determining the premises licence application, unless the objection or representation is considered to be "frivolous or vexatious" (see subs.(3)). This simplification of the objection process is an important step forward. Presently, objectors are required to lodge their objection with the clerk to the licensing board and intimate their objection to the applicant. Objections often fall by the wayside because of a failure to take the latter step, or to take it timeously.

Subsection (4)

A licensing board may reject a notice of objection or representation if it is considered to be frivolous or vexatious. This power is only likely to be invoked in exceptional circumstances. Section 16(6) of the 1976 Act allows a licensing board to find an objector to the renewal of a licence liable in expenses (to the such extent as the board thinks fit) if in its opinion the objection is "frivolous or vexatious". It is doubtful whether this power has ever been invoked.

Subsection (5)

The board may recover the expenses which it has incurred in considering a rejected objection or representation. It is extremely improbable that such a step would ever be taken.

23. Determination of premises licence application

(1) A premises licence application received by a Licensing Board is to be determined in accordance with this section.
(2) The Licensing Board must hold a hearing for the purpose of considering and determining the application.
(3) In considering and determining the application, the Board must take account of the documents accompanying the application under section 20(2)(b).
(4) The Board must, in considering and determining the application, consider whether any of the grounds for refusal applies and-
   (a) if none of them applies, the Board must grant the application, or
   (b) if any of them applies, the Board must refuse the application.
(5) The grounds for refusal are-
   (a) that the subject premises are excluded premises,
   (b) that the application must be refused under section 25(2), 64(2) or 65(3),
   (c) that the Licensing Board considers that the granting of the application would be inconsistent with one or more of the licensing objectives,
   (d) that, having regard to-
      (i) the nature of the activities proposed to be carried on in the subject premises,
      (ii) the location, character and condition of the premises, and
      (iii) the persons likely to frequent the premises,
   the Board considers that the premises are unsuitable for use for the sale of alcohol,
   (e) that, having regard to the number and capacity of-
      (i) licensed premises, or
      (ii) licensed premises of the same or similar description as the subject premises,
   in the locality in which the subject premises are situated, the Board considers that, if the application were to be granted, there would, as a result, be overprovision of licensed premises, or licensed premises of that description, in the locality.
(6) In considering, for the purposes of the ground for refusal specified in subsection (5)(c), whether the granting of the application would be inconsistent-
   (a) with the crime prevention objective, the Licensing Board must, in particular, take into account-
      (i) any conviction notice of which is given by the appropriate chief constable under subsection (4)(b) of section 21,

(ii) any recommendation of the chief constable included in the notice under subsection (5) of that section, and

(b) with any licensing objective, the Licensing Board must take into account any report made by the appropriate chief constable under subsection (3)(b) of section 21.

(7) Where the Licensing Board considers that-

(a) they would refuse the application as made, but

(b) if a modification proposed by them were made to the operating plan for the subject premises accompanying the application, they would be able to grant the application,

the Board must, if the applicant accepts the proposed modification, grant the application as modified.

(8) Where the Licensing Board refuses the application-

(a) the Board must specify the ground for refusal, and

(b) if the ground for refusal is that specified in subsection (5)(c), the Board must specify the licensing objective or objectives in question.

(9) In subsection (5)(e), references to "licensed premises" do not include licensed premises in respect of which an occasional licence has effect.

DEFINITIONS

"premises licence application": see s.20(3) of this Act
"grounds for refusal": see subs.(5)
"excluded premises": see s.123(2) of this Act
"licensing objectives": see s.4(1) of this Act
"alcohol": see s.2 of this Act
"licensed premises": see s.147(1) of this Act
"locality": see s.7(2) of this Act
"crime prevention objective": see s.4(2) of this Act
"appropriate chief constable": see s.147(1) of this Act
"licensing objectives": see s.4(1) of this Act
"operating plan": see s.20(4) of this Act
"applicant": see s.147(1) of this Act
"occasional licence": see s.56(1) of this Act

GENERAL NOTE

This section provides grounds upon which an application for a premises licence must be refused and allows the grant of an application where a modification to the operating plan would permit such a course. If no ground for refusal applies, the application must be granted.

In terms of s.17 of the 1976 Act a licensing board must refuse an application for the grant or provisional grant of a new licence if it "finds":

"(a) that the applicant, or the person on whose behalf the applicant will manage the premises or, in the case of an application to which s.11 of this Act applies, the applicant or the employee or agent named in the application is not a fit and proper person to be the holder of a licence;

(b) that the premises to which the application relates are not suitable or convenient for the sale of alcoholic liquor, having regard to their location, their character or condition, the nature and extent of the proposed use of the premises, and the persons likely to resort to the premises;

(c) that the use of the premises for the sale of alcoholic liquor is likely to cause undue public nuisance or a threat to public order or safety;

(d) that, having regard to -

(i) the number of licensed premises in the locality at the time the application is considered; and

(ii) the number of premises in respect of which the provisional grant of a

new licence is in force,
the board is satisfied that grant of the application would result in the overprovision of licensed premises in the locality."

Otherwise, the board "shall grant the application".

The grounds for refusal set out here largely follow the Nicholson recommendations. Nicholson considered that, broadly speaking, the 1976 Act's grounds for refusal were acceptable (Report, para.6.31). There should, however, be a general ground for refusal that the grant of a particular premises licence would offend the "licensing principles" (as the "licensing objectives" were termed in the Report). The need for the "fit and proper person" ground, which had been criticised by consultees as "vague and ill-defined" (Report, para 6.30), would disappear with the creation of separate premises and personal licences. (See notes to s.22.)

It would not be necessary to provide for a "public nuisance" ground for refusal if provision were to be made for the over-arching "licensing principles" ground (Report, para.6.33).

In relation to the "overprovision" ground (currently the ground most commonly invoked by licensing boards), Nicholson considered that this directed attention to the density of licensed premises in localities "in an unfocused way which is likely to result in no more than a somewhat arid and uncertain arithmetical exercise". Account should be taken not only of the number of licensed premises in a particular area but also their type, size and capacity: "a concentration of a few, very large pubs in a small area might well have a greater consequence in terms of public nuisance and public order than would a concentration of a large number of much smaller establishments" (Report, para.6.35).

Subsection (1)

The premises licence application must be determined in accordance with this section and having regard to any objection or representation which has not been rejected as "frivolous or vexatious" (see s.22(3)(b)).

Subsection (2)

The board must hold a hearing for the purpose of considering and determining an application for a premises licence; and such a hearing must take place at a meeting of the board (s.133(1); Sch.1, para.10(2)(c)). Scottish Minister may by regulations make provision for the procedure to be followed (s.133(2)).

Subsection (3)

The board must take account of the operating plan and layout plan for the subject premises; and the "suitability" certificates specified in s.50(1).

Subsection (4)

Licensing boards are required to give consideration as to whether any of the grounds of refusal set out in subs.(5) apply. If none of them applies, the application must be granted; but if any of them applies, the application must be refused. This requirement probably stems from a concern, as represented to Nicholson by some consultees, that some boards have given no consideration to possible grounds for refusal unless they have been specifically advanced by an objector. Those consultees proposed that there should be a duty on boards to consider every application on its merits, even in the absence of formal objections (Report, para.6.27).

Subsection (5)(a)

"Excluded premises" are those situated at motorway service stations; and (subject to certain exceptions) premises uses as a garage: see s.123.

Subsection (5)(b)

In terms of s.25(2), the refusal of an application for a premises licence prevents a further application being granted for the same premises within the ensuing year, unless the board had directed otherwise at the time of refusal or there had been a material change of circumstances. Section 64(2) requires the refusal of an application which would allow the sale of alcohol for a continuous period of 24 hours unless there are exceptional circumstances. An application may not be granted if the sale of alcohol for consumption off the premises would be permitted before 10 am, after 10 pm or both (s.65(3)).

Subsection (5)(c)

The application must be refused if the grant would be inconsistent with the licensing objectives set out in s.4(1). Since these objectives are very broadly expressed, licensing boards will no doubt be afforded a very wide discretion in their approach to this ground.

The potential impact upon any licensing objective must be considered by reference to the "antisocial behaviour report" which the chief constable is required to provide in terms of s.21(3)(b) (see subs.(6)(b)).

The crime prevention objective

In relation to the "crime prevention objective", the board must take account of any conviction notice given by the chief constable and any recommendation that the application ought to be refused for the purpose of that objective (see subs.6(a)). The chief constable may also object on the ground that the applicant, or, in certain cases, "any connected person", is involved in "serious organised crime" (see s.22(2)).

Securing public safety and preventing public nuisance

The approach to the "securing public safety" and "preventing public nuisance" objectives will no doubt reflect the body of case law generated by s.17(1)(c) of the 1976 Act, except that, under the new regime, public nuisance need not be "undue": Nicholson noted that, by the use of the word "undue", "the legislation appears to be suggesting that a certain amount of public nuisance will not be a ground for refusal, and will simply have to be tolerated by local residents" (Report, para.6.30).

The refusal of an application on the basis of these objectives must have a proper basis in the material before the licensing board. For example, in *Risky Business Ltd v City of Glasgow Licensing Board*, 2000 S.L.T. 923; [2000] 16 SLLP 9 the Board had no basis for concluding that violent conduct of a sexual nature towards woman was a probable consequence of granting an application for an exotic dancing club. A lack of relevant material may not be made good by the invocation of the board's local knowledge and experience: *Risky Business Ltd, cit supra*; *Singh v City of Glasgow Licensing Board* 1998 SCLR 865; *G A Estate Agency Ltd v City of Glasgow Licensing Board*, digested at [2000] 15 SLLP 22. In *Augustus Barnett Ltd v Ross and Cromarty Licensing Board*, Tain Sheriff Court, March 9, 1993, unreported, where a licence was refused on the ground that existing problems in the area would otherwise be exacerbated, the sheriff considered that the board had proceeded upon "no more than a belief based upon an assertion".

The term "public" includes those likely to be affected by the conduct of the premises as well as customers: *Sangha v Bute and Cowal Divisional Licensing Board*, 1990 SCLR 409.

One would have thought that, in considering the public nuisance and public safety objectives, licensing boards would wish to take account of information supplied by the chief constable, such as statistics relating to crimes of disorder in the locality of application premises (provided that this information could be causally related to the operation of licensed premises: see *Pagliocca v Glasgow District Licensing Board*, 1995 S.L.T. 180). However, the chief constable's contribution appears limited to the provision of his "antisocial behaviour report" (see subs.(6)(b)), in which event he will not be able to complain that the grant of an application in a particular locality would place an intolerable strain on the provision of police resources.

Protecting and improving public health

It remains to be seen how licensing boards will approach this entirely novel consideration. Conceivably, the local licensing forum (see ss.10, 11, 12 and Sch.2) may have given advice or made recommendations to the board which are relevant to the pursuit of this objective, although the forum has no locus in relation to any particular case (s.11(3)). The density of licences and wide availability of alcohol in a particular area could have adverse public health consequences, but the overprovision of licences is a matter for consideration in terms of subs.5(e).

Protecting children from harm

A child is a person under the age of 16 (in distinction to a person aged 16 or 17, who is a "young person"): see s.147(1).

A consideration of this objective is likely to overlap with the ground for refusal contained in subs.5(d). Nicholson suggested that a proposal to open licensed premises adjacent to a primary school could fall foul of this objective (Report, para.6.32), as well as having an impact upon the suitability of premises.

In *Scott Catering & Offshore Services Ltd v Aberdeen Licensing Board*, 1987 G.W.D. 22-823 application had been made for a new public house licence in respect of premises which would interconnect with a licensed fish restaurant and take-away. The sheriff upheld a refusal based on the board's conclusion that unaccompanied children and young persons frequenting the existing premises were likely to frequent the public house.

The fact that children and young persons visiting a leisure complex could be "unduly exposed to drink" led to the refusal of an entertainment licence in *Fife Regional Council v Kirkcaldy District Licensing Board (No 2)*, 1991 G.W.D. 18-1110. (The court had previously accepted that the words "unduly exposed to drink" were sufficiently clear: see 1991 G.W.D. 10-611). The first floor of the premises contained a segregated bar area (overlooking the games hall), to which the sale of drink was to be restricted, and a separate cafeteria where alcohol could be consumed. In the opinion of the court:

> "[I]t was plain... that the [board] were satisfied that the premises were not suitable for the sale of alcoholic liquor having regard to the proposed use of the premises and having regard to the fact that children and young persons were likely to resort there. Although it is no doubt true that children under 14 will be prohibited from the actual bar, it is plain that both children under 14 and children above the age of 14 will be entitled to use the refreshment area".

However, the refusal of an off-sale licence was overturned where the board considered that the applicant's grocery premises would attract children and young persons and "unduly expose" them to drink: the board had not considered the fact that off-sale premises do not contain a bar and the "bald assertion" that children would be so exposed could not be supported. Similarly, in *Littlewoods Chain Stores Ltd v Inverclyde District Licensing Board*, Greenock Sheriff Court, 12 May 1995, unreported, the refusal of an off-sale licence on the ground that the juxtaposition of clothing could lead to "young and vulnerable people" being tempted to purchase alcohol was held to be unreasonable.

Subsection (5) (d)

This is a modified re-enactment of the ground for refusal found in s.17(1)(b) of the 1976 Act, introducing a consideration of the activities proposed to be carried on in the premises (replacing the nature and extent of their proposed use).

In relation to "location", the availability of access for police supervision has occupied the attention of the court in a number of cases. (For this Act's provisions in relation to police powers of entry, see s.138). Where it would have proved impossible to gain access to licensed premises without entering private property, the sheriff considered that it was not unreasonable to insist that police access "should depend upon clear right, as opposed to assurances about constant access given at the time of the application", although the *bona fides* of the assurances was not questioned: *University of Glasgow Court v City of Glasgow District Licensing Board*, Glasgow Sheriff Court (unreported, 26 October, 1981).

Per contra, in *Chief Constable of Strathclyde v Glasgow District Licensing Board*, 1988 S.L.T. 128, the Board had been entitled to accept an assurance given by the prospective owners of the city's Princes Square shopping centre that the police would, at all times, enjoy unrestricted access to licensed shops. The First Division agreed with the sheriff that each case required to be considered on its own merits; and that a question to whether the access arrangements were satisfactory was "entirely a matter within the discretion of the Board to decide".

The location of premises may be unsuitable having regard to loss of amenity which may be suffered by surrounding properties: *William Hill (Scotland) Ltd v Kyle and Carrick District Licensing Board*, 1991 S.L.T. 559. Proper weight must, however, be given to the grant of planning consent which has been granted subject to conditions directed at amenity issues: *Leisure Inns (UK) Ltd v Perth and Kinross Licensing Board*, 1993 S.L.T. 796.

Lack of disabled access may be a relevant consideration: *William Hill (Caledonian) Ltd v City of Glasgow Licensing Board*, 2003 S.L.T. 668; [2003] 25 SLLP 12.

Where the "persons likely to frequent the premises" are children, see notes to subs.5(c).

Subsection (5) (e)

This re-working of s.17(1)(d) of the 1976 is intended to allow licensing boards a more focused approach to the overprovision of licensed premises by permitting them to have regard to the capacities of existing premises and their types of operation. As interpreted in *Chung v Wigtown Dis-*

trict Licensing Board, 1993 S.L.T. 1118 and *Caledonian Nightclubs Ltd v City of Glasgow District Licensing Board*, 1996 S.L.T. 451; [1996] 4 SLLP 11, s.17(1)(d) requires a licensing board to select a locality, ascertain the number of licences of each type listed in Sch.1 to the 1976 Act and then examine the facilities which the holders of those types are authorised to provide. It is not, however, relevant to consider the particular manner in which each licence holder is in fact operating the premises or to take into account the particular facilities which an applicant proposes to provide. In the result, licensing boards have been disabled (in theory, at least) from drawing a distinction between, say, an existing nightclub operating under an entertainment licence and a proposed concert hall. See further: Paul Romano, "Explaining Overprovision" [1996] 5 SLLP 16.

It will be possible for licensing boards to invoke the "new" overprovision ground simply having regard to the number and capacity of premises but no doubt that approach will only be adopted in rare cases.

Boards will enjoy a very wide discretion in the selection of a locality: *Lazerdale v Glasgow District Licensing Board* [1996] 4 SLLP 6. That selection must take place *in limine*: *Botterills of Blantyre v Hamilton District Licensing Board*, 1986 S.L.T. 14. The matter of locality may be considered *de novo* when an application is remitted to a licensing board for reconsideration (s.131(5)(a)): *Ross v Moray District Licensing Board*, 1995 S.L.T. 447.

Where a licensing board has declared a locality to be overprovided in terms of a policy promulgated in terms of s.7 there will, in effect, be a rebuttable presumption that an application for a new licence in that locality ought to be refused; but each case will, of course, require to be considered on its own merits.

Subsection (6)

In considering whether grant of a licence would be inconsistent with the licensing objectives, the board must take account of any conviction notice and any refusal recommendation made by the chief constable for the purpose of the crime prevention objective (s.21(4)(b)); and, as respects the other objectives, it must take account of the "antisocial behaviour report" made by the chief constable in terms of s.21(5)

Subsection (7)

The licensing board may, of the applicant's consent, modify an operating plan where they would otherwise be minded to refuse the application. It will no doubt be appropriate to give an applicant a proper opportunity to consider his position in relation to a proposed modification and, if need be, to adjourn the hearing of the application for that purpose.

This provision gives licensing boards powers far more extensive than those currently enjoyed. A modification does not amount to the attachment of a condition (see s.27); but compliance with the operating plan is a condition of the licence (see Sch.3, para 2(1)). A modification becomes, in effect, a condition and the safeguards provided by s.27(7) (*qv*) do not apply. It is to be expected that many licensing boards will use the modification power to impose strict controls on children's access to licensed premises. Presently, licensing boards may only regulate the presence of children under the age of 14 in bars by imposing conditions on children's certificates: this Act allows them to impose controls on access to all parts of on-licensed premises.

Subsection (8)

The ground or grounds for refusal must be specified by the licensing board; and where the refusal is based on a licensing objective, the objective or objectives in question must be specified.

24. Applicant's duty to notify Licensing Board of convictions

(1) This section applies where any of the persons specified in subsection (2) is convicted of a relevant or foreign offence during the period beginning with the making of a premises licence application and ending with determination of the application.

(2) Those persons are-
  (a) the applicant, and
  (b) where-
    (i) the applicant is neither an individual nor a council, or

(ii) the premises in respect of which the licence is sought are used wholly or mainly for the purposes of a club,

any connected person.

(3) The applicant must, no later than one month after the date of the conviction, give notice of the conviction to the Licensing Board to which the application was made.

(4) A notice under subsection (3) must specify-
   (a) the nature of the offence, and
   (b) the date of the conviction.

(5) Where the Licensing Board receives a notice under subsection (3) at any time before they have determined the application, the Board must-
   (a) suspend consideration of the application, and
   (b) give notice of the conviction to the appropriate chief constable.

(6) The appropriate chief constable must, within 21 days of the date of receipt of a notice under subsection (5)(b), respond to the notice by giving the Licensing Board one or other of the notices mentioned in subsection (7).

(7) Those notices are-
   (a) a notice stating that the chief constable is unable to confirm the existence of the conviction or that the conviction does not relate to a relevant offence or foreign offence, or
   (b) a notice confirming the existence of the conviction and that it relates to a relevant offence or foreign offence.

(8) Where the chief constable-
   (a) proposes to give a notice under subsection (7)(b), and
   (b) considers that, having regard to the conviction specified in the notice, it is necessary for the purposes of the crime prevention objective that the application be refused,

the chief constable may include in the notice a recommendation to that effect.

(9) On receipt of the chief constable's notice under subsection (7), the Licensing Board must resume consideration of the application and determine it in accordance with section 23.

(10) For that purpose, that section has effect as if-
   (a) references in it to a notice under section 21(4)(b) included references to a notice under subsection (7)(b) of this section, and
   (b) references in it to a recommendation under section 21(5) included references to a recommendation under subsection (8) of this section.

(11) A person who, without reasonable excuse, fails to comply with subsection (3) commits an offence.

(12) A person guilty of an offence under subsection (11) is liable on summary conviction to a fine not exceeding level 2 on the standard scale.

DEFINITIONS
"relevant offence": see s.129(1) of this Act
"foreign offence": see s.129(2) of this Act
"premises licence application": see s.20(3) of this Act
"applicant": see s.147(1) of this Act
"council": see s.147(1) of this Act
"connected person": see s.147(3) of this Act
"appropriate chief constable": see s.147(1) of this Act
"crime prevention objective": see s.4(2) of this Act

GENERAL NOTE

This section takes account of the possibility that an applicant or a connected person is convicted or a relevant or foreign offence prior to the determination of a premises licence application. The applicant is required to give the licensing board notice of the conviction no later than one month of its date. Failure to do so without reasonable excuse is an offence. Where a notice is received, consideration of the application must be suspended and the board must inform the chief constable of the conviction. The chief constable is then under an obligation to give the board one of two notices: (1) a notice stating that he is unable to confirm the existence of the conviction or that the conviction does not relate to a relevant or foreign offence; or (2) a notice confirming the existence of the conviction and that it relates to such an offence. If the latter notice is given, he may recommend refusal of the application for the purposes of the crime prevention objective.

Upon receipt of a notice from the chief constable, the board must resume consideration of the application and determine it in accordance with s.23

25. Further application after refusal of premises licence application

(1) Subsection (2) applies where a Licensing Board has refused a premises licence application in respect of any premises (such a refusal being referred to in this section as the "earlier refusal").

(2) Subject to subsection (3), the Board must refuse any subsequent premises licence application in respect of the same premises made before the expiry of the period of one year beginning with the date of the earlier refusal.

(3) Subsection (2) does not apply in relation to any subsequent application made during that period if-
   (a) at the time of the earlier refusal, the Board directed that the subsection would not apply to any subsequent application, or
   (b) the Board is satisfied that there has been a material change of circumstances since the earlier refusal.

DEFINITIONS

"premises licence application": see s.20(3) of this Act
"premises": see s.147(1) of this Act
"earlier refusal": see subs.(1)

GENERAL NOTE

This section derives from s.14 of the 1976 Act which prohibits re-application for a new licence in respect of the same premises within two years of a refusal unless the board directed otherwise at the time of refusal; and s.64(9) which prevents re-application for an extension of hours within one year subject to a contrary direction. The rationale of this provisions is to protect objectors from the necessity of having to renew their objections with these periods. Nicholson considered that the provisions of s.14 were "unduly restrictive" and the substitution of one year reflects the Committee's recommendation (Report, para.14.18).

Subsection (2)

Whether a subsequent application is for the "same premises" is a matter for the board, rather than the clerk, to consider: *Kelvinside Community Council v Glasgow District Licensing Board*,1990 S.L.T. 726.

Subsection (3)

The one-year prohibition on re-application for a premises licence following a refusal may be waived by the licensing board by means of a direction at the time of refusal. A further application may also be considered within the one-year period if the board is satisfied that there has been a material change in circumstances.

26. Issue of licence and summary

(1) Where a Licensing Board grants a premises licence application, the Board must issue to the applicant-
   (a) a premises licence-
      (i) in the prescribed form, and
      (ii) containing the information and documents specified in subsection (2), and
   (b) a summary of the licence in the prescribed form.
(2) The information and documents referred to in subsection (1)(a)(ii) are-
   (a) the name and address of-
      (i) the holder of the licence, and
      (ii) the premises manager in respect of the premises to which the licence relates,
   (b) a description of the premises in respect of which the licence is issued,
   (c) the date on which the licence takes effect,
   (d) the conditions to which the licence is subject, or, in relation to any such condition, a reference to another document in which details of the condition can be found,
   (e) the operating plan and layout plan in respect of the premises to which the licence relates, and
   (f) such other information as may be prescribed.

DEFINITIONS
"premises licence application": see s.20(3) of this Act
"applicant": see s.147(1) of this Act
"premises licence": see s.17 of this Act
"prescribed": see s.147(1) of this Act
"premises manager": see s.19(1) of this Act
"operating plan": see s.20(4) of this Act

GENERAL NOTE
Following the grant of a premises licence application, the board must issue to the applicant a premises licence (the form of which will be prescribed) containing specified information and documents, as well as a summary of the licence in a prescribed form.

Conditions of premises licence

27. Conditions of premises licence

(1) Except to the extent that schedule 3 provides otherwise, every premises licence is subject to the conditions specified in that schedule.
(2) The Scottish Ministers may by regulations modify schedule 3 so as-
   (a) to add such further conditions as they consider necessary or expedient for the purposes of any of the licensing objectives, or
   (b) to extend the application of any condition specified in the schedule.
(3) The Scottish Ministers must by regulations prescribe further conditions which Licensing Boards must impose on the granting by them of premises licences falling within subsection (4).

(4) A premises licence falls within this subsection if the operating plan for the premises to which the licence relates specifies that the premises will, on any occasion, be open for a continuous period beginning on one day and ending after 1am on the following day.

(5) The Scottish Ministers may by regulations prescribe further conditions as conditions which Licensing Boards may, at their discretion, impose on the granting by them of premises licences.

(6) Without prejudice to subsection (5), where a Licensing Board grants a premises licence, the Board may impose such other conditions (in addition to those to which the licence is subject by virtue of subsection (1) or (3)) as they consider necessary or expedient for the purposes of any of the licensing objectives.

(7) A Licensing Board may not impose a condition under subsection (6) which-
  (a) is inconsistent with any condition-
    (i) to which the premises licence is subject by virtue of subsection (1), or
    (ii) prescribed under subsection (5),
  (b) would have the effect of making any such condition more onerous or more restrictive, or
  (c) relates to a matter (such as planning, building control or food hygiene) which is regulated under another enactment.

(8) The conditions which may be-
  (a) added under subsection (2)(a),
  (b) prescribed under subsection (5), or
  (c) imposed under subsection (6),

include, in particular, conditions of the kind described in subsection (9).

(9) Those are conditions requiring anything to be done, or prohibiting or restricting the doing of anything, in connection with-
  (a) the sale of alcohol on the premises in respect of which a premises licence has effect, or
  (b) any other activity carried on in such premises.

(10) Where, under any provision of this Act, a Licensing Board has power to make a variation of the conditions to which a premises licence is subject, the power may not be exercised so as to have the effect of imposing a condition which the Board could not have imposed under this section on the granting of the licence.

DEFINITIONS

"premises licence": see s.17 of this Act
"licensing objectives": see s.4(1) of this Act
"operating plan": see s.20(4) of this Act
"prescribe": see s.147(1) of this Act

GENERAL NOTE

All premises licences must be subject to the mandatory conditions set out in Sch.3 ("national conditions"). Mandatory conditions will also be prescribed in relation to premises operating after 1 am ("late-opening conditions").

Otherwise, licensing boards will have a discretion to attach conditions, either drawing from those prescribed by Scottish Ministers ("pool conditions") or by devising their own conditions ("local conditions") for the purposes of any of the licensing objectives.

Local conditions must not be inconsistent with pool conditions, nor with national conditions. They must not have the effect of making any of the pool conditions or national conditions more onerous or more restrictive, nor may they relate to a matter regulated by another enactment.

Subsection (1)

All premises licences must be subject to a set of national conditions intended to achieve consistency in relation to matters such as the irresponsible promotion of alcohol: see notes to Sch.3.

Subsection (2)

In order to meet changing trends, Scottish Ministers may add to the national conditions or extend their application. The Executive's memorandum to the Subordinate Legislation Committee noted "it was very likely, as new practices develop within the licensed trade or as new public order issues arise" there may be a need to prescribe additional conditions.

Subsections (3), (4)

These provisions require Scottish Ministers to prescribe late-opening conditions which must be imposed by a licensing board when granting a premises licence which authorises trading for a continuous period beginning on one day and ending after 1 am on the following day.

They were added at Stage 3 of the Bill in order to accommodate concerns that heavily-invested entertainment premises, deriving most of their revenue from late-night trading, could face competition from premises which had operated under public house licences, producing a downward pressure on alcohol prices. The proponent of this measure, Pauline McNeill MSP, considered that late-opening premises should be prepared to invest in measures relating to public safety and violence reduction (Official Report, col.20707).

The Executive supported the late-opening conditions on the basis that they would be "appropriate and proportionate" and "meet the needs of public safety and tackling crime". They are likely to include a requirement to provide closed circuit television and stewards with first-aid training.

Subsection (5)

Scottish Ministers may prescribe further pool conditions which may be imposed on premises licences at the discretion of the licensing board.

The Policy Memorandum (page 20) indicates it is likely that these conditions will:

1. give licensing boards the power to require separate alcohol displays where alcohol is sold for consumption off the premises where such a step would be appropriate (although, in the case of small corner shops, this would be a "voluntary condition");
2. provide for the regulation of adult entertainment by requiring closed circuit television, the display of rules of behaviour for customers and staff and the provision of showering and changing facilities;
3. require the provision of baby-changing facilities accessible to both sexes unless children under five are not to be admitted to the premises.

The Policy Document indicates that the last condition would be "mandatory", although it is referred to in that part of the document which deals with discretionary conditions.

Subsection (6)

Licensing boards may attach local conditions of their own devising to a premises licence as they consider necessary or expedient for the purposes of any of the licensing objectives. Since breach of a condition may lead to the review of a premises licence (ss.36(3), 37(3)), it ought to be clearly expressed and leave the applicant in no doubt as to the obligations imposed upon him: see *Spook Erection Ltd v City of Edinburgh District Council*, 1995 S.L.T. 107; *R v Hammersmith and Fulham London Borough Council ex parte Earls Court Ltd*, QBD, 15 July 1993, unreported. A condition may not be imposed for an ulterior purpose (see *Gerry Cottle's Circus Ltd v City of Edinburgh District Council*, 1990 S.L.T. 235); but in determining whether a condition is necessary to achieve a particular purpose boards enjoy "a broad range of discretion within which they can operate without fear of interference from the courts" (*Applegate Inns Ltd. v North Lanarkshire Licensing Board* [1997] 7 SLLP 10 at 17).

Subsection (7)

The local conditions which may be imposed under subs.(6) are subject to limitations. They may not be inconsistent with the national conditions set out in Sch.3 or the pool conditions which may be prescribed by virtue of subs.(5); nor may they make any such condition more onerous or more restrictive. For example, it would not be open to a licensing board to attach a condition requiring the price of alcohol to be maintained for a period longer than 72 hours (see Sch.3, para.7).

They may not relate to a matter such as planning, building control or food hygiene which is already regulated under another enactment, a provision is no doubt intended to prevent licensing boards from using the licensing system to pursue non-licensing objectives.

By way of examples:

- A condition should not conflict with or add to a requirement to cater for disabled persons under the Disability Discrimination Act 1995 or under building regulations.
- The DCMS Guidance relative to the analogous provisions of the 2003 Act explains that:

"[I]f other existing law already places certain statutory responsibilities on an employer or operator of premises, it cannot be necessary to impose the same or similar duties on the premises licence holder or club. For example, employers or self-employed persons are required by the Management of Health and Safety at Work Regulations 1999 (SI 1999/3242) to assess the risks to their workers and any others (for example, members of the public visiting the premises) who may be affected by their business so as to identify what measures are needed to avoid or control risks."

- In relation to passenger vessels (see s.126), the safety regime is enforced by the (UK) Maritime and Coastguard Agency who operate a passenger ship certification scheme.

The subsection appears to suffer from a *lacuna*. It does not place any limitations on the imposition of local conditions which would be in conflict with late-opening conditions attached by virtue of subs.(3) or which would make the performance of such a condition more onerous or more restrictive. The terms of subs.(3) may conceivably allow Ministers to overcome this oversight by prescribing conditions which not only must be imposed but which cannot be added to, or derogated from, by virtue of the powers conferred on licensing boards by subs.(6).

Subsections (8), (9)
Any conditions added to the national conditions, the pool conditions and local conditions include conditions relating not only to the sale of alcohol but any other activity carried on in the premises.

Subsection (10)
The variation of conditions attached to a premises licence may not result in the imposition of a condition which could not have been imposed under this section.

Duration of premises licence

28. Period of effect of premises licence

(1) A premises licence-
  (a) takes effect on such date as the Licensing Board issuing it may determine, and
  (b) ceases to have effect on the occurrence of any of the events mentioned in subsection (5).
(2) However, a premises licence is not to be taken to have ceased to have effect under subsection (1)(b) by virtue of the occurrence of any of the events mentioned in paragraphs (c) to (e) of subsection (5) if, within 28 days of the occurrence of the event, an application for the transfer of the licence is made under section 34(1).
(3) If such an application is made but refused, the premises licence ceases to have effect on the refusal.

(4) A premises licence does not have effect for any period during which it is suspended by virtue of any provision of this Act.
(5) The events referred to in subsection (1)(b) are-
   (a) the premises licence is revoked under any provision of this Act,
   (b) the licensed premises in respect of which the licence was issued cease to be used for the sale of alcohol,
   (c) the premises licence holder, being an individual-
      (i) dies, or
      (ii) becomes incapable within the meaning of section 1(6) of the Adults with Incapacity (Scotland) Act 2000 (asp 4),
   (d) the premises licence holder, being an individual, a partnership or a company, becomes insolvent,
   (e) the premises licence holder, being a person other than an individual, a partnership or a company, is dissolved, and
   (f) the appropriate Licensing Board receives from the premises licence holder a notice under subsection (6).
(6) That is a notice-
   (a) accompanied by the premises licence, or where that is not practicable, by a statement of reasons for failure to produce the licence, and
   (b) stating that the licence holder wishes to surrender the licence.
(7) For the purposes of subsection (5)(d)-
   (a) an individual or partnership becomes insolvent on-
      (i) the approval of a voluntary arrangement proposed by the individual or partnership,
      (ii) being adjudged bankrupt,
      (iii) the individual's or partnership's estate being sequestrated,
      (iv) entering into a deed of arrangement made for the benefit of creditors, or
      (v) granting a trust deed for creditors, and
   (b) a company becomes insolvent on-
      (i) the approval of a voluntary arrangement proposed by its creditors,
      (ii) the appointment of an administrator or administrative receiver in respect of it, or
      (iii) going into liquidation.
(8) An expression used in subsection (7) which is also used in the Bankruptcy (Scotland) Act 1985 (c.66) or the Insolvency Act 1986 (c.45) has the same meaning in that subsection as it has in that Act.

DEFINITIONS
"premises licence": see s.17 of this Act
"licensed premises": see s.147(1) of this Act
"alcohol": see s.2 of this Act

GENERAL NOTE
Licences granted under the 1976 Act have a currency of three years. Premises licences will not require renewal and continue in effect indefinitely, save in certain circumstances as set out in subs.(5).
They will be capable of being surrendered on the giving of notice to the licensing board. No provision is made for surrender in the 1976 Act and the practice is well-established; but it has given rise to difficulty where a landlord's interests were prejudiced: *London and Edinburgh Inns Ltd v North Ayrshire Licensing Board*, 2004 S.L.T. 848; [2004] 29 SLLP 30.
Where the premises licence holder dies; or becomes incapable or insolvent; or is dissolved, the licence will not cease to have effect provided that an application for transfer is made under

s.34(1) within 28 days of such an occurrence. However, if a transfer application is refused, the licence immediately ceases to have effect.

Variation of premises licence

29. Application to vary premises licence

(1) A premises licence holder may apply to the appropriate Licensing Board for a variation of the licence.

(2) An application under subsection (1) must be accompanied by-
   (a) the premises licence to which the application relates, or
   (b) if that is not practicable, a statement of the reasons for failure to produce the licence.

(3) An application under subsection (1) which complies with subsection (2) is referred to in this Act as a "premises licence variation application".

(4) Sections 21(1) and (2) and 22 apply in relation to a premises licence variation application (other than one in which the only variation sought is a minor variation) as they apply to a premises licence application.

(5) In this Act, "variation", in relation to a premises licence, means any variation of-
   (a) any of the conditions to which the licence is subject (other than those to which the licence is subject by virtue of section 27(1)),
   (b) any of the information contained in the operating plan contained in the licence,
   (c) the layout plan contained in the licence, or
   (d) any other information contained or referred to in the licence,
and includes an addition, deletion or other modification.

(6) In this Act, "minor variation" means-
   (a) any variation of the layout plan, if the variation does not result in any inconsistency with the operating plan,
   (b) where, under the operating plan contained in the licence, children or young persons are allowed entry to the premises, any variation reflecting any restriction or proposed restriction of the terms on which they are allowed entry to the premises,
   (c) any variation of the information contained in the licence relating to the premises manager (including a variation so as to substitute a new premises manager), and
   (d) any other variation of such description as may be prescribed for the purposes of this subsection.

DEFINITIONS
   "variation": see subs.(5)
   "premises licence": see s.17 of this Act
   "premises licence variation application": see subs.(3)
   "operating plan": see s.20(4) of this Act
   "layout plan": see s.20(2)(b)(ii) of this Act
   "minor variation": see subs.(6)
   "children": see s.147(1) of this Act
   "young persons": see s.147(1) of this Act
   "premises manager": see s.19(1) of this Act

GENERAL NOTE

This section provides for a variation of a premises licence, which may require a hearing (see s.30) unless the variation is "minor". The hearing must take place at a meeting of the board: s.133(1); Sch.1, para.10(2)(d).

Licences granted under the 1976 Act are not capable of being varied, except that the licensing board is empowered to consent to alterations to premises which are not considered "material" (1976 Act, s.35). For example, if an entertainment licence is subject to conditions attached by virtue of s.101(2) prescribing the forms of entertainment which may be offered on the premises, any additional form of entertainment will require an application for a new licence. Such a course would also require to be followed if the licence holder wished to be free from a condition imposed under s.29, which prevents the sale of spirits.

Subsection (2)

A variation application must be accompanied by the premises licence or a statement of the reasons for the failure to produce the licence. Where a premises licence application is granted, the licensing board must make any necessary amendments (s.49(1), (2)). If the board is not in possession of the licence, it may require its production within 14 days; and a licence holder who, without reasonable excuse, fails to comply with that requirement commits an offence (s.49(3), (4)). Application may, however, be made for a replacement licence in certain circumstances (s.53). It may be thought that these provisions, of a type to be found in the 2003 Act, are unnecessarily cumbersome.

Subsection (4)

Sections 21(1), (2) and s.22 apply to variation applications, except where the application is for a minor variation. In the result, the licensing board is obliged to give notice of the application to certain persons and bodies, as it would in the case of an application for a premises licence; and the variation application is opened up to the full procedure for objections and representations. In effect, an application to vary a premises licence, except in the case of a minor variation, takes on the characteristics of an application for a new premises licence and, to that extent at least, confers little advantage over the scheme of the 1976 Act.

Subsection (5)

A variation is required where it is proposed to modify, delete or amend any of the conditions to which the licence is subject; any of the information contained in the operating plan; or any other information contained or referred to in the licence. A variation is also necessary to alter the layout plan of the premises.

A "national condition" (s.27(1), Sch.3.) may not be varied; but, subject to s.27(10), it is possible to vary a "pool condition" (s.27(5)) or a "local condition" (s.26(6)). It seems that there is nothing to prevent the variation of a "late-opening condition" (s.27(3)), although such a condition *must* be imposed on the granting of a premises licence where the premises will operate after 1 am.

Subsection (6)

A variation will be considered "minor" (and therefore must be granted: see s.30(1)) where the variation:

1 would alter the layout plan and not result in any inconsistency with the operating plan;
2 relates to a restriction on the terms on which children or young persons are allowed entry to the premises;
3 concerns the information contained in the licence relating to the premises manager; or
4 is for the substitution of a new premises manager.

Variations of other descriptions may be prescribed by Scottish Ministers.

An inconsistency with the operating plan would result where, for example, it was intended to create a dance floor, although the operating plan did not provide for dancing with the premises.

In relation to variations of type (2), the subsection refers to "any variation reflecting any restriction or proposed restriction" of the terms on which children or young persons are allowed entry. The word "reflecting" is perhaps not happily chosen; but subs.(6)(b) appears intended to ensure that only limitations on children's or young persons' access may be the subject of a minor variation application.

30. Determination of application for variation

(1) A premises licence variation application received by a Licensing Board is to be determined by the Board in accordance with this section.
(2) If the variation sought is a minor variation, the Board must grant the application.
(3) In any other case, the Licensing Board must hold a hearing for the purpose of considering and determining the application.
(4) Where a hearing is held under subsection (3), the Board must consider whether any of the grounds for refusal applies and-
   (a) if none of them applies, the Board must grant the application,
   (b) if any of them applies, the Board must refuse the application.
(5) The grounds for refusal are-
   (a) that the application must be refused under section 32(2), 64(2) or 65(3),
   (b) that the Licensing Board considers that the granting of the application would be inconsistent with one or more of the licensing objectives,
   (c) that, having regard to-
      (i) the nature of the activities carried on or proposed to be carried on in the subject premises,
      (ii) the location, character and condition of the premises, and
      (iii) the persons likely to frequent the premises,
   the Board considers that the premises are unsuitable for use for the sale of alcohol in accordance with the proposed variation,
   (d) that, having regard to the number and capacity of-
      (i) licensed premises, or
      (ii) licensed premises of the same or similar description as the subject premises (taking account of the proposed variation),
   in the locality in which the subject premises are situated, the Board considers that, if the application were to be granted, there would, as a result, be overprovision of licensed premises, or licensed premises of that description, in the locality.
(6) Where the Licensing Board grants the application, the Board may make a variation of the conditions to which the licence is subject.
(7) Where the Licensing Board refuses the application-
   (a) the Board must specify the ground for refusal, and
   (b) if the ground for refusal is that specified in subsection (5)(b), the Board must specify the licensing objective or objectives in question.
(8) In subsection (5)(d), references to "licensed premises" do not include references to licensed premises in respect of which an occasional licence has effect.

DEFINITIONS
  "premises licence variation application": see s.29(3) of this Act
  "variation": see s.29(5) of this Act
  "minor variation": see s.29(6) of this Act
  "licensing objectives": see s.4(1) of this Act

"alcohol": see s.2 of this Act
"capacity": see s.147(1) of this Act
"licensed premises": see s.147(1) of this Act
"occasional licence": see s.56(1) of this Act

GENERAL NOTE

Where an application is made for a minor variation (see 29(6)), it must be granted. Otherwise, a variation application requires to be determined at a hearing and is subject to grounds for refusal which largely mirror those contained in s.23(5) in relation to premises licence applications. The board must take into account objections or representations (s.22(3), as applied by s.29(4)). If no ground for refusal applies, the application must be granted.

The licensing board has no power to adjust the applicant's proposals so that the variation is capable of being granted: cf s.27(7).

Subsection (5)

In terms of s.35(2), the refusal of a premises licence application prevents a further application seeking the same variation in respect of the same premises being granted within the ensuing year, unless the board has directed otherwise at the time of refusal or there has been a material change in circumstances. Section 64(2) requires the refusal of an application which would allow the sale of alcohol for a continuous period of 24 hours unless there are exceptional circumstances. A variation may not be granted if the sale of alcohol for consumption off the premises would be permitted before 10 pm, after 10 pm or both (s.65(3)).

In relation to the grounds for refusal set out in subs.5(b)-(d), see notes to s.23.

Subsection (6)

The purpose of this provision may not be immediately apparent. According to the Explanatory Notes, the subsection "provides a power for licensing boards to make their own additional variations to the licence conditions where it grants the variation applied for". If that is correct, it would be possible to accommodate a difficulty which would be caused by the grant of the variation sought. For example, if a licence holder wished to provide live musical entertainment and dancing, the licensing might accede to that request but vary the licence so as to prohibit the admission of children to the relevant part of the premises which would otherwise have been permitted in terms of the operating plan.

It appears that, in England and Wales, some licensing authorities have employed the analogous provisions of the 2003 Act (ss.34, 35) to carry out what is, in effect, a review of the licence, imposing conditions which are not in the least referable to the subject matter of the variation sought. Such a step is capable of being appealed (2003 Act, Sch.5, para.4); but no such provision is made here, although it may be arguable that the refusal of a board to grant a variation *de plano* is a "refusal" (*cf Wolfson v Glasgow District Licensing Board*, 1981 S.L.T. 136; and General Note to s.131).

The subsection may not, of course, be used to modify a mandatory condition contained in Sch.3 (see s.29(5)); and, by virtue of s.27(10), the variation could not have the effect of imposing a condition which the board could not have imposed on the granting of a premises licence.

31. Variation to substitute new premises manager

(1) This section applies in relation to a premises licence variation application where-
  (a) the variation sought is the substitution of another individual as the premises manager, and
  (b) the applicant requests in the application that the variation should have immediate effect.
(2) Where this section applies, the premises licence to which the application relates has effect during the application period as if it were varied as proposed in the application.
(3) In subsection (2), "the application period" means the period-

(a) beginning when the application is received by the Licensing Board, and
(b) ending-
   (i) when the variation takes effect, or
   (ii) if the application is withdrawn before it is determined, when it is withdrawn.

DEFINITIONS

"premises licence variation application": see s.29(3) of this Act
"variation": see s.29(5) of this Act
"premises manager": see s.19(1) of this Act
"applicant": see s.147(1) of this Act
"premises licence": see s.17 of this Act

GENERAL NOTE

Alcohol may not be sold in licensed premises where there is no premises manager: Sch.3, para.4(1). Section 54 provides a six-week "window" in which an application to substitute a new premises manager may be made. This section allows a new premises manager to take up his post at the premises pending the determination of a substitution application and, during that period, the premises licence is deemed to be varied as proposed.

32. Further application after refusal of application for variation

(1) Subsection (2) applies where a Licensing Board has refused a premises licence variation application (such a refusal being referred to in this section as the "earlier refusal").
(2) Subject to subsection (3), the Board must refuse any subsequent premises licence variation application-
   (a) in respect of the same premises licence, and
   (b) seeking the same variation,
made before the expiry of the period of one year beginning with the date of the earlier refusal.
(3) Subsection (2) does not apply in relation to any subsequent application made during that period if-
   (a) at the time of the earlier refusal, the Board directed that the subsection would not apply to any subsequent application, or
   (b) the Board is satisfied that there has been a material change of circumstances since the earlier refusal.

DEFINITIONS

"premises licence variation application": see s.29(3) of this Act
"earlier refusal": see subs.(1)
"premises licence": see s.17 of this Act
"variation": see s.29(5) of this Act

GENERAL NOTE

Echoing the terms of s.25, this section has the effect of preventing the variation of a premises licence where an application for the same variation has been refused within the preceding year, unless at the time of refusal the board directed otherwise, or there has been a material change in circumstances.

Licensing (Scotland) Act 2005

Transfer of premises licence

33. Transfer on application of licence holder

(1) A premises licence holder may apply to the appropriate Licensing Board for the transfer of the licence to such person as is specified in the application (such person being referred to in this section as the "transferee").

(2) The transferee may not be an individual under the age of 18.

(3) An application under subsection (1) must be accompanied by-
   (a) the premises licence to which the application relates, or
   (b) if that is not practicable, a statement of the reasons for failure to produce the licence.

(4) Where a Licensing Board receives an application under subsection (1), the Board must give notice of it, together with a copy of the application, to the appropriate chief constable.

(5) The appropriate chief constable must, within 21 days of the date of receipt of a notice under subsection (4), respond to the notice by giving the Licensing Board one or other of the notices mentioned in subsection (6).

(6) Those notices are-
   (a) a notice stating that neither-
      (i) the transferee, nor
      (ii) where the transferee is neither an individual nor a council, any connected person,
   has been convicted of any relevant offence or foreign offence, or
   (b) a notice specifying any convictions of-
      (i) the transferee, and
      (ii) where the transferee is neither an individual nor a council, any connected person,
   for a relevant offence or a foreign offence.

(7) Where the appropriate chief constable-
   (a) proposes to give a notice under subsection (6)(b), and
   (b) considers that, having regard to any conviction to be specified in the notice, it is necessary for the purposes of the crime prevention objective that the application for transfer of the licence to the transferee be refused,
the chief constable may include in the notice a recommendation to that effect.

(8) Where the Licensing Board receives a notice under subsection (6)(a) in relation to an application under subsection (1), the Board must grant the application.

(9) Where the Licensing Board receives a notice under subsection (6)(b) in relation to an application under subsection (1), the Board must hold a hearing for the purpose of considering and determining the application.

(10) Where a hearing is held under subsection (9), the Licensing Board must, having regard to the chief constable's notice-
   (a) if satisfied that it is necessary to do so for the purposes of the crime prevention objective, refuse the application, or
   (b) if not so satisfied, grant the application.

DEFINITIONS
"premise licence": see s.17 of this Act
"transferee": see subs.(1)
"appropriate chief constable": see s.147(1) of this Act
"council": see s.147(1) of this Act
"connected person": see s.147(3) of this Act
"relevant offence": see s.129(1) of this Act
"foreign offence": see s.129(2) of this Act
"crime prevention objective": see s.4(2) of this Act

GENERAL NOTE
This section makes provision for the transfer of a premises licence at the instance of the premises licence holder. Under the current system, transfer applications are made by the proposed transferee (1976 Act, s.25): see s.34 for circumstances in which a person other than the licence holder may apply under this Act.

In terms similar to those contained in s.21, provision is made for the intimation by the chief constable of any convictions for a relevant or foreign offence incurred by the proposed transferee or "any connected person". Where the board has received notice from the chief constable that neither the proposed transferee or any connected person has incurred such a conviction, the application must be granted. Otherwise, the transfer application must be the subject of a hearing, at which the board must grant the application unless it is satisfied that it must be refused for the purposes of the crime prevention objective. The hearing must take place at a meeting of the board: s.133(1); Sch.1, para.10(2)(e).

Convictions which are "spent" in terms of the Rehabilitation of Offenders Act 1974 must be disregarded: see s.129(4).

No provision is made for objections, even where the chief constable has reason to believe that the proposed transferee is involved in serious organised crime (cf s.22(2)).

The board may not carry out an overall assessment of the proposed transferee's suitability to hold a licence. The "fit and proper person" test contained in the 1976 Act has been abandoned: see notes to s.22.

34. Transfer on application of person other than licence holder

(1) A person other than-
   (a) the holder of a premises licence, or
   (b) an individual under the age of 18,
(being a person of a prescribed description) may, within 28 days of the occurrence of any of the events specified in subsection (3), apply to the appropriate Licensing Board for the transfer to that person of the licence.

(2) An application under subsection (1) must be accompanied by-
   (a) the premises licence to which the application relates, or
   (b) if that is not practicable, a statement of the reasons for failure to produce the licence.

(3) The events referred to in subsection (1) are-
   (a) the premises licence holder, being an individual-
     (i) dies, or
     (ii) becomes incapable within the meaning of section 1(6) of the Adults with Incapacity (Scotland) Act 2000 (asp 4),
   (b) the premises licence holder, being an individual, a partnership or a company, becomes insolvent,
   (c) the premises licence holder, being a person other than an individual, a partnership or a company, is dissolved, and
   (d) the business carried on in the licensed premises to which the licence relates is transferred (whether by sale or otherwise) to another person.

(4) Subsections (4) to (10) of section 33 apply for the purposes of an application under subsection (1) of this section as they apply for the purposes of an application under subsection (1) of that section, but as if references in them to the transferee were references to the applicant in relation to the application under subsection (1) of this section.

(5) Subsections (7) and (8) of section 28 apply for the purposes of subsection (3)(b) of this section as they apply for the purposes of subsection (5)(d) of that section.

DEFINITIONS
"premises licence": see s.17 of this Act
"prescribed": see s.147(1) of this Act
"licensed premises": see s.147(1) of this Act
"applicant": see s.147(1) of this Act

GENERAL NOTE
Application for the transfer of a premises licence may be made by a person other the licence holder, provided that person is age 18 or over and is a person of a "prescribed description". According to the Scottish Executive's memorandum to the Subordinate Legislation Committee, regulations will set out the required nexus between the transfer applicant and the premises licence holder. For example, "where the licence holder has died, it is envisaged that it will be an executor who makes and application and where a business has been sold it is likely to be the purchaser". The details of the possible permutations "are likely to be intricate and complicated".

Subsection (1)
The application requires to be made within 28 days of the occurrence of the events specified in subs.(3), that is to say, where the licence holder has (a) died, (b) become incapable or insolvent or (c) has been dissolved and the business carried on in the licensed premises is to be transferred (by sale or otherwise) to another person. In terms of s.28, events (a)-(c) result in the premises licence ceasing to have effect unless a transfer application is made under this subsection.

35. Variation on transfer

(1) A person making an application to a Licensing Board under section 33(1) or 34(1) for transfer of a premises licence may also make an application to the Board for a variation of the licence.
(2) Sections 29 and 30 apply in relation to an application under subsection (1) for a variation as they apply to a premises licence variation application.
(3) Where-
  (a) an application is made under subsection (1), and
  (b) the applicant intimates to the Licensing Board that the application under section 33(1) or 34(1) for transfer of the premises licence is contingent on the grant of the application under subsection (1),
the Licensing Board must determine the application under subsection (1) before determining the application for the transfer of the licence.
(4) In such a case, if the Licensing Board refuses the application under subsection (1), the application for the transfer of the licence falls.
(5) In any other case where an application under subsection (1) is made-
  (a) the Licensing Board must first determine the application for transfer of the licence before determining the application under subsection (1), and
  (b) if the application for the transfer of the licence is refused, the application under subsection (1) falls.

DEFINITIONS
"premises licence": see s.17 of this Act
"variation": see s.29(5) of this Act
"premises licence variation application": see s.29(3) of this Act
"applicant": see s.147(1) of this Act

GENERAL NOTE
A person applying for the transfer of a premises licence may make contemporaneous application for a variation of the licence. A transfer will fall if the applicant informs the board that it is dependent upon the grant of the variation and the variation is refused. These provisions will be of assistance to applicants who do not wish to acquire premises under the current licensing arrangements.

Subsections (3), (4)
The transfer applicant may intimate to the licensing board that the variation sought is a precondition of the transfer. In that case, the board must first consider the variation application and, if it is refused, the transfer application falls.

Subsections (3), (4)
Where no intimation is given under subs.(3), the board will first determine the transfer application and, if it refused, the variation application will fall.

Review of premises licence

36. Application for review of premises licence

(1) Any person may apply to the appropriate Licensing Board in respect of any licensed premises in relation to which a premises licence has effect for a review of the licence on any of the grounds for review.

(2) An application under subsection (1) is referred to in this Act as a "premises licence review application".

(3) The grounds for review referred to in subsection (1) are-
   (a) that one or more of the conditions to which the premises licence is subject has been breached, or
   (b) any other ground relevant to one or more of the licensing objectives.

(4) A Licensing Standards Officer may make a premises licence review application on the ground specified in subsection (3)(a) only if-
   (a) in relation to the alleged ground for review, the Officer or any other Licensing Standards Officer has issued to the licence holder a notice under section 14(2)(a)(i), and
   (b) the licence holder has failed to take the action specified in the notice to the satisfaction of the Officer.

(5) A premises licence review application must specify the alleged ground for review, including in particular-
   (a) where the ground is that specified in subsection (3)(a), the condition or conditions alleged to have been breached,
   (b) where the ground is that specified in subsection (3)(b), the licensing objective or objectives to which the alleged ground of review relates.

(6) The Licensing Board may reject a premises licence review application if the Board considers the application-
   (a) is vexatious or frivolous, or
   (b) does not disclose any matter relevant to any ground for review.

(7) Where the Licensing Board rejects a premises licence review application under subsection (6), the Board-
- (a) must give notice of the decision, and the reasons for it, to the applicant, and
- (b) where it is rejected on the ground that it is frivolous or vexatious, may recover from the applicant any expenses incurred by the Board in considering the application.

(8) In any proceedings by a Licensing Board for the recovery of expenses under subsection (7)(b), a copy of any minute of proceedings of the Licensing Board-
- (a) recording the Board's rejection of the application and the grounds for rejection, and
- (b) certified by the clerk of the Board to be a true copy,

is sufficient evidence of the rejection and of the establishment of the grounds for rejection.

DEFINITIONS
"licensed premises": see s.147(1) of this Act
"premises licence review application": see subs.(2)
"premises licence": see s.17 of this Act
"licensing objectives": see s.4(1) of this Act
"applicant": see s.147(1) of this Act

GENERAL NOTE
The 1976 Act affords licensing boards very little control over licences during their currency. Nicholson considered that, as part of "a compliant licensing system", licensing boards should have power "to take appropriate action in cases where licensing terms and conditions are not being properly observed" (Report, para.7.2). This section provides for the review of a premises licence at the instance of "any person", including a licensing standards officer. Separate provision is made for a premises licence review where the holder is convicted of a relevant or foreign offence: see s.44.

Subsection (3)
A review may take place on the ground that one or more of the conditions attached to the premises licence has been breached (see s.27); or on any other ground relevant to one or more of the licensing objectives. Since the licensing objectives are framed in wide terms, the scope for review is extensive.

Subsection (4)
A licensing standards officer may only apply for a review on the ground that licence conditions have been breached if he has given notice requiring the breach to be remedied and the licence holder has not taken action to the satisfaction of the officer.

Nicholson considered that licensing standards officers should co-operate with licence holders in order to assist compliance with the terms and conditions attached to licences and report to the licensing board "any persistent or serious cases of non-compliance" (Report, para.39).

Subsections (6), (7)
A licensing board may reject a premises licence review application on the ground that it (a) is frivolous or vexatious or (b) does not disclose any relevant matter (subs.6), and, in either case, must give notice of its decision, and the reasons for it, to the applicant. (Where a licensing board has considered whether or not to hold a hearing following a complaint made under s.31 of the 1976 Act, which may lead to the suspension of the licence, it must inform the complainer of its decision, but need not provide reasons).

37. Review of premises licence on Licensing Board's initiative

(1) The appropriate Licensing Board in respect of any licensed premises in relation to which a premises licence has effect may, on their own initiative, propose to review the licence on any of the grounds for review.

(2) A proposal under subsection (1) is referred to in this Act as a "premises licence review proposal".

(3) The grounds for review referred to in subsection (1) are those specified in subsection 36(3).

(4) A premises licence review proposal must specify the alleged ground for review, including in particular-
  (a) where the ground is that specified in subsection 36(3)(a), the condition or conditions alleged to have been breached,
  (b) where the ground is that specified in subsection 36(3)(b), the licensing objective or objectives to which the alleged ground of review relates.

DEFINITIONS
"licensed premises": see s.147(1) of this Act
"premises licence review proposal": see subs.(2)

GENERAL NOTE
This section allows a licensing board to review a premises licence on their own initiative. The 1976 Act does not allow licensing boards to consider the possible imposition of sanctions *ex proprio motu*, except that they made order the closure of licensed premises in limited circumstances (1976 Act, s.32).

The grounds for review are the same as those available to third parties in terms of s.36(3).

38. Review hearing

(1) Where a Licensing Board-
  (a) makes a premises licence review proposal, or
  (b) receives a premises licence review application,
the Board must hold a hearing for the purposes of considering and determining the proposal or application unless, in the case of a premises licence review application, the Board has rejected the application under subsection 36(6).

(2) A hearing under subsection (1) is referred to in this Act as a "review hearing".

(3) Where a review hearing is to be held, the Licensing Board must-
  (a) in the case of a premises licence review application, give notice of the hearing to the applicant, and
  (b) give notice of the hearing and a copy of the premises licence review proposal or application to-
    (i) the licence holder, and
    (ii) any Licensing Standards Officer for the area in which the premises concerned are situated, unless, in the case of a premises licence review application, the applicant is such an Officer.

(4) Where a Licensing Standards Officer receives under subsection (3)(b)(ii) a copy of a premises licence review proposal or application-

(a) the Officer must, before the review hearing, prepare and submit to the Licensing Board a report on the proposal or application, and
(b) the Licensing Board must take the report into account at the hearing.

(5) The Licensing Board may, for the purposes of the review hearing-
(a) obtain further information from such persons, and in such manner, as the Board thinks fit, and
(b) take the information into account.

(6) In particular, the Board may-
(a) request-
(i) the attendance at the review hearing of any person for the purpose of providing information, and
(ii) the production at the review hearing by any person of any documents in that person's possession or under that person's control, and
(b) take into account any information relevant to any ground for review even though it is not relevant to any circumstances alleged in the review proposal or application under consideration.

DEFINITIONS
"premises licence review proposal": see s.37(2) of this Act
"premises licence review application": see s.36(2) of this Act
"review hearing": see subs.(2)
"applicant": see s.147(1) of this Act

GENERAL NOTE
A premises licence review proposal or a premises licence review application must be considered at a hearing of the board (s.133(1), Sch.1, para.10(2)(g)), unless the latter has been rejected because it is frivolous or vexatious or does not disclose any relevant matter. The board has extensive powers to obtain further information as it sees fit.

Subsection (3)
Notice of the hearing requires to be given to (a) the applicant, (b) the licence holder and (c) any licensing standards officer for the area (unless the review is to take place at the instance of such an officer). The licence holder and licensing standards officer must also be provided with a copy of the review application or proposal.

Subsection (4)
A licensing standards officer who receives a copy of the application or proposal must, before the hearing, provide the licensing board with a report, which the board must take into account at the hearing.

Subsection (5)
The licensing board is afforded a wide power to obtain further information from such persons, and in such manner, as it sees fit and to take that information into account.

Subsection (6)
In addition to the powers afforded by subs.(5), the board may request (but not compel) the attendance of any person at the hearing for the purpose of providing information and the production of any documents in that person's possession or within their control. Any information obtained by the board may be taken into account even if it does not relate to the circumstances set out in the review proposal or application, so long as it is relevant to one of the grounds for review. The board is thus empowered to carry out a very wide enquiry.

39. Licensing Board's powers on review

(1) At a review hearing in relation to any premises licence, the Licensing Board may, if satisfied that a ground for review is established (whether or not on the basis of any circumstances alleged in the premises licence review proposal or application considered at the hearing) take such of the steps mentioned in subsection (2) as the Board considers necessary or appropriate for the purposes of any of the licensing objectives.

(2) Those steps are-
   (a) to issue a written warning to the licence holder,
   (b) to make a variation of the licence,
   (c) to suspend the licence for such period as the Board may determine,
   (d) to revoke the licence.

(3) On making a variation under subsection (2)(b), the Board may provide for the variation to apply only for such period as they may determine.

DEFINITIONS
"premises licence": see s.17 of this Act
"premises licence review proposal": see s.37(2) of this Act
"premises licence review application": see s.36(2) of this Act
"licensing objectives": see s.4(1) of this Act
"variation": see s.29(5) of this Act

GENERAL NOTE
Licensing boards are afforded a number of options where a ground for review has been established. Nicholson noted that, under the existing law, only a limited number of sanctions are available; and while a licence could be suspended, no provision was made for less serious cases. This section reflects the suggestion made by a number of the Committee's consultees, which was adopted in the Report, that there should be a range of sanctions allowing licensing boards "to mark transgressions of all kinds by the imposition of a penalty or sanction which was commensurate with the seriousness of a particular default" (Report, para.7.10).

Where a licensing board has refused to renew or has suspended a licence under the 1976 Act, there is nothing to prevent the licence holder continuing to trade on the dependency of an appeal. In terms of s.132(7) of this Act, a sanction will come into effect immediately, except that a decision to suspend or revoke a licence may be set aside *pro tem* by the sheriff principal (s.132(8)).

Provision is made in s.84 for a hearing where, in the course of a review hearing, a licensing board makes a finding that a personal licence holder working at the premises "acted in a manner which was inconsistent with any of the licensing objectives".

Subsection (1)
The licensing board may find a ground for review established on the basis of material beyond that set out in the premises licence review application or proposal, no doubt on the basis of information obtained by virtue of the provisions of s.38(6). Where a ground is established the board may take such of the steps set out in subs.(2) for the purpose of any of the licensing objectives.

Subsection (2)
This subsection sets out the available sanctions in ascending order of severity. The variation of a licence could, for example, provide for a reduction in trading hours.

40. Review of Licensing Board's decision to vary or suspend licence

Where a Licensing Board has made a variation under subsection (2)(b) of section 39 or suspended the licence under subsection (2)(c) of that section, the Board may-
- (a) on the application of the licence holder, and
- (b) if satisfied that, by reason of a change of circumstances, the variation or suspension is no longer necessary,

revoke the variation or suspension.

DEFINITIONS
"variation": see s.29(5) of this Act

GENERAL NOTE
Where a licence has been varied or suspended, the licensing board may revoke the variation or suspension on the application of the licence holder if it is satisfied that such a course is justified by reason of a change of circumstances. This provision could, for example, be used by a new licence holder who was able to satisfy the licensing board that the difficulties experienced in relation to the premises were attributable to the faults of his predecessor.

Conviction of licence holder etc. for relevant or foreign offence

41. Duty to notify court of premises licence

(1) Subsection (2) applies where-
- (a) a person who holds a premises licence is charged with a relevant offence, or
- (b) a person charged with a relevant offence is granted a premises licence after the person's first appearance in court in connection with the offence but before-
  - (i) conviction and sentencing for the offence or acquittal, or
  - (ii) where an appeal is brought against conviction, sentence or acquittal, the disposal of the appeal.

(2) The person must, not later than the person's first appearance or, as the case may be, next appearance in court in connection with the offence-
- (a) produce to the court the premises licence, or
- (b) if that is not practicable, notify the court of-
  - (i) the existence of the premises licence,
  - (ii) the identity of the Licensing Board which issued it, and
  - (iii) the reasons why it is not practicable to produce the licence.

(3) A person who, without reasonable excuse, fails to comply with subsection (2) commits an offence.

(4) A person guilty of an offence under subsection (3) is liable on summary conviction to a fine not exceeding level 2 on the standard scale.

DEFINITIONS
"premises licence": see s.17 of this Act
"relevant offence": see s.129(1) of this Act

GENERAL NOTE
Where a premises licence holder is charged with a relevant offence he must produce his premises licence to the court or provide the court with the information set out in subs.(2). A similar

obligation falls upon a person who obtains a personal licence during the currency of criminal proceedings, up to and including the disposal of an appeal.

The purpose of this provision is to alert the court to the obligation imposed upon the clerk in terms of s.42.

42. Court's duty to notify Licensing Board of convictions

(1) This section applies where the clerk of a court in Scotland by or before which a person is convicted of a relevant offence is aware that the person holds a premises licence.

(2) The clerk of the court must, as soon as reasonably practicable after the conviction, give notice of the conviction to the Licensing Board which issued the premises licence held by the person convicted.

DEFINITIONS
"relevant offence": see s.129(1) of this Act
"premises licence": see s.17 of this Act

GENERAL NOTE
In terms of s.129 of the 1976 Act, the clerk of the court is required to transmit a certified extract of a conviction for a licensing offence to the licensing board's clerk with six days of the date of conviction. This section requires the clerk of the court to give notice of a conviction for a relevant offence to the board's clerk as soon as reasonably practicable, where the clerk of the court is aware that the person convicted is the holder of a premises licence.

43. Licence holder's duty to notify Licensing Board of convictions

(1) This section applies where any of the persons specified in subsection (2) is convicted of a relevant or foreign offence.

(2) Those persons are-
   (a) the holder of a premises licence, and
   (b) where-
       (i) the holder of such a licence is neither an individual nor a council, or
       (ii) the premises in respect of which such a licence is held are used wholly or mainly for the purposes of a club,
   any connected person.

(3) The holder of the premises licence must, no later than one month after the date of the conviction, give notice of the conviction to the Licensing Board which issued the premises licence held by the licence holder.

(4) A notice of conviction under subsection (3) must-
   (a) specify-
       (i) the nature of the offence, and
       (ii) the date of conviction, and
   (b) be accompanied by-
       (i) the premises licence held by the licence holder, or
       (ii) if that is not practicable, a statement of the reasons for failure to produce the licence.

(5) A premises licence holder who fails, without reasonable excuse, to comply with subsection (3) commits an offence.

(6) A person guilty of an offence under subsection (5) is liable on summary conviction to a fine not exceeding level 4 on the standard scale.

DEFINITIONS
"relevant offence": see s.129(1) of this Act
"foreign offence": see s.129(2) of this Act
"premises licence": see s.17 of this Act
"council": see s.147(1) of this Act
"connected person": see s.147(3) of this Act

GENERAL NOTE
Where the holder of a premises licence or any connected person is convicted of a relevant or foreign offence, the licence holder must, no later than one month after the date of the conviction, give notice of the conviction to the licensing board. The notice must specify the nature of the offence and the date of conviction and be accompanied by the premises licence or a statement of the reasons as to why the licence has not been produced.

44. Procedure where Licensing Board receives notice of conviction

(1) This section applies where the Licensing Board which issued a premises licence receives a notice of conviction relating to-
   (a) the holder of the licence, or
   (b) where-
      (i) the holder of the licence is neither an individual nor a council, or
      (ii) the premises in respect of which the licence is held are used wholly or mainly for the purposes of a club,
   a connected person.
(2) The Licensing Board must give notice of the conviction to the appropriate chief constable.
(3) The appropriate chief constable must, within 21 days of the date of receipt of a notice under subsection (2), respond to the notice by giving the Licensing Board one or other of the notices mentioned in subsection (4).
(4) Those notices are-
   (a) a notice stating that the chief constable is unable to confirm the existence of the conviction or that the conviction does not relate to a relevant or foreign offence, or
   (b) a notice confirming the existence of the conviction and that it relates to a relevant or foreign offence.
(5) Where the chief constable-
   (a) proposes to give a notice under subsection (4)(b), and
   (b) considers that, having regard to the conviction specified in the notice, it is necessary for the purposes of the crime prevention objective that the premises licence should be varied, suspended or revoked,
the chief constable may include in the notice a recommendation to that effect.
(6) If the Licensing Board receives from the appropriate chief constable a notice under subsection (4)(a), the Licensing Board may not take any further action in relation to the conviction.

(7) If the Licensing Board receives from the appropriate chief constable a notice under subsection (4)(b), the Licensing Board must make a premises licence review proposal in respect of the premises licence.

(8) In this section, "notice of conviction" means a notice under section 42(2) or 43(3).

DEFINITIONS
"premises licence": see s.17 of this Act
"notice of conviction": see subs.(8)
"council": see s.147(1) of this Act
"connected person": see s.147(3) of this Act
"appropriate chief constable": see s.147(1) of this Act
"relevant offence": see s.129(1) of this Act
"foreign offence": see s.129(2) of this Act
"crime prevention objective": see s.4(2) of this Act
"variation": see s.29(5) of this Act
"premises licence review proposal": see s.37(2) of this Act
"notice of conviction": see subs.(8)

GENERAL NOTE

This section applies where the licensing board has received notice of a conviction either from the clerk of court (s.42) or from the holder of a premises licence (s.43). The board must proceed to give notice of the conviction to the chief constable, who is then required to give the licensing board one of two notices within 21 days, either confirming or otherwise that the conviction exists and, if so, that it relates to a relevant or foreign offence.

A notice in the affirmative may be conjoined with the chief constable's recommendation that the licence should be varied, suspended or revoked for the purpose of the crime prevention objection; and, whether or not such a recommendation is made, the board must make a premises licence review proposal.

If the notice is in the negative, no further action may be taken.

Premises under construction or conversion

45. Provisional premises licence

(1) A premises licence application may be made in relation to any premises despite the fact that, at the time the application is made, the premises are yet to be, or are in the course of being, constructed or converted for use as licensed premises.

(2) A premises licence application in respect of any such premises is referred to in this Act as a "provisional premises licence application".

(3) A premises licence issued in respect of any such premises does not take effect unless and until it is confirmed by the Licensing Board which issued it in accordance with section 46.

(4) If a premises licence issued in respect of any such premises is not confirmed before the end of the provisional period, then at the end of that period the licence is treated as revoked.

(5) A premises licence-
   (a) to which subsection (3) applies, and
   (b) which has not been confirmed in accordance with section 46,
is referred to in this Act as a "provisional premises licence".

(6) The provisional period, in relation to a provisional premises licence, is the period of 2 years beginning with the date of issue of the licence.

(7) On the application of the holder of a provisional premises licence made before the expiry of the provisional period, the Licensing Board which issued the licence may, if satisfied as to the matter mentioned in subsection (8), extend the provisional period by such period as the Board considers appropriate.

(8) That matter is that-
  (a) completion of the construction or conversion of the premises to which the licence relates has been delayed, and
  (b) the delay has been caused by factors outwith the premises licence holder's control.

(9) Where the provisional period in relation to any provisional premises licence has been extended under subsection (7), references in this section and section 46 to the provisional period are to that period as so extended.

(10) Section 20 has effect in relation to a provisional premises licence application as if-
  (a) in subsection (2)(b), for sub-paragraph (iii) there were substituted-
       "(iii) the certificate required by section 50(2),", and
  (b) in subsection (4), paragraph (g) were omitted.

(11) In this section, "construct" and "convert" have the same meanings as they have for the purposes of the Building (Scotland) Act 2003 (asp 8).

DEFINITIONS

"premises licence": see s.17 of this Act
"premises": see s.147(1) of this Act
"construct": see subs.(11)
"convert": see subs.(11)
"licensed premises": see s.147(1) of this Act
"provisional premises licence application": see subs.(2)
"provisional premises licence": see subs.(5)

GENERAL NOTE

This section allows application to be made for a provisional premises licence where premises have yet to be, or are in the course of being, constructed or converted for use as licensed premises, adapting the provisional grant mechanism found in s.26 of the 1976 Act. The provisional premises licence does not come into effect until confirmed (s.46). It has an initial currency of two years which may be extended in the event of a delay caused by factors outwith the licence holder's control. (Presently, provisional grants endure initially for one year, subject to renewal where there has been no "unreasonable delay": 1976 Act, s26(8), (9)). The licensing board may choose the period of extension.

The Act does not replicate the 1976 Act's provision for an "outline" provisional grant, which proceeds simply on the basis of a locality plan identifying the site of the proposed premises and a general description of the applicant's proposals (1976 Act, s.26(2)).

Subsection (10)

The applicant requires to comply with the provisions of s.20 in relation to a "full" premises licence application, except that he need only produce a provisional planning certificate, with the requirement for building standards and food hygiene certification being reserved until the confirmation stage (see s.46(2)(d) and s.50(3)); and no information need be provided about the person who is to be the premises manager.

46. Confirmation of provisional premises licence

(1) The holder of a provisional premises licence may, at any time before the expiry of the provisional period in relation to the licence, apply to the Licensing Board which issued the licence for confirmation of the licence.

(2) An application under subsection (1) must be accompanied by-
   (a) the provisional premises licence,
   (b) the operating plan for the premises to which the licence relates,
   (c) the layout plan for the premises, and
   (d) the certificates required by section 50(3).

(3) The operating plan referred to in subsection (2)(b) must, in particular and without prejudice to subsection (4) of section 20, contain a statement of the information specified in paragraph (g) of subsection (4) of that section.

(4) Where a Licensing Board which issued a provisional premises licence receives an application under subsection (1) in respect of the licence, the Board must, if satisfied as to the matters mentioned in subsection (5), confirm the licence.

(5) Those matters are that-
   (a) since the provisional premises licence was issued, or
   (b) if, since that time, an application for a variation of the licence has been granted under section 30, since the last such application was granted,

there has been no variation (other than a minor variation) made to the operating plan or layout plan for the premises to which the licence relates.

(6) Where a Licensing Board confirms a provisional premises licence under subsection (4), the Board may, for the purpose specified in subsection (7), make a variation of the conditions to which the licence is subject.

(7) That purpose is ensuring consistency with any licensing policy statement or supplementary licensing policy statement published since the licence was issued.

DEFINITIONS
"provisional premises licence": see s.45(5) of this Act
"provisional period": see s.45(6) of this Act
"operating plan": see s.20(4) of this Act
"layout plan": see s.20(2)(b)(ii) of this Act
"variation": see s.29(5) of this Act
"minor variation": see s.29(6) of this Act
"supplementary licensing policy statement": see s.6(2) of this Act

GENERAL NOTE
Provision is made here for the confirmation of a provisional premises licence by a procedure not dissimilar to the finalisation procedure found in the 1976 Act.

Subsection (1)
Application for confirmation must be made prior to the expiry of the provisional premises licence.

Subsection (2)
In addition to the provisional premises licence, operating plan and layout plan, the applicant must provide certificates in relation to building standards and food hygiene (see s.50(6), (7)). If the licence holder produced a provisional planning certificate consisting only of outline planning

permission at the time of the application for the provisional premises licence, he must now produce a planning certificate (s.50(4)).

Subsection (3)
The operating plan produced to the board must contain prescribed information about the individual who is to be the premises manager.

Subsections (4), (5)
The licensing board must confirm the provisional premises licence if it is satisfied that, since the licence was issued or last varied, there has been no variation of the operating plan or layout plan, other than a minor variation. Any variation which is not a "minor variation" (as defined in s.29(6)) would require to be authorised by a procedure similar to that for a new licence (see notes to s.29(4)).

Subsections (6), (7)
The licensing board may vary the licence conditions for the purpose of ensuring consistency with a policy statement or supplementary licensing policy statement published since the licence was issued. Conditions to which the licence is subject by virtue of s.27(1) (see Sch.3) may not be varied (s.29(5)(a)).

47. Temporary premises licence

(1) This section applies where any licensed premises (other than premises in respect of which a provisional premises licence or occasional licence has effect) are undergoing, or are to undergo, reconstruction or conversion (referred to in this section as the "principal premises").

(2) The appropriate Licensing Board in relation to the principal premises may-
   (a) on the application of the holder of the premises licence in respect of the premises, and
   (b) if satisfied as to the matters mentioned in subsection (3),
issue to the applicant a premises licence in respect of such other premises within the Licensing Board's area as are specified in the application (such premises being referred to in this section as the "temporary premises").

(3) The matters referred to in subsection (2)(b) are-
   (a) that the temporary premises are suitable for use for the sale of alcohol, and
   (b) that it is necessary to grant the application to enable the applicant to carry on business pending reconstruction or conversion of the principal premises.

(4) A premises licence issued under subsection (2) is referred to in this Act as a "temporary premises licence".

(5) A temporary premises licence-
   (a) has effect for such period of not more than 2 years beginning with the date of its issue as the Licensing Board may determine, and
   (b) is subject to the same conditions as those to which the premises licence in respect of the principal premises is subject at the time the temporary premises licence is issued, with such exceptions or variations (if any) as the Licensing Board considers appropriate.

(6) The Licensing Board may, on the application of the holder of a temporary premises licence, extend the period during which it has effect for such further period of not more than 12 months as they may determine.

(7) In this section-
"conversion" has the same meaning as it has for the purposes of the Building (Scotland) Act 2003 (asp 8), and
"reconstruction" includes alteration, re-erection and extension.

DEFINITIONS
"licensed premises": see s.147(1) of this Act
"provisional premises licence": see s.45(5) of this Act
"occasional licence": see s.56(1)
"principal premises": see subs.(1)
"applicant": see s.147(1) of this Act
"premises": see s.147(1) of this Act
"premises licence": see s.17 of this Act
"temporary premises": see subs.(2)
"alcohol": see s.2 of this Act
"temporary premises licence": see subs.(4)
"conversion": see subs.(7)
"reconstruction": see subs.(7)

GENERAL NOTE
Section 27 of the 1976 Act provides, without elaboration, that a licensing board "may grant a provisional licence to the holder of any licence allowing him to carry on business in temporary premises during the reconstruction of his premises". The economical terms of the section had provided licensing boards with no assistance whatsoever in relation to the procedure which ought to be followed or as to the duration of the licence. This section makes similar provision for the grant of a licence in the circumstances described in s.27 but also sets out the procedure to be followed and also limits the duration of the licence.

Subsection (1)
Application for a temporary premises may not be made where the premises which are undergoing, or are to undergo, reconstruction or conversion are the subject of a provisional premises licence or an occasional licence.

Subsection (3)
The board requires to be satisfied that the premises are suitable for the sale of alcohol. It would be entitled to refuse the application if it considered that the disruption caused by the building works ought not to prevent business continuing at the principal premises.

Subsections (5), (6)
The licensing board may fix the duration of the temporary premises licence, but it must not exceed two years. The licence holder may, however, apply for an extension of the period set by the board - for example, where building works at the principal premises have taken longer than expected - but the extension may not last longer than 12 months.

Updating of licence

48. Notification of change of name or address

(1) A premises licence holder must, not later than one month after the occurrence of any change in-
  (a) the licence holder's name or address, or
  (b) the name or address of the premises manager specified in the licence,
give the appropriate Licensing Board notice of the change.

(2) A notice under subsection (1) must be accompanied by the premises licence or, if that is not practicable, by a statement of the reasons for the failure to produce the licence.
(3) A premises licence holder who fails, without reasonable excuse, to comply with subsection (1), commits an offence.
(4) A person guilty of an offence under subsection (3) is liable on summary conviction to a fine not exceeding level 2 on the standard scale.

DEFINITIONS
"premises licence": see s.17 of this Act

GENERAL NOTE
The premises licence holder must, within one month, give the licensing board notice of a change in the licence holder's name or address or the name and address of the premises manager. A name change may occur upon marriage or where a company changes its name. A change in the *identity* of the premises licence holder must, of course, be the subject of a transfer application (ss.33, 34); and a change of premises manager must be accomplished by a minor variation application (s.29(6)(c)).

The notice must be accompanied by the premises licence or a statement of the reasons for the failure to produce the licence.

49. Licensing Board's duty to update premises licence

(1) Subsection (2) applies where a Licensing Board-
   (a) receives a notice under section 48(1) in relation to a premises licence,
   (b) grants a premises licence variation application or otherwise makes a variation of a premises licence,
   (c) grants an application under section 33(1) or 34(1) for the transfer of a premises licence,
   (d) in relation to a provisional premises licence, grants-
      (i) an application under section 45(7) for an extension of the provisional period, or
      (ii) an application under section 46(1) for confirmation of the licence,
   (e) in relation to a temporary premises licence, grants an application under section 47(6) for an extension of the period during which the licence has effect, or
   (f) on reviewing a premises licence, takes any of the steps referred to in section 39(1).
(2) The Board must make any necessary amendments to the licence and, if necessary, issue a new summary of the licence.
(3) Where a Licensing Board is not in possession of a premises licence and-
   (a) the licence has ceased to have effect under any provision of this Act, or
   (b) the Board requires the licence for the purpose of complying with the duty under subsection (2),
the Board may require the licence holder to produce the licence to the Board within 14 days from the date on which the requirement is notified.
(4) A licence holder who, without reasonable excuse, fails to comply with a requirement made under subsection (3), commits an offence.

(5) A person guilty of an offence under subsection (4) is liable on summary conviction to a fine not exceeding level 2 on the standard scale.

DEFINITIONS

"premises licence": see s.17 of this Act
"premises licence variation application": see s.29(3) of this Act
"variation": see s.29(5) of this Act
"provisional premises licence": see s.45(5) of this Act
"temporary premises licence": see s.47(4) of this Act

GENERAL NOTE

This section sets out the circumstances in which a licensing board must amend a premises licence and, if necessary, issue a new summary of the licence.

In most cases, the licence will be in the licensing board's possession (for example, it will require to have been produced in connection with a transfer application) but if the position is otherwise it may require production of the licence within 14 days.

Provision is made in s.53 for the issue of a replacement licence in certain circumstances.

Miscellaneous

50. Certificates as to planning, building standards and food hygiene

(1) A premises licence application (other than a provisional premises licence application) must be accompanied by-
 (a) a planning certificate,
 (b) a building standards certificate, and
 (c) if food is to be supplied on the premises, a food hygiene certificate,
in respect of the subject premises.

(2) A provisional premises licences application must be accompanied by a provisional planning certificate in respect of the subject premises.

(3) An application under section 46(1) in respect of any premises must be accompanied by-
 (a) if the provisional planning certificate which accompanied the provisional premises licence application in respect of the subject premises consisted of outline planning permission, a planning certificate,
 (b) a building standards certificate, and
 (c) if food is to be supplied on the premises, a food hygiene certificate,
in respect of the subject premises.

(4) A planning certificate is a certificate signed on behalf of the appropriate authority and stating-
 (a) that planning permission under the Town and Country Planning (Scotland) Act 1997 (c.8) (referred to in this section as "the 1997 Act") in respect of any development of the subject premises in connection with their proposed use as licensed premises has been obtained, or
 (b) that no such planning permission is required.

(5) A provisional planning certificate is a certificate signed on behalf of the appropriate authority and stating-
 (a) that planning permission or outline planning permission under the 1997 Act has been obtained in respect of the construction or conversion of the subject premises, or

(b) that no such planning permission is required.
(6) A building standards certificate is a certificate signed on behalf of the appropriate authority and stating-
    (a) that a completion certificate has been accepted under section 18 of the Building (Scotland) Act 2003 (asp 8) (referred to in this section as "the 2003 Act") in respect of any construction or conversion of the subject premises in connection with their proposed use as licensed premises,
    (b) that permission for the temporary occupation or use of the premises has been granted under section 21(3) of the 2003 Act, or
    (c) that no such completion certificate or permission is required.
(7) A food hygiene certificate is a certificate signed on behalf of the appropriate authority and stating that the subject premises comply with the requirements of regulations made under section 16 of the Food Safety Act 1990 (c.16) (referred to in this section as "the 1990 Act") relating to construction, layout, drainage, ventilation, lighting and water supply or concerned with the provision of sanitary and washing facilities.
(8) In this section-
"appropriate authority" means-
    (a) in relation to a planning certificate or provisional planning certificate, the planning authority (within the meaning of the 1997 Act) for the area in which the subject premises are situated,
    (b) in relation to a building standards certificate, the council for that area,
    (c) in relation to a food hygiene certificate, the food authority (within the meaning of the 1990 Act) for that area,

"construction" and "conversion" have the same meanings as they have in the 2003 Act,
"development" has the same meaning as it has in the 1997 Act.

DEFINITIONS
"premises licence application": see s.20(3) of this Act
"provisional premises licence application": see s.45(2) of this Act
"appropriate authority": see subs.(8)
"construction": see subs.(8)
"conversion": see subs. (8)
"development": see subs.(8)

GENERAL NOTE
Modelled on s.23 of the 1976 Act, this section makes provision for the submission of planning, building control and food hygiene certificates in support of an application for a premises licence, a provisional premises licence and confirmation of a provisional premises licence.

51. Notification of determinations

(1) Where a Licensing Board grants or refuses an application under this Part, the Board must give notice of the grant or refusal to-
    (a) the applicant,
    (b) the appropriate chief constable, and
    (c) in the case of the grant or refusal of a premises licence application, any person who gave a notice of objection or representation under section 22(1) in respect of the application.

(2) A person to whom notice is given under subsection (1) may, by notice to the clerk of the Board, require the Board to give a statement of reasons for the grant or refusal of the application.

(3) Where the clerk of a Licensing Board receives a notice under subsection (2), the Board must issue a statement of the reasons for the grant or refusal of the application to-
   (a) the person giving the notice, and
   (b) each other person to whom the Board gave notice under subsection (1).

(4) A statement of reasons under subsection (3) must be issued-
   (a) by such time, and
   (b) in such form and manner,

as may be prescribed.

DEFINITIONS
"applicant": see s.147(1) of this Act
"appropriate chief constable": see s.147(1) of this Act
"premises licence application": see s.20(3) of this Act

GENERAL NOTE
The licensing board is required to give notice of the grant or refusal of an application under this part of the Act to the applicant, the chief constable and, in the cases of a premises licence application, any person who objected or submitted representations. A person who receives such a notice may request a statement of reasons for the board's decision.

Subsection (1)
The applications which may be made under this part of the Act are for: a premises licence (including a provisional premises licence); the variation, transfer or review of a premises licence; confirmation of a provisional premises licence; and a temporary premises licence.

The obligation to notify and give reasons under the following subsections applies only to applications, not a licensing board's decisions (*cf* 1976 Act, s.18).

Subsection (2)
Nicholson considered whether there would be a continuing need for the provision of reasons if, as the Report recommended and the Act provides (s.131(2)), appeals should proceed by way of stated case (see notes to s.131(2)). The Committee took the view that a provision similar to that contained in s.18 of the 1976 Act could still be useful. If a potential appellant was uncertain as to whether or not to proceed with an appeal, he would be in a position to form a clearer view if he knew the reasons for which a decision was taken against him. If, on seeing the reasons, the potential appellant decided not to proceed, unnecessary work and expense would be spared. On the other hand, in the event of an appeal being taken, the board would already have a statement of their reasons which, with any necessary expansion, could be incorporated into the stated case (Report, para.11.11).

Provisions for reasons is also made in ss.61(1) (occasional licences), 70(5) (extended hours applications) and 79(5) (personal licences).

While an objector may require a statement of reasons for the grant or refusal of an application, he has no right of appeal: see s.131, Sch.5.

52. Duty to keep, display and produce premises licence

(1) A premises licence holder must secure that the premises licence, or a certified copy of it, is kept at the premises in respect of which it is issued in the custody or under the control of-
   (a) the licence holder, or
   (b) the premises manager.

(2) A premises licence holder must secure that the summary of the licence, or a certified copy of the summary, is prominently displayed on the premises so as to be capable of being read by anyone frequenting the premises.

(3) A premises licence holder who fails, without reasonable excuse, to comply with subsection (1) or (2) commits an offence.

(4) Any of the persons specified in subsection (5) may require the person in whose custody or under whose control a premises licence (or a certified copy of it) is kept by virtue of subsection (1) to produce the licence (or certified copy) for inspection.

(5) The persons referred to in subsection (4) are-
   (a) a constable, and
   (b) a Licensing Standards Officer for the council area in which the premises are situated.

(6) A person who fails, without reasonable excuse, to comply with a requirement made under subsection (4) commits an offence.

(7) A person guilty of an offence under this section is liable on summary conviction to a fine not exceeding level 3 on the standard scale.

DEFINITIONS
"premises licence": see s.17 of this Act
"certified copy": see s.55 of this Act
"premises manager": see s.19(1) of this Act

GENERAL NOTE
The premises licence or a certified copy must be kept at the premises by the licence holder or premises manager. Either the summary of premises licence or a certified copy requires to be displayed at the premises where it may be read by persons frequenting the premises. The licence or a certified copy must on request be produced to a constable or a licensing standards officer. Failure to comply with these provisions without reasonable excuse is an offence.

There is no obligation to display or produce licences under the 1976 Act, not are licence holders burdened with this sort of administrative offence which appears to have its origins in the 2003 Act.

53. Theft, loss etc. of premises licence or summary

(1) This section applies where the appropriate Licensing Board receives from a premises licence holder an application for a replacement premises licence or a replacement summary.

(2) If satisfied that-
   (a) the premises licence held by the licence holder or, as the case may be, the summary of it has been lost, stolen, damaged or destroyed, and
   (b) where it has been lost or stolen, the licence holder has reported the loss or theft to the police,
the Licensing Board must issue to the licence holder a replacement licence or, as the case may be, a replacement summary.

(3) A replacement licence or a replacement summary is a copy of the licence or summary-
   (a) in the form in which it existed immediately before it was lost, stolen, damaged or destroyed, and
   (b) certified by the Board to be a true copy.

(4) In this Act, references to-

(a) a premises licence include references to a replacement premises licence,
(b) a summary of a premises licence include references to a replacement summary,
issued under this section.

DEFINITIONS
"premises licence": see s.17 of this Act

GENERAL NOTE
Where a premises licence or summary has been lost, stolen, damaged or destroyed, the holder may apply for a replacement. In the case of loss or theft, the matter must have been reported to the police.

54. Dismissal, resignation, death etc. of premises manager

(1) This section applies where any of the events specified in subsection (2) occurs in relation to any licensed premises in respect of which a premises licence has effect.
(2) Those events are-
   (a) the premises manager ceases to work at the premises,
   (b) the premises manager becomes incapable for any reason of acting as premises manager,
   (c) the premises manager dies, or
   (d) the personal licence held by the premises manager is revoked or suspended.
(3) The premises licence holder must, not later than 7 days after the occurrence of the event, give notice of it to the appropriate Licensing Board.
(4) Subsection (5) applies if-
   (a) subsection (3) is complied with, and
   (b) within the period of 6 weeks beginning with the day on which the event occurs, a premises licence variation application is made seeking a variation of the premises licence in respect of the premises so as to substitute another individual as the premises manager.
(5) Any breach of the conditions specified in paragraphs 4 and 5 of schedule 3 in the period beginning with the occurrence of the event and ending with the receipt by the Licensing Board of the application referred to in subsection (4)(b) is, so far as it is attributable to the occurrence of the event, to be disregarded.
(6) If no such application as is mentioned in paragraph (b) of subsection (4) is made within the period mentioned in that paragraph, then, at the end of that period, the Licensing Board must vary the premises licence so that there is no longer any premises manager specified in it.

DEFINITIONS
"licensed premises": see s.147(1) of this Act
"premises licence": see s.17 of this Act
"premises manager": see s.19(1) of this Act
"personal licence": see s.71 of this Act
"premises licence variation application": see s.29(3) of this Act
"variation": see s.29(5) of this Act

GENERAL NOTE

This section provides a "window" of six weeks in which an application may be made to substitute a new premises manager where that person has ceased to work at the premises, has become incapable of acting as premises manager for any reason, has died or has suffered the suspension or revocation of his personal licence.

Notice of the occurrence of any of these events must be given to the licensing board with seven days.

Provided that notice is given *and* a variation application is made within six weeks of the event, any breach of the conditions set out in paras.4 and 5 of Sch.3, beginning with the date of the event and the receipt by the board of the application, are to be disregarded.

If a variation application is not made within the six-week period the board must vary the premises licence so there is no specified premises manager. In such a case, the sale of alcohol at the premises would require to cease: see Sch.3, para.4(1)(a).

See also s.31, which provides for the deemed variation of premises licence where application is made to substitute a new premises manager and the applicant requests that the variation should have immediate effect.

55. Certified copies

Any reference in this Part to a certified copy of a premises licence or of a summary of such a licence is a reference to a copy of the licence or summary certified to be a true copy by-
- (a) the Licensing Board,
- (b) a solicitor or notary public, or
- (c) a person of a prescribed description.

DEFINITIONS
"premises licence": see s.17 of this Act
"prescribed": see s.147(1) of this Act

GENERAL NOTE

This section allows a copy of a premises licence or a summary of such a licence to be certified as a true copy by the licensing board, a solicitor or notary, or a person of a prescribed description.

A copy of the licence kept at the premises as required by s.52(1) or the summary which must be displayed in terms of s.52(2) could be a copy certified by the board or the other specified persons. A replacement licence or a replacement summary must be certified by the board (s.53(3)).

PART 4

OCCASIONAL LICENCES

56. Occasional licence

(1) A Licensing Board may, on the application of any of the persons mentioned in subsection (2) made in relation to any premises (other than licensed premises) within the Board's area, issue to the applicant a licence (referred to in this Act as an "occasional licence") authorising the sale of alcohol on the premises.

(2) Those persons are-
- (a) the holder of a premises licence,
- (b) the holder of a personal licence, and
- (c) a representative of any voluntary organisation.

(3) An application under subsection (1) must contain details of the information which the applicant proposes should be included in the licence under subsection (7)(b).

(4) An application under subsection (1) which complies with subsection (3) is referred to in this Act as an "occasional licence application".

(5) An occasional licence has effect for such period of not more than 14 days as the Licensing Board may determine.

(6) A Licensing Board may issue under subsection (1) in respect of any one voluntary organisation in any period of 12 months-
   (a) not more than 4 occasional licences each having effect for a period of 4 days or more, and
   (b) not more than 12 occasional licences each having effect for a period of less than 4 days,

provided that, in any period of 12 months, the total number of days on which occasional licences issued in respect of the organisation have effect does not exceed 56.

(7) An occasional licence issued by a Licensing Board under subsection (1) must-
   (a) be in the prescribed form, and
   (b) contain the information specified in subsection (8).

(8) That information is-
   (a) the name and address of the holder of the licence,
   (b) a description of the premises in respect of which it is issued,
   (c) a description of the activities to be carried on in the premises,
   (d) a statement of the period during which the licence has effect,
   (e) a statement of the times during which alcohol may be sold on the premises,
   (f) a statement as to whether alcohol may be sold for consumption on the premises, off the premises or both,
   (g) a statement of the times at which any other activities in addition to the sale of alcohol are to be carried on in the premises,
   (h) where alcohol is to be sold for consumption on the premises, a statement as to whether children or young persons are to be allowed entry to the premises and, if they are to be allowed entry, a statement of the terms on which they are allowed entry including, in particular-
      (i) the ages of the children or young persons to be allowed entry,
      (ii) the times at which they are to be allowed entry, and
      (iii) the parts of the premises to which they are to be allowed entry,
   (i) the conditions to which the licence is subject, or, in relation to any such condition, a reference to another document in which details of the condition can be found, and
   (j) such other information as may be prescribed.

(9) Where alcohol is to be sold both for consumption on and for consumption off the premises, the occasional licence for the premises may, under subsection (8)(e), state different times for-
   (a) the sale of alcohol for consumption on the premises, and
   (b) the sale of alcohol for consumption off the premises.

DEFINITIONS
"licensed premises": see s.147(1) of this Act
"applicant": see s.147(1) of this Act
"occasional licence": see subs.(1)

"alcohol": see s.2 of this Act
"premises licence": see s.17 of this Act
"personal licence": see s.71 of this Act
"occasional licence application": see subs.(4)
"prescribed": see s.147(1) of this Act
"children": see s.147(1) of this Act
"young persons": see s.147(1) of this Act

GENERAL NOTE

Sections 33 of the 1976 Act allows the holder of a licence (other than the holder of a refreshment or entertainment licence) to obtain an occasional licence authorising the sale of alcoholic liquor at an event such as a wedding reception) taking place outwith his premises for a period of not more than 14 days. Section 34 makes provision for the grant of occasional permissions to a voluntary organisation (or a branch of such an organisation) authorising the sale of alcohol over a maximum period of 14 days at an event taking place outwith licensed premises which arises from or is related to the activities of the organisation.

This and the following sections set out combined replacement provisions adapted to the new system which are more prescriptive than those contained in the 1976 Act.

Subsection (2)

An application for an occasional licence in respect of unlicensed premises may be made by the holder of a premises or personal licence or by a person representing a voluntary organisation.

The expression "voluntary organisation" is not defined. Nicholson suggested that a definition might be helpful as otherwise there may be room for dispute as to the types of organisation entitled to make an application (Report, para.14.25). Clayson (para.15.04) referred to "an established society or organisation" and cited as an example "a sports club which is not a registered club". By virtue of the condition set out in Sch.4, para 5(2), which must be attached to an occasional licence granted to a voluntary organisation, alcohol may only be sold at an event related to the organisation's activities.

Subsections (5), (6)

An occasional licence has a maximum duration of 14 days.

In the case of a voluntary organisation the grant of occasional licences is subject to quotas. In any twelve month period, the board may not issue more than four licences each lasting four days or more, and not more than 12 licences each lasting less than four days; and during that period the total number of days on which occasional licences have effect must not exceed 56.

Currently, in terms of 34(2) of the 1976 Act, no more than four occasional permissions may be granted in any one year to the same voluntary organisation. Since each application could authorise the sale of alcohol for 14 days, the maximum number of days on which occasional permissions may be operated is 56.

Subsection (8)

This subsection sets out the information which the applicant proposes should be included in the licence (subs.(3)) and which must be contained in the licence issued by the board. This information is much more extensive than that presently required when application is made under s.33 or s.34 of the 1976 Act.

57. Notification of application to chief constable and Licensing Standards Officer

(1) Where a Licensing Board receives an occasional licence application, the Board must give notice of it, together with a copy of the application, to-
  (a) the appropriate chief constable, and
  (b) any Licensing Standards Officer for the area in which the subject premises are situated.

(2) If the chief constable considers that it is necessary for the purposes of the crime prevention objective that the application be refused, the chief constable may, by notice to the Licensing Board given within 21 days of the date of receipt of the notice under subsection (1), make a recommendation to that effect.

(3) A Licensing Standards Officer may, within 21 days of receipt of a notice under subsection (1)(b), prepare and submit to the Licensing Board a report setting out the Officer's comments on the application.

DEFINITIONS
"occasional licence application": see s.56(4) of this Act
"appropriate chief constable": see s.147(1) of this Act
"crime prevention objective": see s.4(2) of this Act

GENERAL NOTE
Notice of an occasional licence application requires to be given by the licensing board to the chief constable and any licensing standards officer for the area. The chief constable may recommend the refusal of the application for the purposes of the crime prevention objective, while a licensing standards officer may "comment" on the application (but is not obliged to do so).

58. Objections and representations

(1) Where an occasional licence application is made to a Licensing Board, any person may by notice to the Licensing Board-
   (a) object to the application on any ground relevant to one of the grounds for refusal specified in section 59(6), or
   (b) make representations to the Board concerning the application, including, in particular, representations-
      (i) in support of the application, or
      (ii) as to conditions which the person considers should be imposed.
(2) Where a Licensing Board receives a notice of objection or representation under subsection (1) relating to any occasional licence application made to the Board, the Board must-
   (a) give a copy of the notice to the applicant in such manner and by such time as may be prescribed, and
   (b) have regard to the objection or representation in determining the application,
unless the Board rejects the notice under subsection (3).
(3) A Licensing Board may reject a notice of objection or representation received by the Board under subsection (1) if the objection or representation is frivolous or vexatious.
(4) Where a Licensing Board rejects a notice of objection or representation under subsection (3), the Board may recover from the person who gave the notice any expenses incurred by the Board in considering the notice.
(5) In any proceedings by a Licensing Board for the recovery of expenses under subsection (4), a copy of any minute of proceedings of the Licensing Board-
   (a) recording the Board's rejection of the notice and the grounds for rejection, and
   (b) certified by the clerk of the Board to be a true copy,

is sufficient evidence of the rejection and of the establishment of the ground for rejection.

DEFINITIONS
"occasional licence application": see s.56(4) of this Act
"applicant": see s.147(1) of this Act

GENERAL NOTE
This section makes provision for objections to an occasional licence application as well as representations in its support or as to the conditions which should be imposed by the licensing board under s.60. Notice of an objection or representation must be given by the board to the applicant, unless it has been rejected as frivolous or vexatious.

Subsection (1)
While "any person" may object, it appears that the chief constable's intervention is limited to the making of a recommendation in terms of s.57(2). The scope for public objections is no doubt limited by the fact that only the chief constable and a licensing standards officer are entitled to receive notice of the application (*cf* s.21(1)).

59. Determination of application

(1) An occasional licence application received by a Licensing Board is to be determined in accordance with this section.
(2) If the Board has not received any-
   (a) notice from the appropriate chief constable under section 57(2),
   (b) report from a Licensing Standards Officer under section 57(3), or
   (c) notice of objection or representation under section 58(1),
relating to the application, the Board must grant the application.
(3) In any other case, the Board must consider whether any of the grounds for refusal applies and-
   (a) if none of them applies, the Board must grant the application, or
   (b) if any of them applies, the Board must refuse the application.
(4) The Board may hold a hearing for the purposes of determining any application which is to be determined in accordance with subsection (3).
(5) Where the Board does not hold a hearing for that purpose, the Board must ensure that, before determining the application, the applicant is given an opportunity to comment on any such notice or report as is referred to in subsection (2).
(6) The grounds for refusal are-
   (a) that the premises to which the application relates are excluded premises,
   (b) that the application must be refused under section 64(2) or 65(3),
   (c) that the Licensing Board considers the granting of the application would be inconsistent with one or more of the licensing objectives,
   (d) that, having regard to-
      (i) the nature of the activities proposed to be carried on in the premises to which the application relates,
      (ii) the location, character and condition of the premises, and
      (iii) the persons likely to frequent the premises,
   the Board considers that the premises are unsuitable for use for the sale of alcohol.
(7) In considering, for the purposes of the ground for refusal specified in subsection (6)(c), whether the granting of the application would be

inconsistent with the crime prevention objective, the Licensing Board must, in particular, take into account any notice given by the appropriate chief constable under section 57(2).
(8) In determining any application which is to be determined in accordance with subsection (3), the Board must take into account any report from a Licensing Standards Officer under section 57(3).

DEFINITIONS
"occasional licence application": see s.56(4) of this Act
"appropriate chief constable": see s.147(1) of this Act
"applicant": see s.147(1) of this Act
"excluded premises": see s.123(2) of this Act
"licensing objectives": see s.4(1) of this Act
"crime prevention objective": see s.4(2) of this Act

GENERAL NOTE
An occasional licence application must be granted in the absence of a refusal recommendation from the chief constable, a licensing standards officer's report or an objection or representation. Otherwise, the board must consider whether any of the grounds for refusal set out in subs.(6) applies. If none applies, the application requires to be granted; if a ground for refusal is established, the application must be refused.

Schedule 1, para.10(1) allows the grant of an application to be delegated, but it may not be granted by the clerk where there is a notice of objection or representations or a notice from the chief constable recommending refusal.

Subsections (4) and (5)
Where the board is not obliged to grant the application by virtue of subs.(2), it may hold a hearing to consider whether any ground for refusal applies. It is not obliged to do so. The conduct of a hearing may not be delegated: see Sch.1, para.10(1), (2). If it decides not to hold a hearing, it must nevertheless ensure that the applicant is given an opportunity to "comment" on a refusal recommendation by the chief constable, a licensing standards officers' report or an objection or representation.

Subsection (6)
For excluded premises, see s.123(2). Section 64(2) requires the refusal of an application which would authorise the sale of alcohol during a continuous period of 24 hours or more unless there are exceptional circumstances. Section 65(3) provides that alcohol must not be sold for consumption off the premises except between 10 am and 10 pm (subject to s.65(4)).

60. Conditions of occasional licence

(1) Except to the extent that schedule 4 provides otherwise, every occasional licence is subject to the conditions specified in that schedule.
(2) The Scottish Ministers may by regulations modify schedule 4 so as—
   (a) to add such further conditions as they consider necessary or expedient for the purposes of any of the licensing objectives, or
   (b) to extend the application of any condition specified in the schedule.
(3) The Scottish Ministers may by regulations prescribe further conditions as conditions which Licensing Boards may, at their discretion, impose on the granting by them of occasional licences.
(4) Without prejudice to subsection (3), where a Licensing Board grants an occasional licence the Board may impose such other conditions (in addition to those to which the licence is subject by virtue of

subsection (1)) as they consider necessary or expedient for the purposes of any of the licensing objectives.

(5) A Licensing Board may not impose a condition under subsection (4) which-
  (a) is inconsistent with any condition-
    (i) to which the occasional licence is subject by virtue of subsection (1), or
    (ii) prescribed under subsection (3),
  (b) would have the effect of making any such condition more onerous or more restrictive, or
  (c) relates to a matter (such as planning, building control or food hygiene) which is regulated under another enactment.

(6) The conditions which may be-
  (a) added under subsection (2)(a),
  (b) prescribed under subsection (3), or
  (c) imposed under subsection (4),

include, in particular, conditions of the kind described in subsection (7).

(7) Those are conditions requiring anything to be done, or prohibiting or restricting the doing of anything, in connection with-
  (a) the sale of alcohol on the premises in respect of which an occasional licence has effect, or
  (b) any other activity carried on in such premises.

DEFINITIONS
"occasional licence": see s.56(1) of this Act
"prescribe": see s.147(1) of this Act
"licensing objectives": see s.4(1) of this Act
"alcohol": see s.2 of this Act

GENERAL NOTE
This section provides for various types of conditions to be attached to occasional licences and echoes the provisions of s.27 which apply to the grant of a premises licence.

Subsection (1)
All occasional licences must be subject to a set of national conditions intended to achieve consistency in relation to matters such as the irresponsible promotion of alcohol.

Subsection (2)
Scottish Ministers may add to the national conditions or extend their application as they may do in relation to the mandatory conditions to be attached to premises licence in terms of s.27(1).

Subsection (3) and (4)
Further conditions may be imposed at the licensing board's discretion, either from a "pool" of conditions prescribed by Scottish Ministers or as may be considered necessary or expedient for the purposes of any of the licensing objectives. There is no provision for mandatory "late-night" conditions where the occasional licence authorises the sale of alcohol after 1 am (cf s.27(3)).

Subsection (5)
The board may not impose conditions of its own devising which are inconsistent with the Sch.4 conditions, which must be attached in each case, nor with the conditions which may be prescribed by Ministers by virtue of subs.(3); nor may they make such a condition more onerous or more restrictive. A condition must not relate to a matter regulated under other legislation.

61. Notification of determinations

(1) Where a Licensing Board grants or refuses an occasional licence application, the Board must give notice of the grant or refusal to-
   (a) the applicant,
   (b) the appropriate chief constable,
   (c) any Licensing Standards Officer for the area in which the subject premises are situated, and
   (d) any person who gave a notice of objection or representation under section 58(1) in respect of the application.

(2) A person to whom notice is given under subsection (1) may, by notice to the clerk of the Board, require the Board to give a statement of reasons for the grant or refusal of the application.

(3) Where the clerk of a Licensing Board receives a notice under subsection (2), the Board must issue a statement of the reasons for the grant or refusal of the application to-
   (a) the person giving the notice, and
   (b) each other person to whom the Board gave notice under subsection (1).

(4) A statement of reasons under subsection (3) must be issued-
   (a) by such time, and
   (b) in such form and manner,
as may be prescribed.

DEFINITIONS
"occasional licence application": see s.56(4) of this Act
"applicant": see s.147(1) of this Act
"appropriate chief constable": see s.147(1) of this Act

GENERAL NOTE
Notice of the licensing board's determination of an occasional licence application must be given to: the applicant, the chief constable, any licensing standards officer and any person who objected to or made a representation in relation to the application. Persons to whom notice is given may require the board to give reasons for its decision, which is open to appeal at the instance of both the applicant and an objector (Sch.5).

PART 5

LICENSED HOURS

General

62. Licensed hours

(1) In this Act, "licensed hours" means, in relation to licensed premises-
   (a) in the case of licensed premises in respect of which a premises licence has effect, the period or periods of time specified for the time being in the operating plan contained in the premises licence as those during which alcohol is to be sold on the premises, and
   (b) in the case of licensed premises in respect of which an occasional licence has effect, the period or periods of time specified in the

licence as those during which alcohol may be sold on the premises,

and a reference to a period of licensed hours is a reference to any of those periods of time.

(2) In this Act-
   (a) in relation to any premises-
      (i) "on-sales hours" means licensed hours applying to the sale of alcohol for consumption on the premises,
      (ii) "off-sales hours" means licensed hours applying to the sale of alcohol for consumption off the premises, and
   (b) in relation to any licensed premises on which alcohol is sold both for consumption on the premises and for consumption off the premises, references to licensed hours are-
      (i) in relation to alcohol sold for consumption on the premises, to be read as references to on-sales hours,
      (ii) in relation to alcohol sold for consumption off the premises, to be read as references to off-sales hours.
(3) Subsection (1) is subject to sections 67(6) and 68(5).

DEFINITIONS
"licensed hours": see subs.(1)
"premises licence": see s.17 of this Act
"operating plan": see s.20(4) of this Act
"alcohol": see s.2 of this Act
"licensed premises" see s.147(1) of this Act
"on-sales hours": see subs.(2)(a)(i)
"off-sales hours": see subs.(2)(a)(ii)

GENERAL NOTE
As explained in the notes to s.64, the Act abolishes the 1976 Act's system of "basic" permitted hours supplemented by extensions and creates "licensed hours" outwith which alcohol may not be sold on, consumed in or taken from licensed premises, including premises which are the subject of an occasional licence (see s.63). The licensed hours will be proposed in the operating plan accompanying an application for a premises licence or in an application for an occasional licence. The board's approach to licensed hours will be set out in its policy statement (see s.6).

Subsection (3)
References to "licensed hours" in the Act include those hours as extended by a general extension of hours (s.67) or hours extended under the provisions of s.68.

63. Prohibition of sale, consumption and taking away of alcohol outwith licensed hours

(1) Subject to subsection (2), a person commits an offence if, outwith licensed hours, the person-
   (a) sells alcohol, or allows alcohol to be sold, on licensed premises,
   (b) allows alcohol to be consumed on licensed premises, or
   (c) allows alcohol to be taken from licensed premises.
(2) It is not an offence under subsection (1) for a person to-
   (a) allow alcohol to be consumed on licensed premises at any time within 15 minutes of the end of any period of licensed hours if the alcohol was sold during that period,

(b) allow alcohol to be taken from licensed premises at any time within 15 minutes of the end of any period of licensed hours if the alcohol-
   (i) was sold during that period, and
   (ii) is not taken from the premises in an open container,
(c) allow alcohol to be consumed on or taken from licensed premises outwith licensed hours if the person consuming or taking the alcohol-
   (i) resides on the premises, or
   (ii) is a guest of a person who resides there,
(d) sell alcohol or allow alcohol to be sold on licensed premises outwith licensed hours if the alcohol is sold to a person who resides on the premises,
(e) allow alcohol to be consumed on licensed premises at a meal at any time within 30 minutes of the end of any period of licensed hours if the alcohol was sold-
   (i) during that period,
   (ii) at the same time as the meal, and
   (iii) for consumption at the meal,
(f) sell alcohol or allow alcohol to be sold on licensed premises outwith licensed hours if the alcohol is sold to-
   (i) a person who is a trader for the purposes of the person's trade, or
   (ii) a person for supply to or on any premises which are occupied for the purposes of the armed forces of the Crown.

(3) It is a defence for a person ("the accused") charged with an offence under subsection (1) of allowing alcohol to be consumed on or taken from any licensed premises outwith licensed hours to prove-
  (a) that the accused, or an employee or agent of the accused, took all reasonable precautions and exercised all due diligence not to commit the offence, or
  (b) that there were no lawful and reasonably practicable means by which the accused could prevent the person consuming or taking the alcohol on or from the premises from so doing.

(4) A person commits an offence if, having been requested by a responsible person not to do so, the person consumes alcohol on, or takes alcohol from, licensed premises outwith licensed hours.

(5) In subsection (4), "responsible person" means-
  (a) in the case of licensed premises in respect of which a premises licence has effect, the premises manager,
  (b) in the case of licensed premises in respect of which an occasional licence has effect, the holder of the licence,
  (c) in either case, any person who works on the premises in a capacity (whether paid or unpaid) which authorises the person to make the request mentioned in subsection (4).

(6) Nothing in this section prevents or restricts-
  (a) the ordering of alcohol for consumption off licensed premises, or
  (b) the despatch of alcohol so ordered by the person selling it.

(7) A person guilty of an offence under this section is liable on summary conviction to a fine not exceeding level 3 on the standard scale.

DEFINITIONS
"licensed hours": see s.62(1) of this Act
"sells": see s.147(1) of this Act

"alcohol": see s.2 of this Act
"licensed premises": see s.147(1) of this Act
"responsible person": see subs.(5)

GENERAL NOTE

Section 54 of the 1976 Act prohibits the sale or consumption of alcohol except during the permitted hours subject to certain exceptions, while s.119 provides for "trading hours" in relation to off-sale licensed premises. The provisions of this section apply to all licensed premises and largely replicate the scheme of s.54, which is adapted to the new system of "licensed hours".

Schedule 3, para.2(1) of this Act provides, as a mandatory condition of a premises licence, that "Alcohol is to be sold on the premises only in accordance with the operating plan contained in the licence". The operating plan will contain the licensed hours.

Section 54(5) of the 1976 Act provides that nothing in that Act requires any premises "to be open for the sale or supply of alcohol during the permitted hours". A similar provision was contained in this Act when it was first introduced. The provision was later removed and, at Stage 3, Bruce Crawford MSP introduced an amendment seeking its reinstatement. In the course of the Stage 3 debate, Mr Crawford expressed concern that businesses could, on occasions, require to remain open when there was patently no demand from customers. In reply, the Deputy Minister for Finance, Public Sector Reform and Parliamentary Business, George Lyon, said that it was

"not in our interest to allow the licensed trade to apply to boards to open their premises for the maximum hours they think the board will agree to, rather than the hours which they intend to open".

He continued:

"In deciding whether there has been a breach [of the operating plan], the board must... take a common sense approach and make allowances for holidays, sickness, bereavement and other such normal business factors before calling a breach of the operating plan".

In the absence of such a "common sense approach", the so-called "duty to trade" could lead to businesses incurring damaging costs by remaining open without custom where it would be patently unreasonable to expect them to do so. As the Scottish Beer and Pub Association pointed out at Stage 3, many factors such as weather, unpredictable emergencies such as a foot-and-mouth outbreak or even the refurbishment of the premises could dictate the closure of premises.

Subsection (1)

In terms very similar to s.54(1) of the 1976 Act, this section provides that it is an offence if, outwith the licensed hours, a person sells alcohol or allows alcohol to be sold on licensed premises; allows its consumption on licensed premises; or allows it to be taken from the premises. It is not an offence under the 1976 Act to allow the consumption or removal of alcohol outwith permitted hours: the offence is committed by the person consuming or taking away the alcohol.

Subsection (2)

Provided that the alcohol was sold during the licensed hours, 15 minutes drinking-time is permitted. Alcohol sold within the licensed hours may taken away within 15 minutes of their conclusion, provided it is not taken away in an open container.

It is not an offence to allow alcohol to be consumed on or taken away from licensed premises outwith the licensed hours if the person consuming or removing the alcohol either resides on the premises (as, for example, a hotel resident) or is a guest of the resident. (While the 1976 Act allows the removal of alcohol by a resident, the dispensation does not, as here, extend to a resident's guest.) Alcohol may be sold at any time to a resident.

The Act does not replicate the provisions of s.139(3) of the 1976 Act, in terms of which a person may be deemed to "reside" in premises even where he occupies sleeping accommodation in an annex or overflow building.

Thirty minutes are added to the licensed hours for the consumption of alcohol at a meal, provided the alcohol was sold during those hours, at the same time as the meal and for consumption at the meal. There is no definition of "meal" in the Act. Whether food constitutes a "meal" may depend on the facts circumstances of the case: see *Miller v MacKnight*, 1954 S.L.T. 251.

Alcohol may be sold outwith the licensed hours to a trader for the purposes of the person's trade or to a person for the supply to or on any premises occupied by the armed forces, provisions which effectively re-enact s.54(3)(i), (j) of the 1976 Act.

Subsection (3)

Where a person is charged with allowing alcohol to be consumed on or taken from the premises outwith the licensed hours, he may prove that either he or his employee or agent took all reasonable precautions and exercised all due diligence not to commit the offence; or that there were no lawful and reasonably practicable means by which the accused could have prevented the consumption or removal of the alcohol.

For a consideration of the "due diligence" defence contained in the 1976 Act, see: *Byrne v Tudhope* 1983 SCCR 337; *Ahmed v MacDonald*, 1995 S.L.T. 1094; and *Gorman v Cochrane* 1997 SCCR (Supp) 185. (It requires to be kept in view that the vicarious responsibility provisions contained in the 1976 Act, with which these cases were concerned, are not replicated here.)

The defence is not available in relation to the offence of allowing the sale of alcohol outwith the licensed hours constituted by subs.(1)(a).

Subsection (4)

In terms of s.54(1)(b) of the 1976 Act, where alcohol is consumed or taken from licensed premises outwith the permitted hours, the offence is committed *simpliciter* by the person consuming or removing the alcohol. This subsection provides that the offence of consuming or taking away is committed only if the person concerned has been requested by a "responsible person" (see subs.(5)) not to do so.

Subsection (6)

This subsection exempts from the licensed hours offences the ordering of alcohol for consumption off licensed premises *or* the despatch of the alcohol so ordered by the person selling it. Its terms are virtually identical to those contained in s.54(3)(f) of the 1976 Act; but that exemption applies only to permitted hours and is not available in relation to off-sale licensed premises which operate under "trading hours" (see 1976 Act, s.119).

The effect of the exemption is perhaps not immediately clear. Alcohol purchased during the licensed hours may be despatched to the customer at any time; and an order placed outwith the licensed hours may be executed during the licensed hours.

The provision does not, however, authorise completed sales outwith the licensed hours. In *Valentine v Bell*, 1930 S.L.T. 685, decided under the corresponding provisions of the Licensing Act 1921, a customer personally ordered and paid for a quantity of wine in a grocer's shop outwith the permitted hours for delivery to her house. The grocer's messenger immediately set off to effect delivery and in fact passed the wine to the customer a short distance from the shop. The court rejected the defence argument that the exemption authorised both the ordering or despatch of liquor outwith permitted hours and held that it only applied to inchoate transactions. See also *Sinclair v Beattie*, 1934 J.C. 24.

For restrictions on late-night deliveries of alcohol, see s.120.

64. 24 hour licences to be granted only in exceptional circumstances

(1) Subsection (2) applies where, in relation to any premises-
   (a) an application of any of the following kinds is made to a Licensing Board in respect of the premises, namely-
      (i) a premises licence application,
      (ii) a premises licence variation application,
      (iii) an occasional licence application, or
      (iv) an extended hours application, and
   (b) if the application were to be granted, the licensed hours in relation to the premises would be such as to allow alcohol to be sold on the premises during a continuous period of 24 hours or more.

(2) The Licensing Board must refuse the application unless the Board is satisfied that there are exceptional circumstances which justify allowing the sale of alcohol on the premises during such a period.

DEFINITIONS
"premises": see s.147(1) of this Act
"premises licence application": see s.20(3) of this Act
"premises licence variation application": see s.29(3) of this Act
"occasional licence application": see s.56(4) of this Act
"extended hours application": see s.68(3) of this Act
"licensed hours": see s.62(1) of this Act

GENERAL NOTE

Nicholson considered that it was appropriate to recognise that a regime of "basic" permitted hours, supplemented by the grant of regular extensions of permitted hours, had outlived its usefulness and was no longer in step with reality. Almost all on-licensed premises in Scotland operate with the benefit of regular extensions. These have generally been approached on the basis of licensing board policies. Thus, in Glasgow, for example, extensions are normally granted having regard to the type of licence and the location of the premises, with longer hours permitted in the city centre than in residential areas.

There was no need for a presumption against 24-hour opening. This has been a theoretical possibility for on-licensed premises since the 1976 Act came into force in 1977; but it was, of course, a step for which licensing boards have demonstrated no appetite. Nevertheless, a mischievous misconstruction of Nicholson which had the capacity to generate alarmist headlines proved irresistible to some newspapers, leading to predictions that there would no hour of the day or night when it would be impossible to purchase alcohol.

Noting that "Sheriff Principal Nicholson has been striving publicly to correct the misinterpretation of his recommendation", Justice Minister Cathy Jamieson told a Parliament debate on the Nicholson Report (17 September 2003):

"My point is that we must work on a premises-by-premises basis. Contrary to what was suggested in some sections of the media, we are not proposing a free-for-all or saying that pubs and other premises could routinely open 24 hours. It is important to get the framework right and to have localised decision making... Routine 24-hour opening is not the way that the Executive intends to go." (Official Report, cols.1741, 1742.)

Guidance which has yet to be issued will set out guidelines on the approach which should be adopted by licensing boards when considering circumstances which may justify 24-hour opening. Boards will be required to set out their policy in relation to licensing hours in the policy statement required by s.6.

Subsection (1)

The drafting of subs.(1) was criticised by Sheriff Principal Gordon Nicholson in his written evidence to the Local Government and Transport Committee at Stage 1 and when he gave oral evidence on 22 March 2005 (Official Report, col.2226). In his written submission he doubted whether the provision "would achieve the desired result". He pointed out that the safeguard "would not be triggered at all if an applicant were to stipulate an opening period of 23 hours and 59 minutes" and suggested that "the trigger point should be a number of hours beyond what might normally be considered as acceptable - say, 18 hours or something around that figure".

65. Licensed hours: off-sales

(1) This section applies where an application specified in subsection (2) is made to a Licensing Board in relation to any premises, but only so far as the application is for-
  (a) a licence authorising the sale of alcohol for consumption off the premises, or
  (b) an extension of off-sales hours in relation to the premises.
(2) That application is-
  (a) a premises licence application,
  (b) a premises licence variation application,

(c) an occasional licence application, or
(d) an extended hours application.

(3) If the off-sales hours proposed in the application are such that alcohol would be sold for consumption off the premises-
  (a) before 10am,
  (b) after 10pm, or
  (c) both,
on any day, the Board must refuse the application.

(4) The Scottish Ministers may by order substitute other times for the times specified in subsection (3).

(5) Where subsection (3) does not apply, in considering whether the granting of the application would be inconsistent with any of the licensing objectives, the Board must, in particular, consider the effect (if any) which the off-sales hours proposed in the application would have on the occurrence of antisocial behaviour.

(6) In subsection (5), "antisocial behaviour" has the same meaning as in section 143 of the Antisocial Behaviour etc. (Scotland) Act 2004 (asp 8).

(7) This section is without prejudice to the generality of sections 23(4), 30(4), 59(3) and 68(1).

DEFINITIONS
"premises licence application": see s.20(3) of this Act
"premises licence variation application": see s.29(3) of this Act
"occasional licence application": see s.56(4) of this Act
"extended hours application": see s.68(3) of this Act
"licensing objectives": see s.4(1) of this Act
"antisocial behaviour": see subs.(6)

GENERAL NOTE
Presently, in terms of s.119 of the 1976 Act, off-sale premises may sell or supply alcohol between 8 am and 10 pm on weekdays and 12.30 pm and 10 pm on Sundays.

Nicholson made no distinction between the flexible setting of trading hours for on- and off-sale premises. In relation to the off-trade, it noted that shopping habits had changed substantially in the past 30 years: some customers who choose to shop in Sunday mornings or very late at night were able to purchase groceries at all hours could not purchase alcohol at the same time (Report, para.2.17).

However, when the Bill was considered by the Local Government and Transport Committee at Stage 2, a majority of members favoured an amendment which would have restricted off-sale opening to the period between 8 am and 11 pm. A subsequent proposal, prior to Stage 3, which would have permitted trading at all hours except between 10 pm and 3 am fuelled fears that customers leaving public houses and nightclubs would seek to purchase further alcohol supplies from off-sales outlets. Although the prospect of licensing boards allowing early morning opening, except in extraordinary circumstances, was, put euphemistically, remote, the Parliament finally agreed to a further proposed amendment which prevents off-sales taking place except between 10 am and 10 pm. It is impossible to divine the logic behind this step.

Subsection (3)
The restriction imposed by subs (3) is without prejudice to the power afforded to licensing boards to stipulate shorter hours when considering a premises licence application. Proposed trading hours will be set out in the operating plan (s.19(4)(b)) and these hours may be modified (s.22(7)). A number of licensing board chairman have already indicated that they may reduce evening hours in cases where the premises are, or are likely to be, a source of antisocial behaviour after, say, 6 pm, an approach legitimised by subs.(5).

Subsection (4)

The power to substitute other times and re-instate at least a degree of the flexibility proposed by Nicholson may well be invoked after the 2007 Parliamentary elections.

Subsection (5)

In considering licensed hours for premises which will be used for off-sales, the licensing board must not only take into the account, as with any application, the licensing objectives, but also the effect which the hours would have on the occurrence of antisocial behaviour.

66. Effect of start and end of British Summer Time

(1) Subsection (2) applies in relation to any period of licensed hours-
   (a) during which, or
   (b) at the end of which,
British Summer Time is due to begin or end.
(2) The beginning or, as the case may be, ending of British Summer Time is to be disregarded for the purpose of determining the time at which that period of licensed hours ends and, accordingly, the period ends at the time it would have ended had British Summer Time not begun or ended.
(3) In this section, "British Summer Time" means the period of summer time for the purposes of the Summer Time Act 1972 (c.6).

DEFINITIONS
"British summer time": see subs.(3)
"licensed hours": see s.62(1) of this Act

GENERAL NOTE

This welcome, sensible and overdue measure will bring to an end the current patchwork approach: in some licensing board areas, licensees are obliged to suffer a loss of an hour in the spring, while gaining in the autumn; in others, a condition attached to the grant of regular extensions of the permitted hours (1976 Act, s.64) effectively nullifies the effect of the clock change.

Subsection (2)

The clock change has no effect on the number of hours during which the premises are authorised to be open.

Occasional extensions

67. Power for Licensing Board to grant general extensions of licensed hours

(1) A Licensing Board may, if they consider it appropriate to do so in connection with a special event of local or national significance, make a determination extending licensed hours by such period as the Board may specify in the determination.
(2) A determination under subsection (1) may apply to-
   (a) the whole of the Licensing Board's area or only to specified parts of the area,
   (b) licensed hours generally or only to specified descriptions of licensed hours, and
   (c) all licensed premises in the Board's area or only to specified descriptions of such premises.

(3) A determination under subsection (1) has effect for such period as the Board may specify in it.
(4) Where a Licensing Board makes a determination under subsection (1), the Board must-
   (a) give notice of the determination to-
      (i) the appropriate chief constable, and
      (ii) the holders of premises licences and occasional licences in respect of premises to which the determination applies, and
   (b) publicise it in such manner as the Board sees fit.
(5) Nothing in this section is to be taken as requiring any licensed premises to be open for the sale of alcohol during the period of any extension of licensed hours specified in a determination under subsection (1).
(6) Except where the context requires otherwise, references in this Act to "licensed hours" are, in relation to any relevant premises to which a determination under subsection (1) applies, to be taken as references to such hours as extended by the determination.
(7) In this section, "specified" means specified in a determination under subsection (1).

DEFINITIONS
"licensed hours": see s.62(1) of this Act
"area": see s.147(1) of this Act
"appropriate chief constable": see s.147(1) of this Act
"premises licence": see s.17 of this Act
"occasional licence": see s.56(1) of this Act
"licensed premises": see s.147(1) of this Act
"alcohol": see s.2 of this Act

GENERAL NOTE
This unprecedented provision abandons the convention that it is the function of licensing boards to receive and consider applications from licence holders. The licensing board may, *ex proprio motu*, by means of a determination, extend licensed hours in connection with a special event of local or national significance, for such as period as it specifies. An application for an extension of hours in connection with such an event may also be made by the holder of a premises licence: see s.68. It is likely that, in practice, determinations will rarely, if ever, be made as licensing boards will wish to consider extensions of hours on a case-by-case basis.

Subsection (2)
In making a determination, the licensing board has a number of options. It may apply to: the whole of its area or only to specified parts; licensed hours generally or only to specified descriptions of licensed hours (for example, on-sales hours only); and all licensed premises or only those of a specified description.

Subsection (4)
Where a determination is made, the licensing board must give notice of it to the chief constable and to the holders of premises licences and occasional licences to which it applies. It must also be publicised in such manner as the board sees fit. The chief constable is not empowered to object to the making of a determination.

Subsection (5)
Where it would be open to a licence holder to trade during the period authorised by the determination, he need not do so.

68. Extended hours applications

(1) The appropriate Licensing Board may-
   (a) on the application of the holder of the premises licence in respect of any licensed premises, and
   (b) if the Board consider it appropriate to do so in connection with-
      (i) a special event or occasion to be catered for on the premises, or
      (ii) a special event of local or national significance,
   extend the licensed hours in respect of the premises by such period as is specified in the application or such other period as the Board consider appropriate.

(2) An extension of licensed hours under subsection (1) has effect for such period as is specified in the application or such other period as the Board consider appropriate; but in either case the period must not exceed one month.

(3) An application under subsection (1) is referred to in this Act as an "extended hours application".

(4) A period of licensed hours which is extended under this section may not be further extended under this section.

(5) Except where the context requires otherwise, references in this Act to "licensed hours" are, in relation to any period of licensed hours extended under this section, to be taken as references to such hours as so extended.

(6) References in this section to "licensed premises" do not include premises in respect of which an occasional licence has effect.

DEFINITIONS
"premises licence": see s.17 of this Act
"licensed premises"; see s.147(1) of this Act
"licensed hours": see s.62(1) of this Act
"extended hours application": see subs.(3)

GENERAL NOTE
Section 64 of the 1976 Act allows an application to be made to the licensing board for an extension of the permitted hours "in connection with any occasion which the board considers appropriate". The grant of such an "occasional extension" authorises the licence holder (or registered club) to sell alcohol in the premises "during such period not exceeding one month and between such hours on such day as may be specified".

This section provides a similar, but much more prescriptive, mechanism, retaining the one-month limit.

Subsection (1)
An extended hours application may be made by the holder of a premises licence (but not an occasional licence: see subs.(6). The hours may be sought in connection with a special event of national or local significance (see s.67 for general extensions in relation those events); or a special event or occasion to be catered for on the premises, such as a wedding reception, birthday party, and so on.

69. Notification of extended hours application

(1) Where a Licensing Board receives an extended hours application, the Board must give notice of it, together with a copy of the application, to-

(a) the appropriate chief constable, and
(b) any Licensing Standards Officer for the area in which the subject premises are situated.
(2) The appropriate chief constable may, within 10 days of receipt of a notice under subsection (1)(a), by notice to the appropriate Licensing Board object to the application if the chief constable considers it necessary to do so for the purposes of the crime prevention objective.
(3) A Licensing Standards Officer must, within 10 days of receipt of a notice under subsection (1)(b), prepare and submit to the Licensing Board a report setting out the Officer's comments on the application.

DEFINITIONS
"extended hours application": see s.68(3) of this Act
"appropriate chief constable": see s.147(1) of this Act
"crime prevention objective": see s.4(2) of this Act

GENERAL NOTE
Notice of the application, with a copy, must be given by the board to the chief constable and any licensing standards officer for the area. The chief constable may object on the basis of the crime prevention objective within ten days of receiving the notice, while the licensing standards officer *must* within a like period prepare and submit a report setting out his comments.

Subsection (2)
The ability of the chief constable to object to an extended hours application demonstrates the Act's inconsistent approach to his participation the licensing process. Apart from this provision, his entitlement to object is restricted to premises licence applications (see s.22(2)).
The effect of the ten-day period is to prevent application being made in respect of a time-sensitive occasion such as a funeral reception taking place before the start of the licensed hours unless appropriate provision has been made in the operating plan.

Subsection (3)
A licensing standards officer *must* prepare a report on an extended hours application: in relation to an occasional licence application that step is optional (s.57(3)).

70. Determination of extended hours application

(1) In determining an extended hours application, the Licensing Board must take into account-
   (a) any notice of objection given by the appropriate Chief Constable under section 69(2), and
   (b) the Licensing Standards Officer's report under section 69(3).
(2) The Board may hold a hearing for the purpose of determining an extended hours application.
(3) Where the Board does not hold a hearing for that purpose, the Board must, before determining the application, ensure that the applicant is given an opportunity to comment on any such notice or report as is mentioned in subsection (1).
(4) Where a Licensing Board grants or refuses an extended hours application, the Board must give notice of the grant or refusal to-
   (a) the applicant,
   (b) the appropriate chief constable, and
   (c) any Licensing Standards Officer for the area in which the subject premises are situated.

(5) A person to whom notice is given under subsection (4) may, by notice to the clerk of the Board, require the Board to give a statement of reasons for the grant or refusal of the application.

(6) Where the clerk of a Licensing Board receives a notice under subsection (5), the Board must issue a statement of the reasons for the grant or refusal of the application to-
   (a) each person giving the notice, and
   (b) each other person to whom the Board gave notice under subsection (4).

(7) A statement of reasons under subsection (6) must be issued-
   (a) by such time, and
   (b) in such form and manner,

as may be prescribed.

DEFINITIONS
"extended hours application": see s.68(3) of this Act
"appropriate chief constable": see s.147(1) of this Act
"applicant": see s.147(1) of this Act

GENERAL NOTE
In determining the application, the licensing board must take into account any notice of objection given by the chief constable and the mandatory licensing standard's officers report. It may hold a hearing, but if it elects not to do so the applicant must be given an opportunity to "comment" on any objection and the report.

Disposal of the application may be delegated: see Sch.1, para.10(1).

The board's determination of the applicant must be communicated to the applicant, the chief constable and any licensing standards officer. Any of those persons may require the board to provide a statement of reasons for the grant or refusal of the application.

PART 6

PERSONAL LICENCES

Introductory

71. Personal licence

In this Act, "personal licence", in relation to an individual, means a licence-
   (a) issued to the individual by a Licensing Board under section 76(1) of this Act, and
   (b) authorising the individual to supervise or authorise the sale of alcohol.

DEFINITIONS
"sale": see s.147(1) of this Act
"alcohol": see s.2 of this Act

GENERAL NOTE
This section introduces the new personal licence which will require to be held by the premises manager. Schedule 3, para.4(1) provides that alcohol may not be sold on the premises when there is no premises manager or the premises manager does not hold a personal licence.

Licensing (Scotland) Act 2005

Grant and renewal of personal licence

72. Application for personal licence

(1) Any individual aged 18 years or more may apply for a personal licence to-
   (a) if the individual is ordinarily resident in the area of any Licensing Board, that Board, or
   (b) in any other case, any Licensing Board.
(2) An application under subsection (1) is referred to in this Act as a "personal licence application".

DEFINITIONS
"personal licence": see s.71 of this Act
"area": see s.147(1) of this Act
"personal licence application": see subs.(2)

GENERAL NOTE

An applicant for a personal licence must be aged 18 or over. Under the current system, a number of licensing boards have required applicants to demonstrate prescribed levels of experience in the licensed trade, effectively preventing the grant or transfer of licences to persons who will qualify for licenceholding under this Act, although the 1976 Act prescribes no minimum age.

73. Notification of application to chief constable

(1) Where a Licensing Board receives a personal licence application, the Board must give notice of it, together with a copy of the application, to the appropriate chief constable.
(2) The appropriate chief constable must, within 21 days of the date of receipt of a notice under subsection (1), respond to the notice by giving the Licensing Board one or other of the notices mentioned in subsection (3).
(3) Those notices are-
   (a) a notice stating that, as far as the chief constable is aware, the applicant has not been convicted of any relevant offence or foreign offence, or
   (b) a notice specifying any convictions of the applicant for any such offence.
(4) Where the chief constable-
   (a) proposes to give a notice under subsection (3)(b), and
   (b) considers that, having regard to any conviction to be specified in the notice, it is necessary for the purposes of the crime prevention objective that the personal licence application be refused,
the chief constable may include in the notice a recommendation to that effect.

DEFINITIONS
"personal licence application": see s.72(2) of this Act
"appropriate chief constable": see s.147(1) of this Act
"applicant": see s.147(1) of this Act
"relevant offence": see s.129(1) of this Act
"foreign offence": see s.129(2) of this Act
"crime prevention objective": see s.49(2) of this Act

GENERAL NOTE
The licensing board is obliged to provide the chief constable with notice of a personal licence application, together with a copy of it. Within 21 days, the chief constable must respond with a notice stating that, so far as he is aware, the applicant has not been convicted of a relevant or foreign offence; or that a notice specifying the applicant's convictions for such an offence.

In the event that the latter notice is given, the chief constable may recommend the refusal of the application for the purposes of the crime prevention objective.

A conviction is to be disregarded if it is spent for the purposes of the Rehabilitation of Offenders Act 1974 (s.129(4)).

Subsection (4)
Although the chief constable may recommend the refusal of the application, he is not empowered to object, although he may object to the grant of a premises licence where the applicant, or a connected person, is believed to be involved in "serious organised crime" (s.22(2)). As explained in the notes to s.22, the Act abandons the "fit and proper test" required by the 1976 Act.

74. Determination of personal licence application

(1) A personal licence application received by a Licensing Board is to be determined by the Board in accordance with this section.
(2) If-
    (a) all of the conditions specified in subsection (3) are met in relation to the applicant, and
    (b) the Board has received from the appropriate chief constable a notice under section 73(3)(a),
the Board must grant the application.
(3) The conditions referred to in subsection (2)(a) are that-
    (a) the applicant is aged 18 or over,
    (b) the applicant possesses a licensing qualification, and
    (c) no personal licence previously held by the applicant has been revoked within the period of 5 years ending with the day on which the application was received.
(4) If any of those conditions is not met in relation to the applicant, the Licensing Board must refuse the application.
(5) If-
    (a) all of those conditions are met in relation to the applicant, and
    (b) the Board has received from the appropriate chief constable a notice under section 73(3)(b),
the Licensing Board must hold a hearing for the purpose of considering and determining the application.
(6) At a hearing under subsection (5), the Licensing Board must, after having regard to the chief constable's notice-
    (a) if satisfied that it is necessary to do so for the purposes of the crime prevention objective, refuse the application, or
    (b) if not so satisfied, grant the application.

DEFINITIONS
"personal licence application": see s.72(2) of this Act
"appropriate chief constable": see s.147(1) of this Act
"applicant": see s.147(1) of this Act
"licensing qualification": see s.91(1) of this Act

GENERAL NOTE
The licensing board is obliged to grant a personal licence application provided the applicant:

1 has not, according to the chief constable's notice, been convicted of a relevant or foreign offence;
2 is aged 18 or over;
3 possesses a licensing qualification; and
4 has not suffered the revocation of a personal licence in the previous five years.

If conditions (2)-(4) are not satisfied, the application must be refused. If all of these conditions are met but the board has received a conviction notice from the chief constable, the board must hold a hearing to determine the application. The "fit and proper person" test, which was applied to applications under the 1976 Act, has been abandoned (see notes to s.22).

Subsection (3)
The nature of licensing qualifications has yet to be prescribed in terms of s.91(1).

Subsection (6)
The conduct of a hearing to consider an application in the light of the applicant's convictions may not be delegated: Sch.1, para.10(2). The board must have regard to the chief constable's notice informing them of convictions (which may, but need not, include a refusal recommendation); and, if it is satisfied that it is necessary to do so for the purposes of the crime prevention objection, must refuse the application. Otherwise, the application must be granted.

75. Applicant's duty to notify Licensing Board of convictions

(1) This section applies where, during the period beginning with the making of a personal licence application and ending with determination of the application, the applicant is convicted of a relevant offence or a foreign offence.
(2) The applicant must, no later than one month after the date of the conviction, give notice of the conviction to the Licensing Board to which the personal licence application was made.
(3) A notice under subsection (2) must specify-
   (a) the nature of the offence, and
   (b) the date of the conviction.
(4) Where the Licensing Board receives a notice under subsection (2) at any time before they have determined the personal licence application, the Board must-
   (a) suspend consideration of the application, and
   (b) give notice of the conviction to the appropriate chief constable.
(5) The appropriate chief constable must, within 21 days of the date of receipt of a notice under subsection (4)(b), respond to the notice by giving the Licensing Board one or other of the notices mentioned in subsection (6).
(6) Those notices are-
   (a) a notice stating that the chief constable is unable to confirm the existence of the conviction or that the conviction does not relate to a relevant offence or foreign offence, or
   (b) a notice confirming the existence of the conviction and that it relates to a relevant offence or foreign offence.
(7) Where the chief constable-
   (a) proposes to give a notice under subsection (6)(b), and
   (b) considers that, having regard to the conviction specified in the notice, it is necessary for the purposes of the crime prevention objective that the personal licence application be refused,

the chief constable may include in the notice a recommendation to that effect.
  (8) On receipt of the chief constable's notice under subsection (6), the Licensing Board must resume consideration of the personal licence application and determine it in accordance with section 74.
  (9) For that purpose, that section has effect as if-
     (a) references in it to a notice under section 73(3)(a) included references to a notice under subsection (6)(a) of this section, and
     (b) references in it to a notice under section 73(3)(b) included references to a notice under subsection (6)(b) of this section.
  (10) A person who, without reasonable excuse, fails to comply with subsection (2) commits an offence.
  (11) A person guilty of an offence under subsection (10) is liable on summary conviction to a fine not exceeding level 3 on the standard scale.

DEFINITIONS
   "personal licence application": see s.72(2) of this Act
   "applicant": see s.147(1) of this Act
   "relevant offence": see s.129(1) of this Act
   "foreign offence": see s.129(2) of this Act
   "appropriate chief constable": see s.147(1) of this Act
   "crime prevention objective": see s.4(2) of this Act

GENERAL NOTE
   Provision is made for the possibility that an applicant for a personal licence may be convicted of a relevant or foreign offence prior to the determination of the application. The applicant must give the licensing board notice of the conviction no later than one month of its date. Failure to do so without reasonable excuse is an offence. Where a notice is received, consideration of the application must be suspended and the board must inform the chief constable of the conviction. The chief constable is then under an obligation to give the board one of two notices: (1) a notice stating that he is unable to confirm the existence of the conviction or that the conviction does not relate to a relevant or foreign offence; or (2) a notice confirming the existence of the conviction and that it relates to such an offence. If the latter notice is given, he may recommend refusal of the application for the purpose of the crime prevention objective.
   Upon receipt of a notice from the chief constable, the board must resume consideration of the application and determine it in accordance with s.74.
   Parallel provision is made in s.24 where an applicant for a premises licence incurs a conviction prior to its determination.

76. Issue of licence

  (1) Where a Licensing Board grants a personal licence application, the Board must issue a personal licence, in the prescribed form, to the applicant.
  (2) A personal licence issued under subsection (1) must specify-
     (a) the name and address of the individual to whom it is issued,
     (b) the Licensing Board issuing the licence,
     (c) the expiry date of the licence,
     (d) any relevant offence or foreign offence of which the applicant has been convicted, and
     (e) such other matters as may be prescribed.
  (3) A personal licence is void if, at the time it is issued under subsection (1), the individual to whom it is issued already holds a personal licence.

DEFINITIONS
"personal licence application": see s.72(2) of this Act
"personal licence": see s.71 of this Act
"relevant offence": see s.129(1) of this Act
"foreign offence": see s.129(2) of this Act
"applicant": see s.147(1) of this Act
"prescribed": see s.147(1) of this Act

GENERAL NOTE
This section sets out the information which must be contained in the personal licence issued to a successful applicant.

Subsection (3)
A personal licence issued under this section is void if, at the time of issue, the individual concerned already holds a personal licence, so that only one personal licence may be held at any time.

77. Period of effect of personal licence

(1) A personal licence has effect, subject to the following provisions of this section, during the period of 10 years beginning with the date on which it is issued.
(2) That period, and any subsequent extension of it under this subsection, is extended for a further period of 10 years if a personal licence renewal application is granted in respect of the licence.
(3) A personal licence does not have effect for any period during which it is suspended by virtue of any provision of this Act.
(4) Subsection (3) does not affect the calculation of the period during which a personal licence has effect by virtue of subsection (1) as read with subsection (2).
(5) A personal licence ceases to have effect if-
  (a) the licence is revoked under any provision of this Part, or
  (b) the Licensing Board which issued the licence receives from the personal licence holder a notice under subsection (6).
(6) That is a notice-
  (a) accompanied by the personal licence or, where that is not practicable, by a statement of reasons for failure to produce the licence, and
  (b) stating that the licence holder wishes to surrender the licence.
(7) The date of expiry of the period during which a personal licence has effect is referred to in this Act as the "expiry date" of the licence.
(8) Not later than 3 months before the expiry date of a personal licence, the Licensing Board which issued the licence must give notice to the licence holder that the licence will cease to have effect on the expiry date unless renewed.

DEFINITIONS
"personal licence": see s.71 of this Act
"personal licence renewal application": see s.78(4) of this Act
"expiry date": see subs.(7)

GENERAL NOTE
Personal licences have a currency of ten years, and may be renewed for a like period. They do not have effect during any period of suspension. Provision for suspension is made in ss.83, 84 and 86.

Licensing (Scotland) Act 2005 123

Subsection (4)
The effect of this subsection is to ensure that any period during which a personal licence is suspended is disregarded for the purpose of calculating the ten-year validity period.

Subsection (8)
The licensing board must give the holder of a personal licence at least three months' notice that his licence will expire on a certain date unless renewed. Under the current system, licensing boards are under no obligation to issue reminders as to the necessity to lodge an application to renew a licence.

78. Renewal of personal licence

(1) The holder of a personal licence may, within the period specified in subsection (2), apply to the Licensing Board which issued the licence for renewal of the licence.
(2) The period referred to in subsection (1) is the period of 2 months beginning 3 months before the expiry date of the licence.
(3) An application under subsection (1) must be accompanied by-
   (a) the personal licence to which it relates, or
   (b) if that is not practicable, a statement of the reasons for failure to produce the licence.
(4) An application under subsection (1) which complies with subsection (3) is referred to in this Act as a "personal licence renewal application".
(5) Sections 73 and 74 apply to a personal licence renewal application as they apply to a personal licence application.
(6) For that purpose, references in those sections to a personal licence application are to be read as if they included reference to a personal licence renewal application.

DEFINITIONS
"personal licence": see s.71 of this Act
"personal licence renewal application": see subs.(4)
"personal licence application": see s.72(2) of this Act

GENERAL NOTE
An application for the renewal of a personal licence may be made to the issuing licensing board within the period of two months beginning three months before the expiry date. It may have been simpler to provide that a renewal application may be made not later than one month prior to the expiry date.

Subsection (3)
A renewal application must be accompanied by the personal licence or, if that is not practicable, a statement of the reasons for the failure to produce it. Provision is made in s.92 for the issue of a replacement licence in certain circumstances.

Subsection (5), (6)
These subsections provide that the procedure which requires to be followed where application is made for the grant of a personal licence also applies to renewal applications.

79. Notification of determinations

(1) This section applies where a Licensing Board grants or refuses-
   (a) a personal licence application, or

(b) a personal licence renewal application.
(2) The Board must give-
    (a) the applicant, and
    (b) the appropriate chief constable,
notice of the grant or refusal of the application.
(3) A person to whom notice is given under subsection (2) may, by notice to the clerk of the Board, require the Board to give a statement of reasons for the grant or refusal of the application.
(4) Where the clerk of a Licensing Board receives a notice under subsection (3), the Board must issue a statement of the reasons for the grant or refusal of the application to-
    (a) the person giving the notice, and
    (b) each other person to whom the Board gave notice under subsection (2).
(5) A statement of reasons under subsection (4) must be issued-
    (a) by such time, and
    (b) in such form and manner,
as may be prescribed.

DEFINITIONS
"personal licence application": see s.72(2) of this Act
"personal licence renewal application": see subs.(4)
"applicant": see s.147(1) of this Act
"appropriate chief constable": see s.147(1) of this Act

GENERAL NOTE
The licensing board is required to give notice of the grant or refusal of a personal licence application or a personal licence renewal application to the applicant and chief constable. Either party may request a statement of reasons for the board's decision.

Conviction of licence holder for relevant or foreign offence

80. Duty to notify court of personal licence

(1) Subsection (2) applies where-
    (a) a person who holds a personal licence is charged with a relevant offence, or
    (b) a person charged with a relevant offence is granted a personal licence after the person's first appearance in court in connection with the offence but before-
        (i) conviction and sentencing for the offence or acquittal, or
        (ii) where an appeal is brought against conviction, sentence or acquittal, the disposal of the appeal.
(2) The person must, no later than the person's first or, as the case may be, next appearance in court in connection with the offence-
    (a) produce to the court the personal licence, or
    (b) if that is not practicable, notify the court of-
        (i) the existence of the personal licence,
        (ii) the identity of the Licensing Board which issued the licence, and
        (iii) the reasons why it is not practicable to produce the licence.
(3) A person who, without reasonable excuse, fails to comply with subsection (2) commits an offence.

(4) A person guilty of an offence under subsection (3) is liable on summary conviction to a fine not exceeding level 2 on the standard scale.

DEFINITIONS
"personal licence": see s.71 of this Act
"relevant offence": see s.129(1) of this Act

GENERAL NOTE
Where the holder of a personal licence is charged with a relevant offence he must produce his personal licence to the court or provide the court with the information set out in subs.(2). A similar obligation falls upon a person who obtains a personal licence during the currency of criminal proceedings, up to and including the disposal of an appeal.

The purpose of this provision is to alert the court to the obligation imposed upon the clerk in terms of s.81.

81. Court's duty to notify Licensing Board of convictions

(1) This section applies where the clerk of a court in Scotland by or before which a person is convicted of a relevant offence is aware that the person holds a personal licence.
(2) The clerk of the court must, as soon as reasonably practicable after the conviction, give notice of the conviction to the Licensing Board which issued the personal licence held by the licence holder.
(3) Where-
   (a) a Licensing Board receives a notice under subsection (2) ("the receiving Board"), and
   (b) that Board has reason to believe that the personal licence holder in respect of whom the notice is given is working in licensed premises situated in the area of another Licensing Board ("the other Board"),
the receiving Board must give notice of the conviction to the other Board.

DEFINITIONS
"relevant offence": see s.129(1) of this Act
"personal licence": see s.71 of this Act

GENERAL NOTE
This section places the clerk of the court under an obligation to give notice of a conviction for a relevant offence to the issuing licensing board as soon as reasonably practicable, where the clerk of the court is aware that the person convicted in the holder of a personal licence.

Where such a notice is received by a licensing board, and the board has reason to believe that the personal licence holder is working in another board's area, it must give notice of the conviction to the other board.

82. Licence holder's duty to notify Licensing Board of convictions

(1) This section applies where a personal licence holder is convicted of a relevant or foreign offence.
(2) The licence holder must, no later than one month after the date of the conviction, give notice of the conviction to-
   (a) the Licensing Board which issued the personal licence held by the licence holder, and

(b) if different, the Licensing Board for the area in which are situated any licensed premises in which the licence holder is working.
(3) A notice of conviction under subsection (2) must-
   (a) specify-
      (i) the nature of the offence, and
      (ii) the date of the conviction, and
   (b) be accompanied by-
      (i) the personal licence held by the licence holder, or
      (ii) if that is not practicable, a statement of the reasons for failure to produce the licence.
(4) Where-
   (a) a Licensing Board receives a notice under subsection (2) ("the receiving Board"), and
   (b) that Board has reason to believe that the personal licence holder in respect of whom the notice is given is working in licensed premises situated in the area of another Licensing Board ("the other Board"),
the receiving Board must give notice of the conviction to the other Board.
(5) A licence holder who fails, without reasonable excuse, to comply with subsection (2) commits an offence.
(6) A person guilty of an offence under subsection (5) is liable on summary conviction to a fine not exceeding level 4 on the standard scale.

DEFINITIONS
"personal licence": see s.71 of this Act
"relevant offence": see s.129(1) of this Act
"foreign offence": see s.129(2) of this Act
"area": see s.147(1) of this Act
"licensed premises": see s.147(1) of this Act

GENERAL NOTE
The holder of a personal licence convicted of a relevant or foreign offence must, no later than one month after the date of the conviction, give notice of the conviction to the licensing board which issued the licence and, if different, the board in whose area the licence holder is working. Where a licensing board receives such a notice and has reason to believe that the licence holder is working in another board's area, it must give notice of the conviction to the other board.

83. Procedure where Licensing Board receives notice of conviction

(1) Subsection (2) applies where the relevant Licensing Board-
   (a) receives a notice of conviction relating to a personal licence holder, or
   (b) becomes aware that a personal licence holder was, during the application period, convicted of a relevant offence or a foreign offence.
(2) The Licensing Board must give notice of the conviction to the appropriate chief constable.
(3) The appropriate chief constable must, within 21 days of the date of receipt of a notice under subsection (2), respond to the notice by giving the Licensing Board one or other of the notices mentioned in subsection (4).
(4) Those notices are-

(a) a notice stating that the chief constable is unable to confirm the existence of the conviction or that the conviction does not relate to a relevant or a foreign offence, or

(b) a notice confirming the existence of the conviction and that it relates to a relevant or a foreign offence.

(5) Where the appropriate chief constable-
   (a) proposes to give a notice under subsection (4)(b), and
   (b) considers that, having regard to the conviction specified in the notice, it is necessary for the purposes of the crime prevention objective that the licence holder's personal licence should be revoked, suspended or endorsed,

the chief constable may include in the notice a recommendation to that effect.

(6) If the Licensing Board receives from the appropriate chief constable a notice under subsection (4)(a), the Licensing Board may not take any further action in relation to the conviction.

(7) If the Licensing Board receives from the appropriate chief constable a notice under subsection (4)(b), the Licensing Board must hold a hearing.

(8) At the hearing, the Licensing Board may-
   (a) having regard to-
      (i) the conviction, and
      (ii) any recommendation contained in the chief constable's notice under subsection (5),
   (b) after giving-
      (i) the licence holder concerned, and
      (ii) the appropriate chief constable,
   an opportunity to be heard, and
   (c) if satisfied that it is necessary to do so for the purposes of the crime prevention objective,

make an order under subsection (9).

(9) That order is an order-
   (a) revoking,
   (b) suspending for such period, not exceeding 6 months, as the Board considers appropriate, or
   (c) endorsing,

the personal licence held by the licence holder concerned.

(10) Where the Licensing Board makes an order under subsection (9), the Board must give-
   (a) the licence holder concerned,
   (b) the appropriate chief constable, and
   (c) if different, the Licensing Board which issued the personal licence,

notice of the order and of the reasons for making it.

(11) In this section-

"the application period" means, in relation to a personal licence holder, the period-
   (a) beginning with the date on which the application for the personal licence held by that licence holder was made, and
   (b) ending with the date on which that application was granted,

"notice of conviction" means a notice under section 81(2) or 82(2), and
"relevant Licensing Board" means, in relation to a personal licence holder-

(a) if the personal licence holder is working as a premises manager at any licensed premises, the Licensing Board for the area in which those premises are situated,

(b) in any other case, the Licensing Board which issued the personal licence held by the licence holder.

DEFINITIONS

"personal licence": see s.71 of this Act
"relevant offence": see s.129(1) of this Act
"foreign offence": see s.129(2) of this Act
"appropriate chief constable": see s.147(1) of this Act
"crime prevention objective": see s.4(2) of this Act
"the application period": see subs.(11)
"notice of conviction": see subs.(11)
"relevant licensing board": see subs.(11)
"premises manager": see s.19(1) of this Act
"area": see s.147(1) of this Act

GENERAL NOTE

This section applies where a personal licence holder is the subject of a conviction for a relevant or foreign offence during its currency or the licensing board becomes aware that such a conviction was incurred during the application process. (Separate provision is made in s.75 for a hearing where the licensing board receives notice of a conviction prior to the determination of an application for a personal licence).

If, after a hearing, the licensing board considers if it necessary to do so for the purpose of the crime prevention objective, it may revoke, suspend or endorse the personal licence. Three endorsements may result in the suspension or revocation of the licence: see s.86.

These and the following provisions largely adopt Nicholson recommendations (Report, para.7.15 *et seq*). The Committee considered that disciplinary measures were more appropriately taken by the licensing board, rather than the court, being better placed to take into account any background such as past misdemeanours which did not amount to the a conviction.

Contrary to a Nicholson recommendation (Report, para.7.20), no provision is made for the premises licence holder to be called to a hearing where a conviction is incurred by a personal licence holder; but a nexus between the two licences is established by s. 84 (*qv*), which requires disciplinary proceedings to be commenced against a personal licence holder as a result of a finding made in the course of a premises licence review.

Neither is provision is made for the consideration of pending criminal charges, which, Nicholson noted, are taken into account by some licensing boards when assessing fitness to hold a licence. Observing that "many people, including in particular many lawyers, have considerable unease about such a practice", the Report recommended that consideration should be give to the formulation of a policy relative to this issue (Report, para.7.20). See further: "Is a public hearing a fair hearing?" (Brian Dunlop), [2002] 22 SLLP 12.

The board's ability simply to endorse a licence reflects the Nicholson proposal that provision should be made for a sanction short of revocation or suspension of a personal licence (Report, para.7.21).

Subsection (1)

The Explanatory Notes are not quite correct in their approach to s.83. They suggest that:

"It is primarily for the licensing board in the area in which the licence holder is working to take action under this section. But if the licence holder is not working in any licensed premises then it will be for the licensing board which issued the personal licence to take action."

Having regard to the definition of "relevant Licensing Board" in subs.11, where the personal licence holder is working as a premises manager, the disciplinary procedures are to be commenced by the licensing board in whose area he is working; but if he is not working *in that capacity* or not working in any licensed premises, then the procedures are invoked by the licensing board which issued the personal licence.

Subsections (2)-(7)

The licensing board must proceed to give notice of the conviction to the chief constable, who is then required to give the board one of two notices within 21 days, either confirming or otherwise that the conviction exists and, if so, that it relates to a relevant or foreign offence.

A notice in the affirmative may be conjoined with the chief constable's recommendation that the personal licence should be revoked, suspended or endorsed for the purpose of the crime prevention objective.

If the notice is in the negative, no further action may be taken. Otherwise, the board must hold hearing.

Subsections (8), (9)

At a hearing, when the licence holder and chief constable must be given an opportunity of being heard, the licensing board must have regard to the conviction and any recommendation made by the chief constable. If it is satisfied that it is necessary to do so for the purposes of the crime prevention objective, it may revoke, suspend or endorse the personal licence. A suspension may last for a period of up to six months.

Subsection (10)

The licensing board must give notice of an order made under subs.(9) and the reasons for it to the licence holder, the chief constable, and, if different, the board which issued the licence. The requirement to give reasons is automatic: in other cases, reasons must be requested (see, for example, s.79(3)).

Conduct inconsistent with licensing objectives

84. Conduct inconsistent with the licensing objectives

(1) This section applies where, in the course of a review hearing in respect of any premises licence, a Licensing Board makes a finding such as is mentioned in subsection (2) in relation to any personal licence holder who is or was working in the licensed premises in respect of which the premises licence was issued ("the licensed premises concerned").

(2) That finding is a finding that the licence holder concerned, while working as mentioned in subsection (1), acted in a manner which was inconsistent with any of the licensing objectives.

(3) The Licensing Board making the finding must-
  (a) if the licence holder concerned is, at the time of the finding, working in licensed premises (whether the licensed premises concerned or other licensed premises) in that Board's area, hold a hearing,
  (b) in any other case, give notice to the relevant Licensing Board of their finding together with a recommendation as to whether the personal licence held by the licence holder concerned should be revoked, suspended or endorsed.

(4) In subsection (3)(b), "relevant Licensing Board" means-
  (a) if the Licensing Board making the finding referred to in subsection (1) has reason to believe that the licence holder concerned is working at licensed premises situated in the area of another Licensing Board, that other Licensing Board,
  (b) in any other case, the Licensing Board which issued the personal licence held by the licence holder concerned.

(5) Where a Licensing Board receives a notice and recommendation under subsection (3)(b), the Board must hold a hearing.

(6) At a hearing under subsection (3)(a) or (5), the Licensing Board may-
  (a) after giving-
    (i) the licence holder concerned, and
    (ii) such other persons as they consider appropriate, an opportunity to be heard, and
  (b) if satisfied that it is necessary to do so for the purposes of any of the licensing objectives,

make an order under subsection (7).

(7) That is an order-
  (a) revoking,
  (b) suspending for such period, not exceeding 6 months, as the Board considers appropriate, or
  (c) endorsing,

the personal licence held by the licence holder concerned.

(8) Where the Licensing Board makes an order under subsection (7), the Board must give-
  (a) the licence holder concerned,
  (b) where the hearing was held in pursuance of a notice given under subsection (3)(b), the Licensing Board which gave the notice, and
  (c) if different, the Licensing Board which issued the personal licence,

notice of the order and of the reasons for making it.

DEFINITIONS
"review hearing": see s.38(2) of this Act
"premises licence": see s.17 of this Act
"personal licence": see s.71 of this Act
"licensed premises": see s.147(1) of this Act
"licensing objectives": see s.4(1) of this Act
"area": see s.147(1) of this Act

GENERAL NOTE
This section forges a nexus between the premises licence and the behaviour of a personal licence holder by making provision for disciplinary proceeding where the review of a premises licence uncovers conduct on the part of the personal licence holder which is inconsistent with any of the licensing objectives.

Nicholson considered that where the holder of a personal licence had not been convicted of an offence but had "failed to carry out his duties in an acceptable manner which was consistent with the 'licensing principles'" it should be open to the licensing board to impose a sanction (Report, para.7.21). The provisions here broadly enact that recommendation.

Subsections (1) and (2)
The catalyst for disciplinary proceedings under this section is a finding made in the course of a premises licence review hearing that the holder of a personal licence has acted in a manner inconsistent with the licensing objectives (rather than, as Nicholson envisaged, a complaint from an external source).

Subsections (3)-(5)
Jurisdiction in relation to disciplinary proceedings depends on a number of variables. The board making the finding must hold a hearing if, at the time of the finding, the licence holder is working in any licensed premises in its area (whether or not as a premises manager (*cf* s.83(11)). Otherwise that board must give notice of the finding to either (a) the licensing board, if any, in whose area the holder is be believed to be working; or in any other case (b) the board which issued the personal licence. The notice is to be conjoined with a recommendation as to whether the licence should be revoked, suspended or endorsed. A board which receives such a notice must hold a hearing.

Subsections (6) and (7)
At a hearing, when the licence holder and such other persons as the board considers appropriate must be given an opportunity of being heard, the licensing board may, if it is satisfied that it is necessary to do so for the purposes of any of the licensing objectives, revoke, suspend or endorse the personal licence. A suspension may last for a period of up to six months.

Subsection (8)
The licensing board must give notice of an order made under subs.(7) and the reasons for it to the licence holder; where applicable, the licensing board from which it received notice of the finding; and, if different, the board which issued the personal licence.

Endorsements

85. Expiry of endorsements

(1) In this section and section 86, "endorsement" means an endorsement made in a personal licence by virtue of an order under-
   (a) section 83(9)(c), or
   (b) section 84(7)(c).
(2) An endorsement expires at the end of the period of 5 years beginning with the date on which the endorsement was made.
(3) The holder of a personal licence containing an endorsement which has expired under subsection (2) may apply to the Licensing Board which issued the licence for removal of the endorsement.
(4) An application under subsection (3) must be accompanied by the personal licence to which it relates.
(5) Where a Licensing Board receives an application under subsection (3) in relation to any personal licence, the Board must amend the licence so as to remove the endorsement from it.
(6) For the purposes of this Act, any endorsement which has expired under subsection (2) is to be disregarded (whether or not the endorsement has been removed under subsection (5)).

DEFINITIONS
"personal licence": see s.71 of this Act

GENERAL NOTE
An endorsement to a personal licence made under the provisions of s.83 or s.84 expires after five years. The licence holder may apply to the issuing licensing board for its removal upon expiry, in which case the licence is to be amended. An expired endorsement is to be disregarded, whether or not it has been removed from the licence.

86. Suspension of licence after multiple endorsements

(1) Where 3 endorsements have been made in any personal licence, the Licensing Board which issued the licence must hold a hearing.
(2) At the hearing, the Licensing Board may-
   (a) after giving-
      (i) the holder of the licence, and
      (ii) such other persons as the Board considers appropriate,
   an opportunity to be heard, and
   (b) if they consider it necessary to do so for the purposes of any of the licensing objectives,

make an order under subsection (3).
- (3) That is an order-
  - (a) suspending the licence for such period, not exceeding 6 months, as the Board considers appropriate, or
  - (b) revoking the licence.
- (4) Where the Licensing Board makes an order under subsection (3), the Board must give the licence holder notice of the order and of the reasons for making it.

DEFINITIONS
"personal licence": see s.71 of this Act

GENERAL NOTE
Where a personal licence has been thrice endorsed, the licensing board which issued the licence must hold a hearing which may result in the licence being suspended or revoked for the purpose of any of the licensing objectives. At the hearing, an opportunity to be heard must be afforded to the licence holder and such other persons as the board considers appropriate. In the event of suspension or revocation, notice must be given to the licence holder, together with the board's reasons.

Licence holder's duty to undertake training

87. Licence holder's duty to undertake training

- (1) The holder of a personal licence must, no later than 3 months after the expiry of-
  - (a) the period of 5 years beginning with the date on which the licence holder's licence was issued, and
  - (b) each subsequent period of 5 years during which the licence has effect,

produce to the Licensing Board which issued the licence evidence in the prescribed form of the licence holder's having complied, during that period, with such requirements as to the training of personal licence holders as may be prescribed.

- (2) A Licensing Board must-
  - (a) in relation to each personal licence issued by it, and
  - (b) no later than 3 months before the expiry of each period mentioned in subsection (1),

give to the holder of the licence notice of the requirement imposed by that subsection.

- (3) If a personal licence holder fails to comply with subsection (1), the Licensing Board which issued the licence held by the licence holder must revoke the licence.
- (4) Regulations under subsection (1) prescribing training requirements may, in particular-
  - (a) provide for accreditation by the Scottish Ministers of-
    - (i) courses of training, and
    - (ii) persons providing such courses,
  - for the purposes of the regulations,
  - (b) prescribe different requirements in relation to different descriptions of personal licence holder, and

Licensing (Scotland) Act 2005 133

(c) require that any person providing training or any particular description of training in accordance with the regulations holds such qualification as may be prescribed in the regulations.

DEFINITIONS
"personal licence": see s.71 of this Act
"prescribed": see s.147(1) of this Act

GENERAL NOTE
This section replaces the current patchwork of training regimes introduced by most licensing boards in recent years and places training on a mandatory footing within a national framework. According to the Policy Memorandum, training is "an important mechanism by which standards can be maintained and indeed raised".

Personal licence holders will require to undertake training every five years and produce to the licensing board evidence of having done so with three months, failing which the board must revoke the licence.

The board is under an obligation to give each person to whom it has issued a personal licence not less than three months' notice of the compliance deadline.

The detail of training requirements has yet to be prescribed by regulations made under subs.(4).

Update of licence

88. Notification of change of name or address

(1) A personal licence holder must, no later than one month after any change in the licence holder's name or address, give the Licensing Board which issued the licence notice of the change.
(2) A notice under subsection (1) must be accompanied by the personal licence or, if that is not practicable, by a statement of the reasons for the failure to produce the licence.
(3) A personal licence holder who fails, without reasonable excuse, to comply with subsection (1) commits an offence.
(4) A person guilty of an offence under subsection (3) is liable on summary conviction to a fine not exceeding level 2 on the standard scale.

DEFINITIONS
"personal licence": see s.71 of this Act

GENERAL NOTE
The holder of a personal licence must notify the issuing licensing board of any change in his name or address within one month of the change occurring and, at the same time, provide the board with the licence or a statement of the reasons why it cannot be produced. Failure to comply with these requirements without reasonable excuse is an offence.

89. Licensing Board's duty to update licence

(1) In this section, the "issuing Licensing Board" means, in relation to a personal licence, the Licensing Board which issued the licence.
(2) Where the issuing Licensing Board grants a personal licence renewal application made in respect of any personal licence, the Board must

make the necessary amendment to the expiry date specified in the licence.
(3) Where a personal licence is suspended by virtue of any provision in this Act, the issuing Licensing Board must amend the licence so as to specify in it-
  (a) the date, and
  (b) period,
of the suspension.
(4) Where the issuing Licensing Board receives a notice of conviction in relation to any personal licence holder, the Board must amend the personal licence held by the licence holder so as to specify in it-
  (a) the date of the conviction, and
  (b) the nature of the offence,
unless the Board has already done so by virtue of any previous such notice.
(5) Where the issuing Licensing Board-
  (a) makes an order under section 83(9)(c) or 84(7)(c) in relation to any personal licence holder, or
  (b) receives notice under section 83(10)(c) or 84(8)(c) of such an order made by another Licensing Board,
the Board must amend the personal licence held by the licence holder so as to include in it a statement that it is endorsed together with the details of the conviction or conduct giving rise to the making of the order.
(6) Where the issuing Licensing Board receives a notice under section 88(1) from a personal licence holder, the Board must amend the personal licence of the licence holder so that it specifies the licence holder's new name or address.
(7) Where the issuing Licensing Board receives evidence of training produced by a personal licence holder in accordance with section 87(1), the Board must amend the personal licence held by the licence holder so as to include in it the prescribed details of the training.
(8) Where the issuing Licensing Board is not in possession of a personal licence and-
  (a) the licence has been revoked under any provision of this Act, or
  (b) the Board requires the licence for the purpose of complying with any duty under this section in relation to the licence,
the Board may require the holder of the licence to produce it to the Board within 14 days from the date on which the requirement is notified.
(9) A personal licence holder who fails, without reasonable excuse, to comply with a requirement made under subsection (8) commits an offence.
(10) A person guilty of an offence under subsection (9) is liable on summary conviction to a fine not exceeding level 2 on the standard scale.
(11) In this section, "notice of conviction" means a notice under section 81(2) or 82(2).

DEFINITIONS
  "issuing licensing board": see subs.(1)
  "personal licence": see s.71 of this Act
  "personal licence renewal application": see s.78(4) of this Act

GENERAL NOTE
  This section makes provision for the amendment of a personal licence by the issuing licensing board where: the licence has been renewed, suspended, or endorsed; the board has received no-

tice of a conviction; or notification has been received of a change to the holder's name or address. An amendment is also required where the board has received evidence of training pursuant to s.87(1).

Miscellaneous

90. Power to specify which Licensing Board is to exercise functions under this Part

(1) The Scottish Ministers may by order provide for any function exercisable under this Part by a Licensing Board of a particular description to be exercisable instead by a Licensing Board of such other description as may be specified in the order.
(2) An order under subsection (1) may-
    (a) modify this Act, and
    (b) make different provision in relation to different functions.

GENERAL NOTE
This provision allows Scottish Ministers to re-determine by order which licensing board is to exercise any function under the Act. Its purpose is opaque, but it would, for example, permit an order modifying the description of licensing board which is to conduct disciplinary proceedings in relation to personal licence holders.

91. Power to prescribe licensing qualifications

(1) In this Act, "licensing qualification" means-
    (a) such qualification, or
    (b) a qualification of such description,
as may be prescribed.
(2) Regulations under subsection (1) may, in particular-
    (a) prescribe qualifications or descriptions of qualifications by reference to whether they are-
        (i) accredited, or
        (ii) awarded by a person who is accredited,
    for the purposes of this section by the Scottish Ministers in accordance with the regulations,
    (b) prescribe qualifications or descriptions of qualifications awarded outwith Scotland (as well as qualifications awarded within Scotland),
    (c) prescribe different qualifications in relation to different licensed premises or licensed premises of different descriptions, and
    (d) prescribe such qualifications as the appropriate licensing qualifications in relation to those descriptions of licensed premises for the purposes of paragraph 4(2) of schedule 3.

DEFINITIONS
  "licensing qualification": see subs.(1)
  "prescribed": see s.147(1) of this Act

GENERAL NOTE
An applicant for a personal licence must be in possession of a "licensing qualification": s.74(3). Nicholson considered that it was desirable that provision should be made for different levels of approved licensing qualification to reflect the range of activities which the qualification

holder would be entitled to undertake (Report, paras.4.8, 4.9). For example, a personal licence holder who was to be the premises manager at a large nightclub would require much more extensive training than, say, the grocer in a small corner shop. The Report's recommendation is reflected in subs.(2)(c). Provision is also made for the accreditation of qualifications and those awarding them.

Subsection (2) (d)

Paragraph 4(1) of Sch.3 provides, as a mandatory condition of a premises licence, that alcohol is not to be sold on the premises if the licensing qualification held by the premises manager is not the appropriate licensing qualification for the premises, by reference to this subsection.

92. Theft, loss etc. of personal licence

(1) This section applies where the Licensing Board which issued a personal licence receives from the holder of the licence an application for a replacement personal licence.

(2) If satisfied that-
   (a) the personal licence held by the applicant has been lost, stolen, damaged or destroyed, and
   (b) where it has been lost or stolen, the applicant has reported the loss or theft to the police,
the Licensing Board must issue to the applicant a replacement personal licence.

(3) A replacement personal licence is a copy of the personal licence held by the applicant-
   (a) in the form in which it existed immediately before it was lost, stolen, damaged or destroyed, and
   (b) certified by the Board to be a true copy.

(4) In this Act, references to a personal licence include references to a replacement personal licence issued under this section.

DEFINITIONS
"personal licence": see s.71 of this Act

GENERAL NOTE
Where a personal licence has been lost, stolen, damaged or destroyed, the holder may apply for a replacement to the issuing licensing board. In the case of loss or theft, the matter must have been reported to the police.

93. Licence holder's duty to produce licence

(1) This section applies where the holder of a personal licence is working at any licensed premises.

(2) A constable or Licensing Standards Officer may, at any time when the licence holder is on the licensed premises, require the licence holder to produce the licence for examination.

(3) A person who fails, without reasonable excuse, to comply with a requirement made under subsection (2) commits an offence.

(4) A person guilty of an offence under subsection (3) is liable on summary conviction to a fine not exceeding level 2 on the standard scale.

DEFINITIONS
"personal licence": see s.71 of this Act
"licensed premises": see s.147(1) of this Act

GENERAL NOTE
Where a personal licence holder is working at any licensed premises, a constable or licensing standards officer may require production of the licence. Failure to comply with this requirement without reasonable excuse is an offence.

Subsection (2)
Production of the licence may only be required when the holder is on the premises and not in his absence.

PART 7

CONTROL OF ORDER

Exclusion of violent offenders

94. Exclusion orders

(1) This section applies where a person is convicted of a violent offence committed on, or in the immediate vicinity of, any licensed premises in respect of which a premises licence has effect (referred to in this section and section 96 as "the licensed premises concerned").

(2) The court by or before which the person is convicted of the offence may, in addition to any sentence imposed or other disposal in respect of the offence, make an order prohibiting the person from entering-
   (a) the licensed premises concerned, and
   (b) such other licensed premises (if any) as the court may specify in the order,
except with the appropriate consent.

(3) The holder of the premises licence in respect of the licensed premises concerned may, by summary application to the sheriff of the appropriate sheriffdom made no later than 6 weeks after the date of the conviction, seek an order prohibiting the person convicted from entering the licensed premises concerned except with the appropriate consent.

(4) On such an application, the sheriff, if satisfied that-
   (a) there is a substantial risk that the person convicted will commit a further violent offence on, or in the immediate vicinity of, the licensed premises concerned, and
   (b) an order has not been made under subsection (2) in relation to the person in respect of the same conviction,
may grant the order sought.

(5) For the purposes of an application under subsection (3), where the sheriff is satisfied that the person to whom the application relates has been convicted as mentioned in subsection (1), it is to be presumed, unless the contrary is proved, that the risk referred to in subsection (4)(a) exists.

(6) An order under subsection (2) or (4) is referred to in this Act as an "exclusion order".

(7) An exclusion order has effect, subject to section 95(3), for such period, being not less than 3 months and not more than 2 years, as is specified in the order.

(8) In this section-

"the appropriate consent" means, in relation to any licensed premises, the express consent of-
  (a) the premises licence holder in respect of the premises, or
  (b) a person authorised by the premises licence holder to give consent for the purposes of this section,

"the appropriate sheriffdom" means the sheriffdom in which the licensed premises concerned are situated,

"violent offence" means any offence involving violence or the threat of violence.

DEFINITIONS

"premises licence": see s.17 of this Act
"licensed premises": see s.147(1) of this Act
"the appropriate consent": see subs.(8)
"the appropriate sheriffdom": see subs.(8)
"violent offence": see subs.(8)

GENERAL NOTE

The provisions of this section and the two sections following attempt to address the inadequacies of the Licensing Premises (Exclusion of Certain Persons) Act 1980 ("the 1980 Act"), in terms of which an exclusion order lasting not less than three months and not more than two years may be imposed following a conviction for an offence committed on licensed premises, where the court is satisfied that the person convicted "resorted to violence or offered or threatened to resort to violence". (For a consideration of the Act's defects, see "Problems Over Exclusion Orders" [1990] 1 LR 12.) The 1980 Act is repealed by Sch.7.

The effect of an order is to prevent the offender from entering the licensed premises *in quo* or any other specified premises without the express consent of the licenceholder or a member of his staff.

Nicholson noted the 1980 Act's weaknesses (Report, paras.14.10, 14.11). Little use has been made of the powers available to the court because, the Committee was told, procurators fiscal fail to suggest to sheriffs that consideration might be given to the making of an appropriate order. In terms of Nicholson recommendation 64, the 1980 Act ought to be amended so as to extend to all licensed premises (off-sales are currently excluded); and consideration should be given to the introduction of a procedure allowing a licenceholder to apply for an exclusion order where such an order had not been sought at the time of conviction.

Daniels supported these proposals (Report, para.4.32) and also suggested that (a) provision should be made for exclusion in respect of disorder in or associated with licensed premises; and (b) as a stop-gap measure, appropriate guidance or training should be provided to prosecutors, judges and justices to raise their awareness of the 1980 Act. Unhappily, no notice has been taken of the latter suggestion.

Broadly speaking, s.94 enacts the Nicholson recommendation; but it does not give effect to concerns expressed by Sheriff Principal Nicholson in his written evidence to the Local Government and Transport Committee (see Note to subs.(3)).

Subsection (1)

An order may be made where a violent offence has been committed on, or in the vicinity, of any licensed premises which are the subject of a premises licence. Presently, the conviction must relate to an offence committed "on licensed premises" other than premises in respect of which an off-sale licence is in force.

Subsection (2)
A failure to specify the premises from which the offender is excluded will render the order incompetent: *Nicolson v Mackenzie*, 1993 G.W.D. 7-476.

Subsection (3)
In his written evidence to the Local Government and Transport Committee, Sheriff Principal Nicholson indicated that he had taken a revised view as to the desirability of allowing an application for an exclusion order to made post conviction. He expressed concern that a sheriff would have no means of knowing whether or not the judge in the original court considered the making of an exclusion order and deliberately chose not to do so, possibly for good reasons. His suggestion that an application for an order could, in most cases, be made to the court which was dealing with the offender was not adopted.

Subsection (7)
Otherwise the order cannot be extended or reviewed.

Subsection (8)
In *Stephen v McKay* 1997 SCCR 444; [1997] 8 SLLP 22, it was held that the subject of an exclusion order under the 1980 Act had "resorted to violence or offered or threatened to resort to violence" where he had shouted and sworn at and struggled with the police officers who were carrying our his arrest.

95. Breach of exclusion order

(1) A person who enters licensed premises in breach of an exclusion order commits an offence.
(2) A person guilty of an offence under subsection (1) is liable on summary conviction to-
  (a) a fine not exceeding level 4 on the standard scale,
  (b) imprisonment for a term not exceeding one month, or
  (c) both.
(3) The court by or before which a person is convicted of an offence under subsection (1) of breaching an exclusion order made under section 94(2) may, if it thinks fit, terminate the exclusion order or vary it so as to delete any licensed premises specified in it.
(4) Where, in relation to any licensed premises, an authorised person reasonably suspects a person of having entered the premises in breach of an exclusion order, the authorised person may-
  (a) remove the person from the premises, and
  (b) if necessary for that purpose, use reasonable force.
(5) A constable must, if-
  (a) asked by an authorised person to assist in exercising a power conferred by subsection (4), and
  (b) the constable reasonably suspects the person to be removed of having entered the premises in breach of an exclusion order,
provide the assistance asked for.
(6) In this section, "authorised person" means, in relation to licensed premises, any of the following persons, namely-
  (a) the premises licence holder,
  (b) the premises manager, and
  (c) any other person who-
    (i) works on the premises, and
    (ii) is authorised by the premises licence holder or the premises manager for the purposes of this section.

DEFINITIONS
"exclusion order": s.94(6)
"licensed premises": see s.147(1) of this Act
"authorised person": see subs.(6)
"premises manager": see s.19(1) of this Act

GENERAL NOTE
This section provides that it is an offence for a person who is the subject of an exclusion order to breach that order and sets out the consequences of such a breach.

Subsection (2)

A similar penalty is provided for by s.2(1) of the 1980 Act. In his written evidence to the Local Government and Transport Committee, Sheriff Principal Gordon Nicholson doubted the wisdom of this approach:

> "Given what has often been said by the Appeal Court regarding the undesirability of short prison terms, I venture to doubt whether the imprisonment option is ever likely to be attractive to the courts. In any event, I suspect that most judges would be with me in thinking that a one month term is unlikely to be adequate in the event of repeat offending. I respectfully suggest that the prescribed maximum term of imprisonment should be three months."

Subsection (3)

This provision more or less replicates the terms of s.2(2) of the 1980 Act.

Subsection (4)

The use of "reasonable force" on the part of a licenceholder or member of his staff is not a step specifically sanctioned by the 1980 Act, although they are empowered to "expel from the premises" any person reasonably suspected of having entered the premises in breach of an order.

In the course of the Local Government and Transport Committee's consideration of the Bill, this provision was referred to by a committee member as "the Rambo Provision" because of a concern that the power "could be used disproportionately" (Official Report, col.2424). Giving oral evidence to the Committee, the Scottish Executive's solicitor, John St Clair, defended the measure because "a pub cannot be run without a publican having the right to use reasonable force to keep an orderly house" (Official Report, col.2582).

It may be wise for an "authorised person" to seek police assistance (see subs.(5)) rather than face a debate as to whether the force used was "reasonable" in the context of an assault prosecution, although licenceholders are often reluctant to involve the police for fear that it may constitute a "black mark" against them.

96. Exclusion orders: supplementary provision

(1) References in section 94 to a person's being convicted of an offence are, in the case mentioned in subsection (2), to be read as references to the court's being satisfied that the person committed the offence.

(2) That case is the case where-
  (a) the person is charged with the offence before a court of summary jurisdiction, and
  (b) the court, without proceeding to conviction, discharges the person absolutely under section 246(3) of the Criminal Procedure (Scotland) Act 1995 (c.46).

(3) Where-
  (a) a court or the sheriff makes an exclusion order, or
  (b) a court makes an order terminating or varying an exclusion order,

Licensing (Scotland) Act 2005

the clerk of the court or, as the case may be, the sheriff clerk must send a copy of the order to the premises licence holder in respect of the licensed premises concerned.

DEFINITIONS
"exclusion order": see s.94(6) of this Act
"premises licence": see s.17 of this Act
"licensed premises": see s.147(1) of this Act

GENERAL NOTE
This section has the effect of allowing an exclusion order to be made in terms of s.94 where the person concerned has not been convicted of an offence, but has been absolutely discharged. Parallel provision is made in the 1980 Act. It also provides that an exclusion order, or an order terminating or varying the order, must be sent by the clerk or court or sheriff clerk to the holder of the premises licence at the premises concerned.

Closure of premises

97. Closure orders

(1) A Licensing Board may-
   (a) on the application of a senior police officer relating to any licensed premises situated within the Board's area, and
   (b) if satisfied that, by reason of the likelihood of disorder on, or in the vicinity of the premises, closure of the premises is necessary in the interests of public safety,
make a closure order in relation to the premises.

(2) A senior police officer may, if the officer reasonably believes that-
   (a) there is, or is likely imminently to be, disorder on, or in the vicinity of, any licensed premises,
   (b) closure of the premises is necessary in the interests of public safety, and
   (c) the risk to public safety is such that it is necessary to do so immediately and without making an application under subsection (1),
make a closure order in relation to the premises.

(3) A closure order is an order requiring the licensed premises to which it relates to be closed for such period, beginning with the coming into force of the order, as may be specified in the order.

(4) A closure order made by a senior police officer under subsection (2) is referred to as an "emergency closure order".

(5) The period of closure specified in an emergency closure order must not exceed 24 hours.

(6) A closure order comes into force in relation to any licensed premises to which it relates when a constable gives notice of it to a responsible person.

(7) Any responsible person who allows any licensed premises to be open in breach of a closure order commits an offence.

(8) A person guilty of an offence under subsection (7) is liable on summary conviction to-
   (a) a fine not exceeding £20,000,
   (b) imprisonment for a term not exceeding 3 months, or
   (c) both.

DEFINITIONS
"senior police officer": see s.147(1) of this Act
"licensed premises": see s.147(1) of this Act
"area": see s.147(1) of this Act
"closure order": see subs.(3)
"emergency closure order": see subs.(4)
"responsible person": see s.101 of this Act

GENERAL NOTE
Under s.89 of the 1976 Act, a sheriff may order the closure of licensed premises "if riot or tumult happens or is expected to happen". Such an order has never been made.

A licensing board may restrict the permitted hours upon receipt of a complaint, but must first hold a hearing (1976 Act, s.65).

A temporary restriction of the permitted hours may be imposed on application to the licensing board by a police officer of the rank of chief inspector or above (1976 Act, s.66). The licence holder has no right to be advised of the application nor to be heard. The invocation of this emergency power is almost unknown.

This section modernises and extends the 1976 Act's provisions. A licensing board may make a closure order in respect of any licensed premises (including premises which are the subject of an occasional licence) on the application of a senior police officer, if the board is satisfied that such a step is necessary in the interests of public safety by reason of the likelihood of disorder on, or in the vicinity of, the premises. The period of closure requires to be specified in the order.

Where the risk to public safety is such that immediate closure is required, a senior police officer may order the closure of premises at his own hand by means of an "emergency closure order" lasting no more than 24 hours (but subject to extension by virtue of s.99).

"Any responsible person" who allows any licensed premises to be open in breach of a closure order commits an offence.

Additionally, in terms of s.26 of the Antisocial Behaviour etc (Scotland) Act 2004 (asp 8) a senior police officer may authorise the service of a closure notice prohibiting access to premises by any person other than a person who habitually resides there or the owner of the premises. Authorisation may only be given where the officer has reasonable grounds for believing that at any time during the immediately preceding three months a person has engaged in antisocial behaviour on the premises; and the use of the premises is association with the occurrence of "relevant harm" (as defined in s.40).

A closure order made under s.26 may be appealed (2004 Act, s.36). There is no appeal against the imposition of a closure order under this Act.

98. Termination of closure orders

(1) A senior police officer must terminate a closure order (whether or not an emergency closure order) relating to any licensed premises if the officer is satisfied that it is no longer necessary in the interests of public safety for the premises to be closed.

(2) Where a senior police officer terminates a closure order relating to any licensed premises, the officer must ensure that notice of the termination is given by a constable to-
   (a) a responsible person, and
   (b) in the case of a closure order made by a Licensing Board, the Board.

(3) A Licensing Board may-
   (a) on the application of the holder of the premises licence or, as the case may be, occasional licence in respect of any licensed premises to which a closure order made by the Board relates, and
   (b) if satisfied that it is no longer necessary in the interests of public safety for the premises to be closed,

terminate the closure order.

DEFINITIONS
"senior police officer": see s.147(1) of this Act
"closure order": see s.97(3) of this Act
"emergency closure order": see s.97(4) of this Act
"licensed premises": see s.147(1) of this Act
"responsible person": see s.101 of this Act
"premises licence": see s.17 of this Act
"occasional licence": see s.56(1) of this Act

GENERAL NOTE
This section places a senior police officer under an obligation to terminate an closure order, whether an emergency order, extended emergency order (see s.99) or an order made by the board, if he is satisfied that the closure is no longer required in the interests of public safety. An order may also be terminated by the licensing board on application by the holder of the premises licence or occasional licence if the board is similarly satisfied.

Subsection (3)
Following the termination of a closure order by a senior police officer, he is required to ensure that a constable gives notice to: the premises licence holder or premises manager; or, in the case of an occasional licence, its holder; or a person working the premises who is authorised to close them. Where the order was made by the board, it must also be given notice.

99. Extension of emergency closure order

(1) Where an emergency closure order is in effect in respect of any licensed premises, a senior police officer may-
   (a) before the expiry of the period during which the order has effect (referred to in this section as the "original closure period"), and
   (b) if the officer reasonably believes that the conditions mentioned in subsection (2) are met in relation to the premises,
extend the original closure period for a further period not exceeding 24 hours.
(2) The conditions referred to in subsection (1)(b) are-
   (a) that there continues to be, or is likely to continue to be, disorder on, or in the vicinity of, the premises,
   (b) that extending the original closure period is necessary in the interests of public safety, and
   (c) the risk to public safety continues to be such that it is necessary to extend the original closure period immediately and without making an application under section 97(1).
(3) An extension under subsection (1) has no effect in relation to any licensed premises unless a constable has, before expiry of the original closure period, given notice of the extension to a responsible person.

DEFINITIONS
"emergency closure order": see s.97(4) of this Act
"licensed premises": see s.147(1) of this Act
"senior police officer": see s.147(1) of this Act
"original closure order": see subs.(1)
"responsible person": see s.101 of this Act

GENERAL NOTE
An emergency closure order may be extended for a further period not exceeding 24 hours where a senior police officer reasonably believes that continuing disorder poses a risk to public

safety which must be addressed immediately without application for closure being made to the board. Only the original closure period may be extended under this provision.

Subsection (3)

An extended emergency closure order is of no effect unless notice of the extension is given to a responsible person before the original order expires.

100. Regulations as to closure orders

The Scottish Ministers may by regulations make further provision as to the procedure to be followed in connection with the making of closure orders and extensions to closure orders including, in particular, provision-
- (a) as to the form and manner in which-
  - (i) any application under section 97(1)(a) or 98(3)(a) is to be made,
  - (ii) any notice under section 97(6), 98(2) or 99(3) is to be given,
- (b) as to the form of closure orders,
- (c) for the holding of hearings by Licensing Boards before making closure orders or extensions to them.

DEFINITIONS
"closure order": see s.97(3) of this Act

GENERAL NOTE
This section makes provision for regulations in relation to closure orders and extensions to them. The expression "closure orders" includes emergency closure orders.

Paragraph (c)

It is likely that regulations will require a hearing before a closure order is made by the licensing board following an application made in terms of s.97(1). The reference to the extension of closure orders in the context of licensing board hearings suggests that regulations may make procedural provision for the extension of orders by the board itself.

101. Interpretation of sections 97 to 100

In sections 97 to 100 "responsible person" means-
- (a) in the case of premises in respect of which a premises licence has effect-
  - (i) the premises licence holder, or
  - (ii) the premises manager,
- (b) in the case of premises in respect of which an occasional licence has effect, the person who holds the occasional licence, and
- (c) in either case, any person working at the premises in a capacity (whether paid or unpaid) which authorises the person to close the premises.

DEFINITIONS
"premises licence": see s.17 of this Act
"premises manager": see s.19(1) of this Act
"occasional licence": see s.56(1) of this Act

GENERAL NOTE
The effect of this provision is to define the "responsible person" who:

- must receive notice as a pre-condition of a closure order coming into force (s.97(6));
- commits an offence by allowing premises to be open in breach of an order (s.97(7));

- is to receive notice of the termination of an order (s.98(2); and who
- must receive notice of an extension to an emergency closure order as a pre-condition of the extension having effect.

PART 8

OFFENCES

Offences relating to children and young people

102. Sale of alcohol to a child or young person

(1) A person who sells alcohol to a child or a young person commits an offence.
(2) It is a defence for a person charged with an offence under subsection (1) (referred to in this section as "the accused") to show that-
　(a) the accused believed the child or young person to be aged 18 or over, and
　(b) either-
　　(i) the accused had taken reasonable steps to establish the child's or young person's age, or
　　(ii) no reasonable person could have suspected from the child's or young person's appearance that the child or young person was aged under 18.
(3) For the purposes of subsection (2)(b)(i), the accused is to be treated as having taken reasonable steps to establish the child's or young person's age if and only if-
　(a) the accused was shown any of the documents mentioned in subsection (4), and
　(b) that document would have convinced a reasonable person.
(4) The documents referred to in subsection (3)(a) are any document bearing to be-
　(a) a passport,
　(b) a European Union photocard driving licence, or
　(c) such other document, or a document of such other description, as may be prescribed.
(5) A person guilty of an offence under subsection (1) is liable on summary conviction to-
　(a) a fine not exceeding level 5 on the standard scale,
　(b) imprisonment for a term not exceeding 3 months, or
　(c) both.

DEFINITIONS
　"sells": see s.147(1) of this Act
　"alcohol": see s.2 of this Act
　"child": see s.147(1) of this Act
　"young person": see s.147(1) of this Act "prescribed": see s.147(1) of this Act

GENERAL NOTE
　The provisions of the 1976 Act which are intended for the protection of children and young persons are expressed in complex terms and poorly understood. (See Cummins, Chapter 14.)

Their access to on-licensed premises will now be governed by the terms of the operating plan. This and the following sections provide a more extensive system of control in relation to sale, consumption and delivery offences and benefit from a clear drafting style.

Subsection (1)

The sale of alcohol to a person under the age of 18 is an offence. This marks a significant enlargement of the 1976 Act, s.68(1), in terms of which it is an offence for the holder of a licence or his employee or agent to sell alcohol to such a person *in licensed premises*.

Subsections (2)-(4)

It is a defence for a person charged under subsection (1) to show that he believed the person to whom the alcohol was sold was aged 18 or over and he had taken "reasonable steps" to establish the purchaser's age.

Those "reasonable steps" will only have been taken if the accused was shown a document bearing to be a passport, European Union photocard driving licence or another prescribed document; and that document would have convinced a reasonable person. Some allowance is therefore made for the production of documents which have been forged or subjected to tampering. The exposure of retailers to this sort of fraud was recognised by Nicholson. The Report noted that the "due diligence" defence provided by the 1976 Act in relation to under-age sales is often invoked on the basis of a proof-of-age card having been produced and recommended the introduction of a national card, which could be used in relation to "any other official document such as a passport" (Report, para.7.16 *et seq*).

In the alternative, the accused may prove that he believed the purchaser to be aged 18 or over and no reasonable person could have suspected from the child's or young person's appearance that child or young person was aged under 18.

Subsection (5)

The sale of alcohol to a person under 18 presently attracts a maximum (level 3) fine of £1,000. This subsection makes provision for substantially increased penalties: a maximum (level 5) fine of £5,000 and/or three months' imprisonment.

103. Allowing the sale of alcohol to a child or young person

(1) Any responsible person who knowingly allows alcohol to be sold to a child or a young person on any relevant premises commits an offence.
(2) A person guilty of an offence under subsection (1) is liable on summary conviction to-
   (a) a fine not exceeding level 5 on the standard scale,
   (b) imprisonment for a term not exceeding 3 months, or
   (c) both.

DEFINITIONS
"responsible person": see s.122 of this Act
"alcohol": see s.2 of this Act
"sold": see s.147(1) of this Act
"child": see s.147(1) of this Act
"young person": see s.147(1) of this Act
"relevant premises": see s.122 of this Act

GENERAL NOTE

The 1976 Act established a system of vicarious responsibility in terms of which proceedings may be instituted against a licence holder where an offence was committed by "an employee or agent", subject to the defence that the offence was committed without the licence holder's "knowledge or connivance" and "all due diligence" was used to prevent its occurrence (1976 Act, s.67(3)).

This Act takes a different approach, possibly because of a concern that vicarious responsibility and the obligation to prove due diligence may not be compatible with the presumption of innocence guaranteed by Art.6(2) of the ECHR. (Such a concern is probably unfounded: see Agnew and Baillie, p.44. See also *McLean v Carnegie*, 2006 S.L.T. 40 for a consideration of the ECHR compatibility of the 1976 Act's s.71 defence).

In this Act, a number of offences are committed where a person "allows" or "knowingly allows" something to be done. The offence of "allowing" is found in ss.63(1), 97(7), 108 and 115; and the offence of "knowingly allowing" in ss.1(3), 103, 106, 107, 120, 121, 127 and 128. Where the offence is of "knowingly allowing" no defence is provided; but the "allowing" offences are conjoined with "reasonable precautions" or similar defences (except those contained in s.63(1)(a) and s.97(7)).

There is plainly a difference between "allowing" and "knowingly allowing" (Gordon, para. 8.33; *Thornley v Hunter*, 1965 S.L.T. 206, per Lord Justice-Clerk Grant at p.207); but, no doubt confusingly, "permitting" (or "allowing") per se may involve "wilful blindness", which is a form of notional or constructive knowledge (see *Mackay Brothers & Company v Gibb*, 1969 J.C. 26; 1969 S.L.T. 216; and Gordon, paras 8.23 and 8.81 *et seq*).

This section provides for the offence of "knowingly allowing" the sale of alcohol to a person under the age of 18 on "relevant premises", that is to say: licensed premises, exempt premises (see s.124) or premises used for the sale of alcohol to trade. The offence is committed by a "responsible person" as defined in s.122(3) so that a premises manager (for example) may be answerable for an offence committed by a fellow employee, as an exception to the principle that one "servant" is not vicariously responsible for the act or omissions of another: *Shields v Little*, 1954 J.C. 25; 1954 S.L.T. 146. (For the purposes of Part 8 of this Act (ss. 102-122), a person aged 18 or over who works on the premises in a paid or unpaid capacity is a "responsible person" if authorised to sell alcohol; or, in relation to any offence of "allowing" something to be done, authorised "to prevent the doing of the thing").

There is no "reasonable steps" or "reasonable precautions" defence, which is available in relation to certain other offences: see, for example, s.63(3)(a), in terms of which a person charged with "allowing" alcohol to be consumed or taken away from licensed premises outwith licensed hours may prove by way of defence that he, or his "employee or agent", "took all reasonable precautions and exercised all due diligence not to commit the offence".

In *Noble v Heatly*, 1967 J.C. 5; 1967 S.L.T. 26 (presaged by *Thornley v Hunter*, *cit. supra*) a certificate holder was charged under the provisions of the Licensing (Scotland) Act 1959 with "knowingly permitting" drunkenness in a public house. He had delegated the management of the premises to an experienced supervisor, who had appointed a manager. The manager was in sole charge of the premises at the relevant time. Because the offence was for a "breach of certificate" the manager could not be charged. The certificate holder was not present. Quashing his conviction, a full bench held that "knowingly" must "mean what it says" and "unless there is express statutory warrant for holding it to mean something else an offence is not committed where knowingly is of the essence unless there is personal knowledge on the part of the accused person".

The Court also disapproved of *dicta* in the earlier case of *Greig v Macleod* (1907) 5 Adam 445; 1908 S.C. (J.) 14; (1908) 15 S.L.T. 620, although the result in that case appeared to be "sound in the light of the facts proved". In *Greig*, the holder of a public house certificate was charged with knowingly allowing an assistant to sell exciseable liquor to a person under the age of 14. No notice had been displayed in the premises reminding staff to observe the provisions of the relevant Act. The certificate holder had not given sufficient instructions as to the prohibited supply of liquor to underage persons; and, although he had no personal knowledge of the sale, his conviction was upheld.

The Court in *Noble* did not overrule *Greig*, possibly because it considered that the failure in the latter case to institute a system designed to prevent breach of the statute provided sufficient *mens rea* to constitute "knowingly permitting" and the certificate holder had demonstrated "wilful blindness". (See the discussion of the two cases in Gordon, para.8.23, under explanation that the narration of the facts in Greig ought to proceed on the basis that the liquor was sold *outwith* the certificate holder's presence and actual personal knowledge.)

Certainly, in *Noble* the Burgh Court had found it proved or admitted that the supervisor engaged by the certificate holder had given instructions to the actual manager (the person *de facto* in control of the premises at the time of the offence) in regard to compliance with licensing laws; and there was available on the premises "General Instructions for Managers" in terms of which any person who appeared to be acting under the influence of alcohol or drugs should not be allowed to remain on the premises. In *Greig*, Lord McLaren said that: "In the absence of [instructions not to supply children under 14 with liquor], I think it is consistent with a sound construction of the statute to hold that if the appellant does not instruct his assistant to give obedience to the requirements of the statute, he must be taken as assenting to what is done under his authority". That analysis may encounter the difficulty that in *Noble* the High Court appears to have paid no regard to any precautionary measures taken by management: the Crown failed to found on the provisions of s.187 of the 1959 Act, in terms of which, where it was proved that any person was drunk on the premises, "it shall lie on the holder of the certificate or licence to prove that he and the persons employed by him "took all reasonable steps to prevent drunkenness".

It may be considered that an attempt to reconcile *Greig* and *Noble* involves difficult jurisprudential acrobatics; and one is left with the clear statement in the latter that there must be "personal knowledge" on the part of a person charged with "knowingly permitting" (as well as the exclusion from Scots Law of the English doctrine of "delegation", in terms of which knowledge could be imputed where the management of premises has been devolved to others). Perhaps that requirement for "personal knowledge" and the concomitantly high degree of mens rea serves to explain the absence of any statutory defence in the Act where "knowledge" is of the essence.

Paradoxically, it was the decision in *Noble* which lead to the system of vicarious responsibility in the 1976 Act, so that the approach to the accountability of licence holders has turned full circle. *Clayson* noted that, following *Noble*, the Secretary of State received representations from, among others, the Association of Chief Police Officers (Scotland) "seeking legislation to establish the absolute vicarious responsibility of the certificate holder for the actings of his staff" (Report, paras.10.11, 10.12). While the majority of the Clayson Committee favoured that approach (*Clayson*, para 10.23), Parliament effectively enacted the minority view by proving the "due diligence" defence which appears in the 1976 Act.

In relation to "knowingly allowing" (and "allowing"), see further: Gordon, Ch.8.

104. Sale of liqueur confectionery to a child

(1) A person who sells liqueur confectionery to a child commits an offence.
(2) It is a defence for a person charged with an offence under subsection (1) (referred to in this section as "the accused") to show that-
　(a) the accused believed the child to be aged 16 or over, and
　(b) either-
　　(i) the accused had taken reasonable steps to establish the child's age, or
　　(ii) no reasonable person could have suspected from the child's appearance that the child was aged under 16.
(3) For the purposes of subsection (2)(b)(i), the accused is to be treated as having taken reasonable steps to establish the child's age if and only if-
　(a) the accused was shown evidence of the child's age, and
　(b) that evidence would have convinced a reasonable person.
(4) A person guilty of an offence under subsection (1) is liable on summary conviction to a fine not exceeding level 2 on the standard scale.

DEFINITIONS
　"sells": see s.147(1) of this Act
　"child": see s.147(1) of this Act
　"liqueur confectionery": see s.147(1) of this Act
　"young person": see s.147(1) of this Act

GENERAL NOTE
　Alcohol contained in "liqueur confectionery" (as defined in s.147(1)) may be sold without a licence and is not "alcohol" for the purpose of the Act (s.2(1)(b)). Save for this provision, the sale

of liqueur confectionery to a person under the age of 16 would not be an offence in terms of s.102(1), which prohibits the sale of alcohol to a child or young person.

Liqueur confectionery which falls within the definition may be sold to or purchased by persons aged 16 or 17; but liqueur confectionery which does not conform to the definition and comestibles containing alcohol of a strength exceeding 0.5 per cent fall to be treated as "alcohol" for the purposes of the Act.

Subsections (2), (3)

A person charged with this offence may show that he believed the child to be aged 16 or over and he had taken reasonable steps to establish the child's age. Those "reasonable steps" will only have been taken if the accused was shown evidence of the child's age and that evidence (the nature of which is not prescribed) would have convinced a reasonable person.

In the alternative, he may show that he believed the child to be aged 16 or over and no reasonable person would have suspected from the child's appearance that the child was under 16.

105. Purchase of alcohol by or for a child or young person

(1) A child or young person who buys or attempts to buy alcohol (whether for himself or herself or another person) commits an offence.

(2) It is not an offence under subsection (1) for a child or young person to buy or attempt to buy alcohol if the child or young person is authorised to do so by the chief constable for the purpose of determining whether an offence is being committed under section 102.

(3) A chief constable may authorise a child or young person to buy or attempt to buy alcohol as mentioned in subsection (2) only if satisfied that all reasonable steps have been or will be taken to avoid any risk to the welfare of the child or young person.

(4) A person other than a child or young person who knowingly buys or attempts to buy alcohol-
  (a) on behalf of a child or young person, or
  (b) for consumption on relevant premises by a child or young person,
commits an offence.

(5) Subsection (4)(b) does not apply to the buying of beer, wine, cider or perry for consumption by a young person along with a meal supplied on relevant premises.

(6) A child or young person guilty of an offence under subsection (1) is liable on summary conviction to a fine not exceeding level 1 on the standard scale.

(7) A person guilty of an offence under subsection (4) is liable on summary conviction to-
  (a) a fine not exceeding level 5 on the standard scale,
  (b) imprisonment for a term not exceeding 3 months, or
  (c) both.

DEFINITIONS
"child": see s.147(1) of this Act
"young person": see s.147(1) of this Act
"alcohol": see s.2 of this Act
"relevant premises": see s.122 of this Act

GENERAL NOTE
This section makes provision for the following offences:

- the purchase or attempted purchase of alcohol by a child or young person;

- "agency" purchases or attempted purchases of alcohol by a person aged 18 or over on behalf of a child or young person; and
- the purchase of alcohol by a person over 18 for a child's or young person's consumption on "relevant premises", except where certain drinks (other than spirits) are to be consumed by a young person with a meal.

So-called "test-purchasing" is authorised by subs.(2). This measure, introduced at Stage 3, is designed to underpin the Act's so-called "no proof, no sale" provisions" and tackle "the underage drinking that bedevils many communities" (Official Report, col.20733).

As a result of the Licensing (Scotland) Act 2005 (Commencement No 2 and Transitional Provisions) Order 2006 (SSI 2006/ 286) ("the Commencement No 2 Order"):

- Subsections (1)-(3) and (6) of this section are in force (Art.2).
- Section 68(2) of the 1976 Act is now in the following terms: "A person under 18 shall not consume alcoholic liquor in a bar." (Art.2.) The offence of purchasing by such a person is now constituted by subs.(1) of this Act.)
- In the period until s.102 of the Act comes into force, s.105(2) has effect as if the words "of selling alcoholic liquor to a person under 18 is being committed under section 68(1) of the Licensing (Scotland) Act 1976" were substituted for the words "is being committed under section 102". (Art.3.)
- Until provision is made to the contrary by means of an order under s.145 of this Act, only the Chief Constable of Fife police force may authorise a child or young person to buy or attempt to buy alcohol for the purpose of determining whether an offence is being committed under subs.(2). The Fife test-purchasing pilot, which will last for twelve months, started on 30 June 2006. According to the Scottish Executive, it is designed to allow "common procedures" to be developed for use by other police forces when test-purchasing is extended to other parts of the country.
- Until s.68(4) of the 1976 Act is repealed, a person aged 16 or over may, despite the terms of s.105(1), purchase beer, wine, made-wine, porter, cider or perry for consumption at a meal in a part of premises set aside for meal service. (Art. 6 of the Commencement No. 2 Order revokes the Licensing (Scotland) Act 2005 (Commencement No. 1 and Transitional Provisions) Order 2006 (SSI 239/2006) which would have criminalised such purchases.)
- Subsection (1) makes it an offence for a child or young person to buy or attempt to buy "alcohol". The definition of "alcohol" is to be found in s.2, which has not yet been commenced (although "alcohol" appears in the index of defined expressions (s.148, which came into force on Royal Assent)). The offence of selling "alcoholic liquor" to a person under 18 (the "mirror", so to speak, of the s.105(1) offence) is contained in s.68(1) of the Act, which remains in force *pro tem*. The expression "alcoholic liquor" is defined in s.139(1) of the 1976 Act. In the result a child or young person commits an offence by purchasing or attempting to purchase "alcohol"; a licence holder or his employee or agent commits an offence by selling "alcoholic liquor" to a person under 18. "Alcohol", even if the s.2 definition applied, is not the same as "alcoholic liquor" as defined in the 1976 Act.

For other difficulties with the partial initiation of test-purchasing, see notes to s.109.

Subsection (1)

The analogous offence contained in the 1976 Act relates to the purchase of alcohol by persons under 18 in licensed premises (1976 Act, s.68(2)). The offence is extended so as to be capable of being committed anywhere.

Subsection (2) and (3)

In the absence of statutory provision, the test-purchasing of alcohol involves the commission of an offence by the children employed for the purpose (subs.(1)). These subsections provide the necessary authority. The Scottish Executive has promised to put in place appropriate guidance to ensure that the protection of the child is "at the heart" of their approach (Official Report, col.20734).

Subsection (4)

This subsection effectively re-enacts s.68(3) of the 1976 Act, which provides that it is an offence for a person knowingly to act as an agent for a person under 18 in the purchase of alcoholic liquor (wherever that purchase may take place).

The offence of purchasing alcohol for consumption by such a person is, however, extended. Section s.68(3) simply strikes at an alcohol purchase which is to be consumed by a person under 18 *in a bar*. As Clayson observed (para.11.23): "It is... possible for an adult to buy a drink in a bar of a public house and give it to someone under 18 to drink elsewhere on the premises which is not a bar". The 1976 Act did not correct that oddity. This Act abandons the distinction between "bars" and other parts of licensed premises (a "poorly defined distinction", *pace* Nicholson, Report, para.13.6) and provides that an offence is committed where an adult purchases alcohol for consumption by a child or young person in any part of relevant premises (subject to subs.(5)).

Subsection (5)

No offence is committed under subs.(4) where a person purchases beer, wine, cider or perry for consumption by a person aged 16 or over along with a meal supplied on the premises. This is a modification of s.68(4) of the 1976 Act which, provides *inter alia* that a person who has attained the age of 16 may himself purchase beer, wine, made-wine, porter, cider or perry for consumption at a meal in a part of the premises set apart for the service of meals (or in bar at any time when it is set apart for that purpose).

Subsection (7)

This subsection makes provision for penalties which are more severe than those available to the court in relation to the analogous offences contained in the 1976 Act.

106. Consumption of alcohol by a child or young person

(1) A child or young person who knowingly consumes alcohol on any relevant premises commits an offence.

(2) Any responsible person who knowingly allows a child or young person to consume alcohol on any relevant premises commits an offence.

(3) Subsections (1) and (2) do not apply to the consumption of beer, wine, cider or perry by a young person along with a meal supplied on relevant premises.

(4) A child or young person guilty of an offence under subsection (1) is liable on summary conviction to a fine not exceeding level 3 on the standard scale.

(5) A person guilty of an offence under subsection (2) is liable on summary conviction to-
 (a) a fine not exceeding level 5 on the standard scale,
 (b) imprisonment for a term not exceeding 3 months, or
 (c) both.

DEFINITIONS
 "child": see s.147(1) of this Act
 "young person": see s.147(1) of this Act
 "alcohol": see s.2 of this Act
 "relevant premises": see s.122 of this Act
 "responsible person": see s.122 of this Act

GENERAL NOTE

Section 16 of the Children and Young Persons (Scotland) Act 1937 (which is repealed by s.149 and Sch.5 of this Act) provides that: "If any person gives, or causes to be give to any child under the age of five years any alcoholic liquor, except upon the order of a duly qualified medical practitioner, or in the case of sickness, apprehended sickness, or other urgent cause, he shall, on summary conviction, be liable to a fine not exceeding level 1 on the standard scale".

Otherwise, the consumption of alcohol by a person over the age of five is largely unregulated. An offence is committed where (a) the licenceholder or his employee or agent allows a person under 18 to consume alcoholic liquor *in a bar* (1976 Act, s.68(1)); or (b) a person under 18 consumes alcoholic liquor in a bar (*ibid.*, s.68(2)). Consumption in any part of licensed premises which is not a bar is perfectly lawful. (See also note to s.104(5), *supra*.)

These remarkably narrow restrictions are removed by this section, so that consumption by a child or young person *in any part* of licensed premises is an offence. A responsible person who "knowingly allows" such consumption also commits an offence. (For a consideration of "knowingly allows", see notes to s.103.) An exception is made for the consumption of beer, wine, cider or perry with a meal.

107. Unsupervised sale of alcohol by a child or young person

(1) Any responsible person who knowingly allows alcohol to be sold, supplied or served by a child or young person on any relevant premises commits an offence.

(2) Subsection (1) does not apply to-
   (a) any sale by a child or young person of alcohol for consumption off the premises, or
   (b) any supply or service by a child or young person of alcohol for consumption on the premises along with a meal supplied on relevant premises,

if the condition in subsection (3) is satisfied.

(3) That condition is that the sale, supply or service is specifically authorised by-
   (a) a responsible person, or
   (b) any other person of or over 18 years of age who is authorised by a responsible person for the purposes of this section.

(4) A person guilty of an offence under subsection (1) is liable on summary conviction to a fine not exceeding level 1 on the standard scale.

DEFINITIONS
"responsible person": see s.122 of this Act
"alcohol": see s.2 of this Act
"child": see s.147(1) of this Act
"young person": see s.147(1) of this Act
"relevant premises": see s.122 of this Act

GENERAL NOTE
The 1976 Act contains provisions which prohibit: (a) the employment of persons under 18 in the bar of licensed premises (s.72), subject to a very limited exception; (b) the service of alcohol by persons under 18 in refreshment-licensed premises (s.73); and (c) sales of alcohol in off-sale licensed or wholesale premises by persons under 18 which have not been specifically approved by a person over that age (ss.97A and 90A(3)).

This section prohibits a responsible person from allowing alcohol to be sold, supplied or served on relevant premises by a person under 18, subject to two exceptions, namely, where alcohol is (1) sold for consumption off the premises, or (2) supplied or served for consumption along with a meal, subject to specific authorisation by a responsible person or a person aged 18 or over who is authorised by such a person.

108. Delivery of alcohol by or to a child or young person

(1) This section applies where alcohol is sold on any relevant premises for consumption off the premises.

(2) Any responsible person who allows the alcohol to be delivered by a child or young person commits an offence.

(3) Any responsible person who-
   (a) delivers the alcohol, or
   (b) allows it to be delivered,
to a child or young person commits an offence.

(4) Subsections (2) and (3) do not apply to the delivery of the alcohol by or to a child or young person who works on the relevant premises or at the place where the delivery is made in a capacity (whether paid or unpaid) which involves the delivery of alcohol.

(5) It is a defence for a person charged with an offence under subsection (2) or (3)(a) (referred to in this subsection and subsection (6) as "the accused") to show that-
   (a) the accused believed the child or young person to be aged 18 or over, and
   (b) either-
      (i) the accused had taken reasonable steps to establish the child's or young person's age, or
      (ii) no reasonable person could have suspected from the child's or young person's appearance that the child or young person was aged under 18.

(6) For the purposes of subsection (5)(b)(i), the accused is to be treated as having taken reasonable steps to establish the child's or young person's age if and only if-
   (a) the accused was shown any of the documents mentioned in subsection (7), and
   (b) that document would have convinced a reasonable person.

(7) The documents referred to in subsection (6)(a) are any document bearing to be-
   (a) a passport,
   (b) a European Union photocard driving licence, or
   (c) such other document, or a document of such other description, as may be prescribed.

(8) It is a defence for a person charged with an offence under subsection (3)(b) ("the accused") to prove that the accused took all reasonable precautions and exercised due diligence not to commit the offence.

(9) A person guilty of an offence under this section is liable on summary conviction to a fine not exceeding level 3 on the standard scale.

DEFINITIONS
"alcohol": see s.2 of this Act
"sold": see s.147(1) of this Act
"relevant premises": see s.122 of this Act
"responsible person": see s.122 of this Act
"child": see s.147(1) of this Act
"young person": see s.147(1) of this Act

GENERAL NOTE
Where alcohol is sold for consumption off the premises, this section prohibits its delivery by or to persons under 18, except where the person delivering or taking delivery of the alcohol works in a capacity involving alcohol deliveries.

Subsection (4)
The offences constituted by subs.(2) and (3) are not committed where the alcohol delivery is made or accepted by a person under 18 who words in a paid or unpaid capacity involving alcohol deliveries.
Section 68(5) of the 1976 Act contains similar prohibitions relative to off-sale deliveries to persons under 18, subject to a broader exception which allows deliveries to the "residence or working place of the purchaser".

Subsections (5)-(7)
Where a responsible person is charged with allowing alcohol to be delivered by a child or young person or with delivering alcohol to such a person, it will be a defence for him to show that he believed the child or young person was aged 18 or over and he had taken "reasonable steps" to establish the purchaser's age.
Those "reasonable steps" will only have been taken if the accused was shown a document bearing to be a passport, European Union photocard driving licence or another prescribed document; and that document would have convinced a reasonable person. Similar provision is made in s.102(2)-(4).
In the alternative, the accused may prove that he believed the person effecting or accepting the delivery to be aged 18 or over and no reasonable person could have suspected from the child's or young person's appearance that child or young person was aged under 18.

Subsection (8)
A separate defence is provided where a person is charged with allowing the delivery of alcohol to person under 18, namely that he took all reasonable precautions and exercised all due diligence not to commit the offence.

109. Sending a child or young person to obtain alcohol

(1) Any person who knowingly sends a child or young person to obtain alcohol sold or to be sold on any relevant premises for consumption off the premises commits an offence.
(2) It is immaterial for the purposes of subsection (1) whether the child or young person is sent to obtain the alcohol from the relevant premises where it is sold or from some other place from which it is to be delivered.
(3) Subsection (1) does not apply where the child or young person works on the relevant premises or at the place where the alcohol is to be delivered in a capacity (whether paid or unpaid) which involves the delivery of alcohol.
(4) A person guilty of an offence under subsection (1) is liable on summary conviction to-
 (a) a fine not exceeding level 5 on the standard scale,
 (b) imprisonment for a term not exceeding 3 months, or
 (c) both.

DEFINITIONS
"child": see s.147(1) of this Act
"young person": see s.147(1) of this Act
"alcohol": see s.2 of this Act
"sold": see s.147(1) of this Act
"relevant premises": see s.122 of this Act

GENERAL NOTE

These provisions have their origins in s.68(5) of the 1976 Act, the relevant part of which makes it an offence for "any person" knowingly to "send a person under 18 for the purpose of obtaining alcoholic liquor sold or to be sold [sc for consumption off the premises] from the licensed premises or other premises from which the liquor is delivered in pursuance of a sale".

(Section 68(5) is in turn derived from s.145 of the Licensing (Scotland) Act 1959, indexed in Purves, *The Scottish Licensing Laws* (8th edn by Walker), p.156, as "sending child to buy liquor an offence".)

This section may cause a difficulty for test-purchasing. Section 105(2) provides that a child or young person who buys or attempts to buy alcohol does not commit an offence in terms of s.105(1) where that purchase or attempted purchase has been authorised by the chief constable. It goes no further. (See notes to s.105(1)-(3).) A question therefore arises as to whether a police officer commits an offence in terms of s.109(1) by knowingly sending "a child or young person to obtain alcohol sold or to be sold on any relevant premises for consumption off the premises".

Subsection (3)

An exception is provided in relation to children or young persons working on the relevant premises or at the premises where the alcohol is to be delivered in a paid or unpaid capacity which involves alcohol deliveries (*cf* proviso to 1976 Act, s.68(5)).

110. Duty to display notice

(1) This section applies in relation to any relevant premises.
(2) The notice mentioned in subsection (3) must be displayed-
   (a) at all times,
   (b) at each place on the premises where sales of alcohol are made, and
   (c) in a position where it is readily visible to any person seeking to buy alcohol.
(3) That is a notice in the prescribed form and of the prescribed dimensions containing the following statements, namely-

"It is an offence for a person under the age of 18 to buy or attempt to buy alcohol on these premises.

It is also an offence for any other person to buy or attempt to buy alcohol on these premises for a person under the age of 18.

Where there is doubt as to whether a person attempting to buy alcohol on these premises is aged 18 or over, alcohol will not be sold to the person except on production of evidence showing the person to be 18 or over.".

(4) If the requirement in subsection (2) is not met in relation to any premises, the person specified in subsection (5) commits an offence.
(5) That person is, in relation to any relevant premises-
   (a) in the case of licensed premises-
      (i) the premises licence holder, and
      (ii) the premises manager,
   (b) in the case of premises in respect of which an occasional licence has effect, the holder of the licence, and
   (c) in the case of other relevant premises, the person having the management and control of the premises.
(6) A person guilty of an offence under subsection (4) is liable on summary conviction to a fine not exceeding level 3 on the standard scale.

DEFINITIONS
  "relevant premises": see s.122 of this Act
  "alcohol": see s.2 of this Act

"prescribed": see s.147(1) of this Act
"licensed premises": see s.147(1) of this Act
"premises licence": see s.17 of this Act
"premises manager": see s.19(1) of this Act
"occasional licence": see s.56(1) of this Act

GENERAL NOTE

In fortification of the Act's "no proof, no sale" approach to potential alcohol purchases by persons under the age of 18, this section requires a notice to be displayed in relevant premises at all times and at each alcohol sale point where it must readily visible by those proposing to buy alcohol.

While the wording of the notice is set out in subs.(3), its form and dimensions have yet to be prescribed by regulations.

Failure to comply with these requirements is an offence.

Drunkenness and disorderly conduct

111. Drunk persons entering or in premises on which alcohol is sold

(1) A person who, while drunk, attempts to enter any relevant premises (other than premises on which the person resides) commits an offence.

(2) A person commits an offence if the person, while drunk-
   (a) is on any relevant premises, and
   (b) is incapable of taking care of himself or herself.

(3) A constable may arrest without warrant any person committing an offence under this section.

(4) A person guilty of an offence under this section is liable on summary conviction to a fine not exceeding level 1 on the standard scale.

DEFINITIONS

"relevant premises": see s.122 of this Act

GENERAL NOTE

The "drunkenness" and disorderly conduct offences found in this and the next three sections mirror those contained in ss.74 to 77 of the 1976 Act.

This section excludes persons who are drunk from relevant premises and renders them liable to arrest without a warrant. Attempted entry is an offence except in the case of a resident. A person who is drunk and incapable of taking care of himself or herself commits an offence by being in licensed premises.

Subsection (2)

While no offence is committed by a drunken person who attempts to enter premises in which he is residing, no other exceptions are made for residents in relation to drunkenness offences. In *Thompson v McKenzie* [1908] 1 KB 905 drunkenness was found to have permitted where a hotel guest was found drunk in a public room.

Subsection (3)

A person who is drunk and incapable is in a condition considerably more serious than drunkenness: see *Dunning v Cardle* 1981 SCCR 136.

112. Obtaining of alcohol by or for a drunk person

(1) A person who, on any relevant premises, obtains or attempts to obtain alcohol for consumption on the premises by a person who is drunk commits an offence.
(2) A person who, on any relevant premises, helps a person who is drunk to obtain or consume alcohol on the premises commits an offence.
(3) A person guilty of an offence under this section is liable on summary conviction to a fine not exceeding level 3 on the standard scale.

DEFINITIONS
"relevant premises": see s.122 of this Act
"alcohol": see s.2 of this Act

GENERAL NOTE
An offence is committed by any person who, on any relevant premises, obtains or attempts to obtain alcohol for consumption on the premises by a drunken person; or who aids a drunken person to obtain or consume alcohol on the premises.

Subsection (1)
While the parallel provision in the 1976 Act (s.75) simply strikes at the procurement or attempted procurement of alcohol "for consumption by a drunken person", this subsection restricts itself to consumption on the premises.

113. Sale of alcohol to a drunk person

(1) Any responsible person who, on any relevant premises, sells alcohol to a person who is drunk commits an offence.
(2) A person guilty of an offence under subsection (1) is liable on summary conviction to a fine not exceeding level 3 on the standard scale.

DEFINITIONS
"responsible person": see s.122 of this Act
"relevant premises": see s.122 of this Act
"alcohol": see s.2 of this Act

GENERAL NOTE
The sale of alcohol by a responsible person to a drunken person on any relevant premises is an offence. It remains to be discovered whether the prosecution of this offence receives a higher degree of priority than the similar offence contained in s.76 of the 1976 Act.

On 2 June 2003, answering a Scottish Parliamentary question which sought the most recent annual figures for successful prosecutions under s.76, the Solicitor General revealed that no such prosecutions had been brought during the year 2002-2003.

On 26 May 2005, the Lord Advocate replied to a Parliamentary question asking what plans the Scottish Executive had "to encourage the police and courts to make more use of the existing law about not serving alcohol to people who are drunk, as part of the campaign against binge drinking". He answered that the matter was taken seriously by the police, the Crown Office and the Procurator Fiscal Service, while "the proposals in the Licensing (Scotland) Bill will further strengthen the powers that are available to local licensing boards, as well as to the police and the courts, to control irresponsible drinks promotions and to deal with those who fail to comply with their licence conditions".

The Lord Advocate also informed the questioner that, in the past year, 19 charges had been reported to the procurator fiscal. Of those, nine were prosecuted on summary complaint, six were dealt with by way of alternatives to prosecution and no proceedings were taken in four cases.

114. Premises manager, staff etc. not to be drunk

(1) Any responsible person in relation to any relevant premises who is drunk while on the premises commits an offence.

(2) A person guilty of an offence under this section is liable on summary conviction to a fine not exceeding level 3 on the standard scale.

DEFINITIONS
"responsible person": see s.122 of this Act
"relevant premises": see s.122 of this Act

GENERAL NOTE

An offence is committed by any responsible person (such as the premises manager) who is drunk on any relevant premises. It is of no consequence that the premises are closed to the public or that the consumption of alcohol leading to drunkenness took place elsewhere.

115. Disorderly conduct

(1) A person on relevant premises who, while drunk-
   (a) behaves in a disorderly manner, or
   (b) uses obscene or indecent language to the annoyance of any person,
commits an offence.

(2) Any responsible person in relation any relevant premises who allows-
   (a) a breach of the peace,
   (b) drunkenness, or
   (c) other disorderly conduct,
to take place on the premises commits an offence.

(3) It is a defence for a person charged with an offence under subsection (2) ("the accused") to prove-
   (a) that the accused, or an employee or agent of the accused, took all reasonable precautions and exercised due diligence not to commit the offence, or
   (b) that there were no lawful and reasonably practicable means by which the accused could prevent the conduct giving rise to the offence.

(4) A person guilty of an offence under subsection (1)(a) is liable on summary conviction to-
   (a) a fine not exceeding level 3 on the standard scale,
   (b) imprisonment for a term not exceeding 60 days, or
   (c) both.

(5) A person guilty of an offence under subsection (1)(b) or (2) is liable on summary conviction to a fine not exceeding level 3 on the standard scale.

DEFINITIONS
"relevant premises": see s.122 of this Act
"alcohol": see s.2 of this Act

GENERAL NOTE

In modernised terms broadly similar to those of s.78 of the 1976 Act, this section provides that an offence is committed by a drunken person in relevant premises who behaves in a disorderly manner or uses obscene or indecent language to the annoyance of any person.

An offence is also committed by any responsible person who allows a breach of the peace, drunkenness or other disorderly conduct to take place on the premises, subject to the defence provided by subs.(3).

Subsection (3)

A person charged with an offence under subs.2 may prove that he, or his employee or agent, took all reasonable precautions and exercised due diligence not to commit the offence; or there were no lawful or reasonably practicable means by the which he could prevent the conduct giving rise to the offence.

In *Soutar v Auchinachie*, (1909) S.L.T. 663 the High Court held that all reasonable steps had been taken for the prevention of drunkenness where a person in a state of intoxication had been refused alcoholic liquor. He was supplied with a bottle of soda water and allowed to remain the premises for about 15 minutes with two sober friends who had undertaken to escort him home.

Similarly, in *Townsend v Arnold* (1911) 75 JP 423 a licensee was properly acquitted of "permitting drunkenness" where he took steps to revive a man who had, without his knowledge, consumed a companion's whisky which had not been sold on the premises.

116. Refusal to leave premises

(1) A person on any relevant premises who-
   (a) behaves in a disorderly manner, and
   (b) refuses or fails to leave the premises on being asked to do so by a responsible person or a constable,

commits an offence.

(2) A person on any relevant premises who, after the end of any period of licensed hours, refuses or fails to leave the premises on being asked to do so by a responsible person or a constable commits an offence.

(3) Where a person refuses or fails to leave any relevant premises as mentioned in subsection (1) or (2), an authorised person may-
   (a) remove the person from the premises, and
   (b) if necessary for that purpose, use reasonable force.

(4) A constable must, if-
   (a) asked by an authorised person to assist in exercising a power conferred by subsection (3), and
   (b) the constable reasonably suspects the person to be removed of having refused or failed to leave as mentioned in subsection (1) or (2),

provide the assistance asked for.

(5) A person guilty of an offence under this section is liable on summary conviction to a fine not exceeding level 3 on the standard scale.

(6) In this section, "authorised person" means, in relation to any relevant premises, any of the following persons, namely-
   (a) a responsible person, and
   (b) any other person who-
      (i) works on the premises, and
      (ii) is authorised by a responsible person for the purposes of this section.

DEFINITIONS

"relevant premises": see s.122 of this Act
"responsible person": see s.122 of this Act

"licensed hours": see s.62(1) of this Act
"authorised person": see subs.(6)

GENERAL NOTE

This section makes provision for the expulsion from relevant premises of persons who either (a) behave in a disorderly manner and who refuse or fail to leave when asked to do so by a responsible person or police officer or (b) refuse or fail to leave when so asked at the end of a period of licensed hours.

Subsection (3)

Where a person refuses to leave the premises as required in the circumstances set out in subs.(1) and (2), an authorised person may effect his removal and, if necessary, use reasonable force for that purpose. For concerns regarding the use of "reasonable force" by licence holders or their staff, see notes to s.95(4).

The corresponding provision contained in the 1976 Act (s.79) gave the licence holder no such authority and simply provides that: "A constable may assist in expelling from any [licensed] premises any person who refuses or neglects to leave the premises" (s.79(3)).

Subsection (3)

A constable must provide assistance where an authorised person is empowered to remove a person from the premises, provided that the constable reasonably suspects the person concerned of having refused or failed to leave by virtue of subs.(1) or (2). (*cf* 1976 Act, s.79(3): see note to subs.(3), *supra*.)

Miscellaneous offences

117. Offences relating to sale of alcohol to trade

(1) A person who sells alcohol to trade otherwise than from premises which are used exclusively for the purpose of the selling of goods (whether solely alcohol or not) to trade commits an offence.
(2) A person guilty of an offence under subsection (1) is liable on summary conviction to a fine not exceeding level 5 on the standard scale.

DEFINITIONS
"alcohol": see s.2 of this Act
"premises": see s.147(1) of this Act
"selling to trade": see s.147(2) of this Act

GENERAL NOTE

The scheme of the 1976 Act involves a distinction between retail and wholesale sales, which is absent from this Act: see notes to s.1. In terms of this section, a person who sells alcohol to trade otherwise from premises used exclusively for the purpose of the selling of goods (whether solely alcohol or not) to trade commits an offence. As a result, having regard to the definition of "selling to trade" (s.147(2)), a premises licence will be required for a cash-and-carry warehouse which allows entry to members of the public who are not purchasing goods for trade purposes. Presumably no offence is committed in respect of premises which are licensed under the Act (*cf* 1976 Act, s.90A).

118. Prohibition of unauthorised sale of alcohol on moving vehicles

(1) A person who knowingly sells alcohol on or from a vehicle at a time when the vehicle is not parked (whether permanently or temporarily)

Licensing (Scotland) Act 2005 161

commits an offence, unless the selling of alcohol on or from the vehicle at such a time is expressly authorised by a premises licence or occasional licence in respect of the vehicle.

(2) A person guilty of an offence under subsection (1) is liable on summary conviction to-
   (a) a fine not exceeding £20,000,
   (b) imprisonment for a term not exceeding 3 months, or
   (c) both.

DEFINITIONS
"alcohol": see s.2 of this Act
"vehicle": see s.147(1) of this Act
"premises licence": see s.17 of this Act
"occasional licence": see s.56(1) of this Act

GENERAL NOTE
The sale of alcohol from an unlicensed moving vehicle attracts a potential penalty of a maximum fine of £20,000 and/or three months' imprisonment (*cf* s.1, which provides for a similar financial penalty and/or six months' imprisonment where alcohol is sold on unlicensed premises).

The Act does not repeat the provisions of s.92 of the 1976 Act, which it makes it an offence for the holder of a public service vehicle licence to permit the carriage of alcohol in certain circumstances. Explaining the removal of an appropriate clause in the Bill, the Minister in charge of licensing reform, George Lyon, told the Local Government and Transport Committee:

> "The original intention of the provisions was to control the carriage of alcohol on football supporters' buses. However, since the 1976 Act was passed, additional legislation has been introduced to deal with that problem. Under the Criminal Law (Consolidation) (Scotland) Act 1995 [s.19, as amended by the Crime and Punishment (Scotland) Act 1997, s.61(1), Sch.1, para.18(4)], it is an offence for persons to be in possession of alcohol on PSVs or trains that are conveying passengers to and from designated sporting events. The Association of Chief Police Officers in Scotland has been consulted on the removal of the provision from the Bill and is content with that."

For a consideration of the licensing of vehicles, see notes to s.126.

119. Delivery of alcohol from vehicles etc

(1) A person who, pursuant to a sale of alcohol by that person, delivers the alcohol from a vehicle or receptacle without the information mentioned in subsection (2) having been entered, before the despatch of the alcohol, in-
   (a) a day book kept on the premises from which the alcohol is despatched, and
   (b) a delivery book or invoice carried by the person delivering the alcohol,
commits an offence.

(2) The information referred to in subsection (1) is-
   (a) the quantity, description and price of the alcohol, and
   (b) the name and address of the person to whom it is to be delivered.

(3) A person who carries in a vehicle or receptacle in use for the delivery of alcohol pursuant to a sale of the alcohol by that person any alcohol the quantity, description and price of which was not entered as mentioned in subsection (1) commits an offence.

(4) A person who, pursuant to a sale of alcohol, delivers the alcohol to an address not entered as mentioned in subsection (1) commits an offence.
(5) A person who refuses to allow a constable or a Licensing Standards Officer to examine-
   (a) any vehicle or receptacle in use for the delivery of alcohol, or
   (b) any-
      (i) day book kept as mentioned in subsection (1)(a), or
      (ii) delivery book or invoice carried as mentioned in subsection (1)(b),
   commits an offence.
(6) A person guilty of an offence under this section is liable on summary conviction to a fine not exceeding level 3 on the standard scale.
(7) In this section, "alcohol" does not include any alcohol being delivered to a trader for the purposes of that person's trade.

DEFINITIONS
"alcohol": see s.2 of this Act
"vehicle": see s.147(1) of this Act

GENERAL NOTE
No doubt with a view to preventing door-to-door or other opportunistic sales of alcohol taking place under the guise of order fulfilment, this section contains detailed provisions regulating vehicle deliveries in pursuance of a sale. Its terms are similar to those contained in s.91 of the 1976 Act, save that under the former provisions the licence holder is vicariously responsible for offences committed by an employee or agent.

The words "pursuant to a sale of alcohol by that person" occurring in subs.(1) and (3) have the effect of absolving any employee of, or contractor engaged by, the seller from responsibility, with the exception of the obligations to delivery alcohol only to recorded addresses (subs.4) and to allow a constable or licensing standards officer to examine the delivery vehicle and prescribed documentation (subs.5). See Agnew and Baillie, p.156.

120. Prohibition of late-night deliveries of alcohol

(1) This section applies where alcohol is sold on any relevant premises for consumption off the premises.
(2) A responsible person commits an offence if the person knowingly delivers the alcohol to any premises (other than licensed premises) between the hours of midnight and 6am.
(3) A responsible person who knowingly allows the alcohol to be so delivered commits an offence.
(4) A person guilty of an offence under this section is liable on summary conviction to a fine not exceeding level 3 on the standard scale.

DEFINITIONS
"relevant premises": see s.122 of this Act
"responsible person": see s.122 of this Act

GENERAL NOTE
The reason for this provision is unclear, but anecdotal evidence suggests that it originates from problems associated with late-night alcohol deliveries in one part of Scotland. Its effect is to prohibit the delivery of alcohol to any premises (except licensed premises) between midnight and 6 am.

See notes to s.63(6) for circumstances in which deliveries pursuant to a sale are otherwise permitted outwith licensed hours.

Subsections (2), (3)
For a consideration of "knowingly allows", see notes to s.103.

121. Keeping of smuggled goods

(1) Any responsible person who knowingly keeps or allows to be kept on licensed premises any goods which-
   (a) have been imported without any duty payable on their importation having been paid, or
   (b) have otherwise been unlawfully imported,
commits an offence.
(2) A person guilty of an offence under subsection (1) is liable on summary conviction to a fine not exceeding level 3 on the standard scale.
(3) The court by or before which a person is convicted of an offence under subsection (1) may order the goods in question to be-
   (a) forfeited, and
   (b) destroyed or otherwise dealt with in such manner as the court may order.

DEFINITIONS
"responsible person": see s.122 of this Act
"licensed premises": see s.147(1) of this Act

GENERAL NOTE
The 1976 Act provides that the occupier or keeper of any licensed premises commits an offence by knowingly permitting "to be deposited in the premises goods which he has reasonable grounds for believing to be stolen goods" (s.80), but makes no provision for smuggled goods.

Subsection (1)
The Crown will require to establish that the accused knew the goods were liable to duty or had been otherwise unlawfully imported: *McQueen v McCann*, 1945 J.C. 151.
For a consideration of "knowingly allows", see notes to s.103.

Interpretation of Part

122. Interpretation of Part 8

(1) This section has effect for the purpose of the interpretation of this Part.
(2) "Relevant premises" means-
   (a) any licensed premises,
   (b) any exempt premises on which alcohol is sold, and
   (c) any premises used for the selling of alcohol to trade.
(3) "Responsible person" means, in relation to relevant premises-
   (a) in the case of licensed premises in respect of which a premises licence has effect, the premises manager,
   (b) in the case of licensed premises in respect of which an occasional licence has effect, the holder of the licence,
   (c) in the case of other relevant premises, the person having management and control of the premises, and

(d) in any of those cases, any person aged 18 or over who works on the premises in a capacity (whether paid or unpaid) which-
  (i) authorises the person to sell alcohol, or
  (ii) in relation to any offence under this Part of allowing something to be done, authorises the person to prevent the doing of the thing.

DEFINITIONS
"relevant premises": see subs.(2)
"licensed premises": see s.147(1) of this Act
"exempt premises": see s.124 of this Act
"alcohol": see s.2 of this Act
"sold": see s.147(1) of this Ac
"premises": see s.147(1) of this Act
"selling to trade": see s.147(2) of this Act
"responsible person": see subs.(3)
"premises licence": see s.17 of this Act
"premises manager": see s.19(1) of this Act
"occasional licence": see s.56(1) of this Act

GENERAL NOTE
This section provides definitions of the expressions "relevant premises" and "responsible person" occurring in this part of the Act.

Subsection (2)
The expression "relevant premises" includes not only licensed premises but also premises such as an airport examination station for which a licence is not required (see ss.1 and 124) and premises used for the sale of alcohol to traders (see ss.1, 117 and 147(2)).

Subsection (3)
The inclusion of "exempt premises" in the expression "relevant premises" could, for example, result in "the person having management and control" of a railway vehicle being a "responsible person" by virtue of this subsection who would be entitled to remove a disorderly person from the train (s.116(2)).

PART 9

MISCELLANEOUS AND GENERAL

Excluded and exempt premises

123. Excluded premises

(1) No premises licence or occasional licence has effect to authorise the sale of alcohol on excluded premises.
(2) For the purposes of this Act, "excluded premises" means-
  (a) premises on land-
    (i) acquired or appropriated by a special roads authority, and
    (ii) for the time being used,
  for the provision of facilities to be used in connection with the use of a special road provided for the use of traffic of class 1 (with or without other classes), and
  (b) subject to subsection (5), premises used as a garage or which form part of premises which are so used.

(3) For the purposes of subsection (2)(a)-
   (a) "special road" and "special roads authority" have the same meanings as in the Roads (Scotland) Act 1984 (c.54), and
   (b) "class 1" means class 1 in Schedule 3 to that Act, as varied from time to time by an order under section 8 of that Act, but, if that Schedule is amended by such an order so as to add to it a further class of traffic, the order may adapt the reference in this section to traffic of class 1 so as to take account of the additional class.
(4) For the purposes of subsection (2)(b), premises are used as a garage if they are used for one or more of the following-
   (a) the sale by retail of petrol or derv,
   (b) the sale of motor vehicles, or
   (c) the maintenance of motor vehicles.
(5) Despite subsection (2)(b), premises used for the sale by retail of petrol or derv or which form part of premises so used are not excluded premises if persons resident in the locality in which the premises are situated are, or are likely to become, reliant to a significant extent on the premises as the principal source of-
   (a) petrol or derv, or
   (b) groceries (where the premises are, or are to be, used also for the sale by retail of groceries).
(6) The Scottish Ministers may by order amend the definition of "excluded premises" in subsection (2) so as to include or exclude premises of such description as may be specified in the order.

DEFINITIONS
"premises licence": see s.17 of this Act
"occasional licence": see s.56(1) of this Act
"sale": see s.147(1) of this Act
"alcohol": see s.2 of this Act
"excluded premises": see subs.(2)
"special roads authority": see subs (3)
"special road": see subs.(3)
"class 1": see subs.(3)

GENERAL NOTE
This section repeats the disqualification of premises situated at motorway service areas contained in s.9(5) of the 1976 Act and, subject to a limited exemption, also prevents the grant of licences for garages and garage shops.

Subsections (2) (b), (4) and (5)
A number of licensing boards are generally unwilling to grant off-sale licences for petrol filling station shops on the view that, as a matter of public policy, no association should be made between the consumption of alcohol and the driving of motor vehicles.
That approach, which currently has no statutory foundation, has largely been supported by the court: *Lamb & Gardiner Ltd v Perth and Kinross District Licensing Board* [1998] 10 SLLP 22; *South Inch Filling Station Partnership v Perth and Kinross Licensing Board* [1996] 3 SLLP 7.
It has, on occasions, involved an examination of the physical size of the shop proposed to be licensed and the facilities offered in relation to the petrol sales element of the business: *Texaco Ltd v City of Glasgow Licensing Board* [1999] 12 SLLP 9; *Sood Enterprises Ltd v City of Glasgow Licensing Board*, 1991 S.L.T. (Sh Ct) 51; [1999] 12 SLLP 14; *BP Express Shopping Ltd v Perth and Kinross Licensing Board*, 2005 S.L.T. 862; [2005] 31 SLLP 34. Boards have conducted an enquiry as to whether the sale of fuel is ancillary to groceries sales, or *vice versa*: *Safeway Stores plc v City of Glasgow Licensing Board*, 2001 S.L.T. 1115; [2001] 20 SLLP 16; *BP Express Shopping Ltd*, cit. supra.

(See further: Tom Johnston, "Should unleaded mean unlicensed?" [1998] 10 SLLP 31; and Paul Romano, "Petrol stations and off-sale licences: cross-border comparisons" [1998] 14 SLLP 39; "Driving through the petrol smokescreen", [1997] 13 LR 13; and "Steering a route to garage licences" [2004] 56 LR 11.)

Nicholson noted the antipathy of some licensing boards to the licensing of petrol filling station shops and the dependency of some rural communities on a village shop with a petrol pump at the roadside. On balance, it was considered neither desirable nor necessary to have a standard licensing provision to deal with the matter; and "as at present, it should be left to licensing boards and, if necessary, the courts to deal with each case on its own merits and by reference to its own particular circumstances" (Report, para.14.23). (The Report did, however, recommend retention of the prohibition on the grant of a licence for motorway service stations.)

The White Paper canvassed the public's views on the issue, noting that the Westminster Government had already legislated against the granting of licences for premises "used primarily as a garage for the sale of petrol" (see below). A "key argument" for this decision "is that it is important not to give any encouragement to motorists to drink and drive". However, there was "clearly an important rural dimension to be considered in some parts of Scotland where a local garage may be the only available shop".

An analysis of responses to the White Paper consultation, which was prepared for the Scottish Executive, recorded that 79 respondents offered an opinion. The "vast majority" considered that "premises selling petrol should be allowed to sell alcohol if their primary function was as a community shop, but petrol stations or motorway service stations should not". Others observed that "there is no connection between drink-driving and petrol station purchases and that to refuse licences to shops selling petrol would be illogical given that alcohol can be purchased by drivers at other outlets".

The Bill, as introduced, more or less replicated the provisions of s.176 of the 2003 Act, albeit with a drafting error which was later corrected. (Section 176 excludes premises used *"primarily"* as a garage.) The absence of any exception for rural garages prompted a number of those who gave written evidence on the Bill to express their concerns. For example:

- Highland Council pointed out that there was no "empirical evidence" to support the claim that the purchase of alcohol at garages encouraged drink-driving offences. In many Highland communities garages were often the "local shop" and to proceed with the Bill as framed would "penalise the local community" and have "a financial impact on many fragile businesses".
- The Scottish Grocers Federation pointed out that many garages would be regarded as "primarily" used for the sale of motor fuels because of the high cost of petrol and suggested that "the measure of the primary function of the garage should be based on profit of the licensed shop premises as a percentage of the whole profit".
- The Convention of Scottish Local Authorities pointed out that rural garages are considered more as community facilities and the loss of licences "would be seen as a significant loss to rural areas, especially where alternative options such as supermarkets and off-sales premises are not likely to be operating".

At Stage 2, the Scottish Executive bowed to these anxieties and amended the Bill by providing for the exemption set out in subs.(5), thus ensuring that "the vital existence of rural petrol stations is not compromised". It also recognised that the benefit of subs.(5) might be obtained by garages other than those in rural areas "because there might be cases in urban or other areas in which the community is reliant on the local shop" (Official Report, col.2928).

Off-sale licensed petrol filling station shops have no automatic right of passage to the new licensing system and face exclusion unless an applicant for a premises licence can successfully negotiate this sections "limbo pole". According to the Scottish Executives Regulatory Impact Assessment, there are at present "over 165 petrol station forecourt shops which hold an off-sales [*sic*] licence".

124. Exempt premises

(1) Each of the following are exempt premises for the purposes of this Act-
   (a) an examination station at an airport designated for the purposes of this section in an order made by the Scottish Ministers,
   (b) an approved wharf at a port or hoverport so designated,
   (c) an aircraft, a hovercraft or a railway vehicle while engaged on a journey,
   (d) a vessel while engaged on-
      (i) an international journey, or
      (ii) a journey (other than an international journey) forming part of a ferry service, and
   (e) premises which are occupied (whether indefinitely or temporarily) for the purposes of the armed forces of the Crown, except while being used for other purposes.

(2) The Scottish Ministers may make an order under subsection (1) designating an airport, port or hoverport for the purposes of this section only if it appears to them to be one at which there is a substantial amount of international passenger traffic.

(3) For the purpose of subsection (1), the period during which an aircraft, hovercraft, railway vehicle or vessel is engaged in a journey includes-
   (a) any period ending with its departure when preparations are being made for the journey, and
   (b) any period after its arrival at its destination when it continues to be occupied by those (or any of those) who made the journey (or any part of it).

(4) In this section-
   "approved wharf" has the meaning given in section 20A of the Customs and Excise Management Act 1979 (c.2),
   "examination station" has the meaning given in section 22A of that Act,
   "ferry service" means a service the principal purpose of which is the transport of passengers or goods over water,
   "international journey" means a journey with-
      (a) a point of departure,
      (b) a destination, or
      (c) at least one port of call,
   outside the United Kingdom, and includes any part of such a journey.

DEFINITIONS
"examination station": see subs.(4)
"approved wharf": see subs.(4)
"railway vehicle": see s.147(1) of this Act
"vessel": see s.147(1) of this Act
"ferry service": see subs.(4)
"premises": see s.147(1) of this Act
"international journey": see subs.(4)

GENERAL NOTE
The 1976 Act exempts from its scope:

● Theatres erected before 1 January 1904 (s.138(1)(b)), which are treated "as if an

entertainment licence were in force" (s.121).
- Service canteens held "under the authority of the Secretary of State" (s.138(1)(a)).
- The sale of supply of alcohol to aircraft passengers while the aircraft is airborne (s.138(1)(c)).
- Railway passenger vehicles, provided that "passengers can be supplied with food" (s.138(1)(c)).
- Passenger vessels while in the course of being navigated (s.138(1)(c)), subject to a restriction on the Sunday permitted hours (s.93).

Nicholson considered that the exemption for theatres of a certain age, "of obscure origin", was no longer appropriate; and the Act adopts the Report's recommendation that they should in future fall under the general licensing system (Report, para.14.44).

In relation to aircraft, trains and vessels, the Report considered that the provisions of the 1976 Act are "almost incapable of sensible comprehension" and identified a number anomalies, recommending that "appropriate provision should be made in relation to the sale and supply of alcohol on aircraft, on passenger trains, and on sea-going vessels" (Report, para.14.54).

This section takes a fresh approach to exemptions based largely on the policy adopted by the 2003 Act.

It requires to be kept in view that "exempt premises" are not totally disconnected from the licensing system:

- "exempt premises" on which alcohol is sold are "relevant premises" for the purpose of the provisions of Part 8 of the Act; and
- reflecting the Scottish Executive's intention to "ensure that under-18s are prevented from buying alcohol on trains, aeroplanes, ships and boats" (White Paper), the offence of selling alcohol to those persons is no longer restricted to licensed premises (see s.102).

Subsection (1) (a)

An examination station at an airport is, in effect, the area beyond security controls.

The 1976 Act does not provide a parallel exemption, simply providing for the exemption of examination stations from the permitted hours and off-sales trading hours (s.63) at airports where there is a significant amount of international passenger traffic. Presently, the examination stations at Aberdeen, Edinburgh, Glasgow, Prestwick and Sumburgh airports are the subject of orders made under s.63.

Subsection (1) (c)

The decision to exempt aircraft, without further elaboration, was taken on the view expressed in the White Paper that "there was no case for imposing further regulations on flights as internal journeys tended to be relatively short thereby limiting the opportunity for misuse"; and "although such problems could arise on long haul flights, there were already firm laws with serious penalties to cope with those who caused disorder on aeroplanes".

The exemption for railway vehicles (without the outdated requirement that food should be available) was explained by the Scottish Executive to the Local Government and Transport Committee at Stage 1:

"It is difficult to license trains because they are not just moveable, but composed of a number of carriages. A train is not a static item that can be licensed, and trains also tend to travel through various different licensing board areas. We have tried to introduce some controls - for example, we hope that such exempt premises will still have to comply with the no proof, no sale requirements of the Bill although they will not have to be licensed." (Official Report, col.2608).

(Trains and other exempt premises on which alcohol is sold will require, *inter alia*, to display the notice referred to in s.110.)

By way of safeguard, a sheriff may make an order prohibiting the sale of alcohol on a railway vehicle: see s.127.

The definition of "railway vehicle" contained in s.147(1) is intended to remove any doubt "about the treatment of underground trains and trams (Official Report, col.2932). The definition originally proposed in the Bill would have opened up the (now removed) possibility of trams becoming exempt premises, no matter how bizarre that possibility might appear. The fact that underground trains are apparently exempt premises is equally bizarre.

Subsection (1) (d)
The definition of premises contained in s.147(1) includes a "vessel", a term defined in that subsection as including "a ship, boat, raft or other apparatus constructed or adapted for floating on water". Vessels which are not encompassed by this exemption will require to be the subject of a premises licence if alcohol is to be sold (s.1): see also s.126.

The Bill as introduced allowed no exemption for ferry services. Unsurprisingly, representations were made to the Local Government and Transport Committee by two Scottish operators, NorthLink and Caledonian MacBrayne. The former company pointed out that ferry operators had not been involved in "'cruising' or similar activities which in the past have led to the tragic loss of life which it could be argued was partly alcohol related"; the latter pointed out that the viability of services could be affected by the costs associated with licensing and alcohol was only a "small part" of their offer.

Account was taken of these concerns, with the result that ferry vessels engaged on domestic journeys are exempt premises, subject to the safeguard provided by s.128.

Subsection (1) (e)
This exemption effectively repeats and enlarges that contained in s.138(1)(a) in relation to service canteens.

Subsection (2)
An exemption order in relation to airport examination stations, ports or hoverports by virtue of subs.(1) may only be made where there is a substantial amount of international passenger traffic, so that orders are likely to be made in relation to, *inter alia*, examination stations at the airports mentioned in the notes to s.(1)(a).

Special provision for certain clubs

125. Special provisions for certain clubs

(1) The provisions of this Act mentioned in subsection (2) do not apply in relation to premises which are used wholly or mainly for the purposes of any club of such description as may be prescribed.

(2) Those provisions are-
 (a) section 7 (assessments of overprovision),
 (b) section 20(4)(g) (requirement for operating plan to contain information as to the premises manager),
 (c) section 23(5)(e) (ground of refusal of premises licence application relating to overprovision),
 (d) section 26(2)(a)(ii) (requirement for name and address of premises manager to be specified in premises licence),
 (e) section 30(5)(d) (ground of refusal of premises licence variation application relating to overprovision),
 (f) in schedule 3-
  (i) paragraph 4 (requirement for there to be a premises manager for licensed premises), and
  (ii) paragraph 5 (requirement for sales of alcohol under premises licence to be authorised by a personal licence holder), and
 (g) in schedule 4, paragraph 4 (requirement for sales of alcohol under certain occasional licences to be authorised by a personal licence holder).

(3) Different descriptions of clubs may be prescribed under subsection (1) in relation to different provisions specified in subsection (2).

(4) The Scottish Ministers may by regulations provide for this Act to apply in relation to-
   (a) clubs of such descriptions as may be prescribed in the regulations, or
   (b) premises used wholly or mainly for the purposes of such clubs,
subject to such further modifications as may be so prescribed.

(5) Regulations under subsection (1) or (4) may prescribe a description of club by reference to-
   (a) requirements as to the constitution of the club, including, in particular, requirements as to-
      (i) membership of the club, and
      (ii) the rules of the club, and
   (b) such other factors as the Scottish Ministers consider appropriate.

DEFINITIONS
"premises": see s.147(1) of this Act
"prescribed"; see s.147(1) of this Act
"operating plan": see s.20(4) of this Act
"premises manager": see s.19(1) of this Act
"premises licence application": see s.20(3) of this Act
"premises licence variation application": see s.29(3) of this Act
"licensed premises": see s.147(1) of this Act
"alcohol": see s.2 of this Act
"personal licence": see s.71 of this Act
"occasional licence": see s.56(1) of this Act

GENERAL NOTE
While members' clubs are brought within the mainstream licensing system for the first time, the Scottish Executive appears to have recognised that it would be reasonable, in certain cases, to exempt them from some of the Act's provisions. Nicholson considered that there was an "overwhelming case" for subjecting clubs to the enhanced supervisory system to be operated by licensing boards, but the Report also suggested that different provisions might be appropriate to recognised their "special character" (Report, Chapter 9). This section affords Ministers considerable latitude in their approach to the dispensations which might be afforded.

Subsection (1)
The approach to the determination of the descriptions of clubs to which the provisions set out in subs.(2) will not apply is perhaps signposted in the Policy Document:
   "We recognise that for a number of small clubs, bar facilities and the supply of alcohol is [sic] a minor part of their activities and it would not be feasible for them to undergo the cost of training attached to appointing a premises manager... The decision to exempt would be subject to further detailed discussion with clubs but could be based, for example, on bar turnover or the number of club members."

Vessels, vehicles and moveable structures

126. Vessels, vehicles and moveable structures

(1) A vessel which is not permanently moored or berthed is to be treated for the purposes of this Act as premises situated in the place where it is usually moored or berthed.

(2) Where a vehicle or moveable structure which is not permanently situated in any place is, or is to be, used for the sale of alcohol while parked at or set in any place-
   (a) it is to be treated for the purposes of this Act as premises situated at that place, and
   (b) each such place at which it is, or is to be, so used is to be treated as separate premises.
(3) The following provisions of Part 3 (which relate to the provision of certificates as to planning, building standards and food hygiene and to notifications of applications) do not apply in relation to premises (other than exempt premises) consisting of a vessel, namely-
   (a) section 20(2)(b)(iii),
   (b) section 21(1)(a) and (e),
   (c) section 29(4) (so far as it applies section 21(1)(a) and (e)),
   (d) section 45(10)(a),
   (e) section 46(2)(d), and
   (f) section 50.
(4) This Act applies in relation to premises consisting of a vehicle or other moveable structure which is, or is to be, used for the sale of alcohol while not parked or permanently situated in any place (referred to in this section as "moving premises") subject to the modifications in subsections (5) to (9).
(5) Section 18 does not apply and instead, in Part 3 and this section, "appropriate Licensing Board" means in relation to moving premises or a premises licence or occasional licence issued in respect of such premises-
   (a) the Licensing Board in whose area the premises are used or to be used for the sale of alcohol, or
   (b) where the premises are used or to be used in the area of more than one Licensing Board-
      (i) the Board in whose area they are used or to be used to the greater or greatest extent, or
      (ii) if neither or none of those Boards falls within sub-paragraph (i), such of those Boards as is, in the application for a premises licence or, as the case may be, occasional licence in respect of the premises, nominated as the appropriate Licensing Board in respect of the premises.
(6) The following provisions of Part 3 do not apply in relation to moving premises, namely-
   (a) section 20(2)(b)(iii),
   (b) section 21(1)(a), (b), and (e),
   (c) section 29(4) (so far as it applies section 21(1)(a), (b) and (e)),
   (d) section 45(10)(a),
   (e) section 46(2)(d), and
   (f) section 50.
(7) Section 21(1) applies in relation to moving premises as if for paragraph (c) there were substituted-
      "(c) the relevant council,".
(8) References to the locality in which premises are situated are, in relation to moving premises, to be taken as references to the area of the appropriate Licensing Board.
(9) For the purposes of Part 4, moving premises are to be treated as premises situated within the area of the appropriate Licensing Board.

(10) The Scottish Ministers may by regulations provide for this Act to apply in relation to vessels, vehicles and moveable structures subject to such further modifications as they consider necessary or expedient.

DEFINITIONS
"vessel": see s.147(1) of this Act
"vehicle": see s.147(1) of this Act
"premises": see s.147(1) of this Act
"exempt premises": see s.124 of this Act
"moving premises": see subs.(4)
"appropriate licensing board": see subs.(5)
"premises licence": see s.17 of this Act
"occasional licence": see s.56(1) of this Act
"area": see s.147(1) of this Act
"relevant council": see s.147(1) of this Act

GENERAL NOTE
While licences have been obtained for the sale of alcohol on vessels while berthed, passenger vessels are currently outwith the scope of the licensing system (1976 Act, s.138(1)(c), subject to s.93: see General Note to s.124). "Premises" for the purposes of this Act means "any place and includes a vehicle, vessel or moveable structure" (s.147(1)); and a licence is now required for the sale of alcohol on vessels, unless they are engaged on an international journey or on a journey forming part of a ferry service (see s.124).

The licensing of vessels addresses the potential safety issues raised by so-called "booze cruises" and "mobile parties". As the White Paper noted, in his report following the Marchioness disaster in 1989, Lord Justice Clarke said:

"If we are to retain liquor licensing laws and require premises to be licensed to sell alcohol, then the reasons that commend themselves to require such premises on land to be licensed seem to me to apply with at least equal force in respect of vessels. Indeed it might be said that safety concerns demand even higher standards for those in charge of serving alcohol on board boats".

The licensing of vehicles stems from supervisory concerns arising from the supply of alcohol to passengers by limousine and other operators of hired vehicles. Some licensing boards have been content to grant off-sale licences for the hirer's business premises; and, in those cases, alcohol consumed in the vehicles has been legitimately purchased from the licensed premises by the hirer's customer (see: "Driven to drink", [2003] 24 SLLP 8). Questions have no doubt arisen as to whether, in some cases, alcohol is in fact being sold from the vehicle itself. This section makes provision for the licensing of vehicles and moveable structures while parked (subs.(2)) and while not parked or permanently situated in any place (subs.(4)).

Subsection (1)
Where a vessel is not permanently moored or berthed it is to be treated as premises situated in the place where it usually moored or berthed and will therefore come within the jurisdiction of the licensing board for the area (s.18).

Subsection (2)
The effect of this subsection is to require a separate premises licence to be obtained for each place at which a vehicle or moveable structure used for the sale of alcohol is parked or set.

The nature of the "moveable structures" embraced by this section is not entirely clear. The Policy Memorandum refers to a "tent or inflatable building". Structures of this kind in which alcohol is sold presently require to be licensed, normally by means of an occasional licence: for example, a marquee in the grounds of a hotel used to host a wedding reception.

Subsection (3)
In relation to vessels, this subsection disapplies the requirement to:

- produce planning, building control and food hygiene certificates with an application

for a premises licence (s.20(2)(b)(iii));
- give notice of a premises licence application to "each person having a notifiable interest in neighbouring land" (s.21(1)(a)) or to the enforcing authority under the Fire (Scotland) Act 2005 (s.21(1)(e));
- give similar notice in connection with an application to vary a premises licence (s.21(1)(a) and (e), otherwise applied by s.29(4));
- produce a provisional planning certificate with an application for a provisional premises licence (s.45(10)(a));
- produce, in certain circumstances, a planning certificate in connection with an application to confirm a provisional premises licence (s.46(2)(d));
- produce a building standards or food hygiene certificate in connection with an application to confirm a provisional premises licence (s.46(2)(d)).

Section 50 is generally disapplied.

Subsection (4)

The whole provisions of the Act are applied to vehicles or other moveable structures which are, or are to be, used for the sale of alcohol while not parked or permanently situated in any place (termed "moving premises"), subject to modifications contained in subs.(5)-(9).

For the offence of selling alcohol on or from an unlicensed moving vehicle, see s.118.

Subsection (5)

Jurisdiction in relation to moving premises lies with the licensing board in whose area the premises are to be used for the sale of alcohol. Where alcohol will be sold in the premises in more than one board's area the appropriate licensing board will be either (a) the board in whose area in which the greater or greatest extent of use occurs; or (b) in other cases, the board nominated by the applicant for a premises licence or occasional licence.

Subsection (6)

In relation to moving premises, this subsection disapplies the requirement to:

- produce planning, building control and food hygiene certificates with an application for a premises licence (s.20(2)(b)(iii));
- give notice of a premises licence application to "each person having a notifiable interest in neighbouring land" (s.21(1)(a)); or to any community council (s.21(1)(b); or to the enforcing authority under the Fire (Scotland) Act 2005 (s.21(1)(e));
- give similar notice in connection with an application to vary a premises licence (s.21(1)(a), (b) and (e), otherwise applied by s.29(4));
- produce a provisional planning certificate with an application for a provisional premises licence (s.45(10)(a));
- produce, in certain circumstances, a planning certificate in connection with an application to confirm a provisional premises licence (s.46(2)(d));
- produce a building standards or food hygiene certificate in connection with an application to confirm a provisional premises licence (s.46(2)(d)).

Section 50 is generally disapplied.

Subsection (7)

The effect of this subsection is to require a licensing board to give notice of a premises licence application for moving premises to the relevant council, rather than, in the case of other premises, the council within whose area the premises are situated. The relevant council is for whose area the board is established; or, in the cases of a divisional licence board, the council for the area of which the division forms part (s.147(1)).

127. Power to prohibit sale of alcohol on trains

(1) A sheriff may-

(a) on the application of a senior police officer, and
(b) if satisfied that it is necessary to do so to prevent disorder,

make an order under subsection (2).

(2) That is an order prohibiting, during such period as may be specified in the order, the sale of alcohol on any railway vehicle-
   (a) at such station or stations within the sheriff's sheriffdom as may be so specified, or
   (b) whilst travelling between such stations as may be so specified, at least one of which is in that sheriffdom.

(3) An order under subsection (2) has no effect in relation to any railway vehicle unless a copy of it has been given by a senior police officer to the train operator (or each train operator) responsible for the vehicle.

(4) A person who knowingly-
   (a) sells or attempts to sell alcohol in breach of an order under subsection (2), or
   (b) allows the sale of alcohol in breach of such an order,

commits an offence.

(5) A person guilty of an offence under subsection (4) is liable on summary conviction to-
   (a) a fine not exceeding £20,000,
   (b) imprisonment for a term not exceeding 3 months, or
   (c) both.

(6) In this section-
   "station" has the meaning given in section 83 of the Railways Act 1993, and
   "train operator" means a person authorised by a licence under section 8 of that Act to operate railway assets (within the meaning of section 6 of that Act).

DEFINITIONS
"senior police officer": see s.147(1) of this Act
"alcohol": see s.2 of this Act
"railway vehicle": see s.147(1) of this Act
"station": see subs.(6)
"train operator": see subs.6

GENERAL NOTE
A licence is not required for the sale of alcohol on a railway vehicle while it is engaged on a journey (s.124(1)(c)). This section addresses concerns that, on occasions, such sales could lead to nuisance and disorder. It also ensure cross-border consistency: similar provision is made in s.157 of the 2003 Act.

Subsection (2)-(3)
An order made by a sheriff under subs.(1) may prohibit the sale of alcohol on any railway vehicle at a specified station or stations within his sheriffdom; or on a railway vehicle travelling between specified stations, at least one of which is within the sheriffdom. An order has no effect unless a copy of it has been given by a senior police officer to the train operator or operators concerned. An offence is committed by a person who sells or attempts to sell alcohol in breach of an order or allows its sale.

128. Power to prohibit sale of alcohol on ferries

(1) This section applies to any vessel which is exempt premises by virtue of section 124(1)(d)(ii) (vessels engaged in ferry services).

Licensing (Scotland) Act 2005

(2) A sheriff may-
   (a) on the application of a senior police officer, and
   (b) if satisfied that it is necessary to do so to prevent disorder,
make an order under subsection (3).
   (3) That is an order prohibiting, during such period as may be specified, the sale of alcohol on any vessel to which this section applies while engaged on-
   (a) any journey to or from a specified place within the sheriff's sheriffdom, or
   (b) a specified journey to or from such a place.
   (4) An order under subsection (3) has no effect in relation to any vessel unless a copy of it has been given by a senior police officer to the operator of the vessel.
   (5) A person who knowingly-
   (a) sells or attempts to sell alcohol in breach of an order under subsection (3), or
   (b) allows the sale of alcohol in breach of such an order,
commits an offence.
   (6) A person guilty of an offence under subsection (5) is liable on summary conviction to-
   (a) a fine not exceeding £20,000,
   (b) imprisonment for a term not exceeding 3 months, or
   (c) both.
   (7) Subsection (3) of section 124, so far as applying to a vessel, applies for the purposes of subsection (3) of this section as it applies for the purpose of subsection (1) of that section.
   (8) In this section, "specified" means, in relation to an order under subsection (3), specified in the order.

DEFINITIONS
"vessel": see s.147(1) of this Act
"exempt premises": see s.124 of this Act
"senior police officer": see s.147(1) of this Act
"alcohol": see s.2 of this Act

GENERAL NOTE
This section makes provision for the prohibition of alcohol sales on domestic ferry services, mirroring the provisions of s.127 which apply to trains.

Relevant and foreign offences

129. Relevant offences and foreign offences

(1) In this Act, "relevant offence" means-
   (a) such offence, or
   (b) an offence of such description,
as may be prescribed.
   (2) In this Act, "foreign offence" means any offence-
   (a) under the law of any place other than Scotland, and
   (b) which is similar in nature to any relevant offence.
   (3) Regulations under subsection (1) may provide, in relation to any offence or description of offence prescribed in them, that a person is to be treated, for the purposes of such provisions of this Act as may be

specified in the regulations, as having been convicted of the offence only if the person-
(a) accumulates such number of separate convictions for the offence, or
(b) is convicted of committing the offence on such number of separate occasions,

as may be so specified.

(4) For the purposes of this Act, a conviction for a relevant offence or a foreign offence is to be disregarded if it is spent for the purposes of the Rehabilitation of Offenders Act 1974 (c.53).

DEFINITIONS
"relevant offence": see subs.(1)
"prescribed": see s.147(1) of this Act
"foreign offence": see subs.(2)

GENERAL NOTE
As explained in the notes to s.22, the Act abandons the "fit and proper person" test used to measure the suitability of applicants and licence holders under the 1976 Act. By virtue of this section, Scottish Ministers will make regulations specifying relevant or foreign offences; and a conviction for such an offence may lead to:

- the refusal of an application for a premises licence (s.23(6)) or a personal licence (s.71(6);
- the variation, suspension or revocation of a premises licence (s.44(7)); or
- the revocation, suspension or endorsement of a personal licence (s.83(8)).

The holders of, and those in the process of making an application for, premises and personal licences are under an obligation to notify the licensing board of a conviction for a relevant or foreign offence (ss.24, 43, 75, 82). Where a person charged with a relevant or foreign offence is the holder or a premises or personal licence or is granted a licence during the currency of the criminal proceedings, he must produce the licence to the court or notify the court of its existence (ss.41 and 80). The clerk of court is under an obligation to give notice of a premises or personal licence holder's conviction to the licensing board (ss. 42 and 81).

Subsection (1)
The list of relevant offences is likely to be extensive and include offences committed under the Smoking, Health and Social Care (Scotland) Act 2005 (asp.13). Under the parallel provisions of the 2003 Act, relevant offences have ranged from robbery to the possession and sale of unmarked tobacco (see 2003 Act, Sch.4).

Subsection (3)
Regulations may provide that any offence or description of offence is only to be regarded as a relevant offence where it has been persistently committed.

Subsection (4)
In terms of the Rehabilitation of Offenders Act 1974 (c.53), with certain exceptions, a conviction becomes spent after a period of rehabilitation according to the sentence imposed (1974 Act, s.5(2)). No evidence of a spent conviction is admissible in any proceedings before a "judicial authority" (an expression which has been held to include a licensing authority), except where the authority is satisfied at "any stage" that justice cannot otherwise be done (*ibid.*, s.7(3)).

Spent convictions are admissible under the present licensing regime, provided that an appropriate procedure is followed: see *O'Doherty v Renfrewshire Council* 1998, S.L.T. 327; [1997] 7 SLLP 6.

This subsection provides that a conviction for a relevant or foreign offence is to be disregarded if it is spent in terms of the 1974 Act.

130. Effect of appeal against conviction for relevant or foreign offence

(1) The fact that any conviction of any person for a relevant offence or foreign offence is subject to appeal does not affect the taking of any action by a Licensing Board which the Board is entitled or required to take in connection with the conviction by virtue of any provision of this Act.

(2) The Licensing Board may, however, postpone the taking of the action for such period as the Board considers appropriate pending the appeal.

(3) Where the conviction is overturned on appeal-
   (a) any action taken by the Licensing Board in reliance on the conviction is to be treated as having no effect, and
   (b) accordingly, the Licensing Board must take such steps as are necessary to return any applicant or licence holder adversely affected by the action to the position the applicant or licence holder would have been in had the action not been taken.

(4) A conviction is subject to appeal for the purposes of subsection (1) if-
   (a) the period during which an appeal may be taken against the conviction has not yet expired, or
   (b) an appeal is taken against the conviction and the appeal has not yet been determined.

DEFINITIONS
"relevant offence": see s.129(1) of this Act
"foreign offence": see s.129(2) of this Act

GENERAL NOTE
An appeal against a conviction for a relevant or foreign offence is to be disregarded for the purposes of the Act, but the licensing board has a discretion to postpone the taking of any action for such period as it considers appropriate pending the disposal of the appeal.

Subsection (3)
Where a conviction is overturned on appeal, the applicant or licence holder is entitled to *restitutio in integrum*: any action taken by the board is to be treated as having no effect and the board must return the person whose appeal has been successful to the position in which he otherwise have been had the board's action not been taken.

Appeals

131. Appeals

(1) A decision of a Licensing Board specified in the left-hand column of schedule 5 may be appealed by the person specified in the right-hand column of that schedule.

(2) An appeal under this section is to be made by way of stated case, at the instance of the appellant, to-
   (a) where the decision appealed is specified in Part 1 of schedule 5, the sheriff principal, or
   (b) where the decision appealed is specified in Part 2 of that schedule, the sheriff,
of the appropriate sheriffdom.

(3) The grounds on which a Licensing Board's decision may be appealed under this section are-
  (a) that, in reaching the decision, the Licensing Board-
    (i) erred in law,
    (ii) based their decision on an incorrect material fact,
    (iii) acted contrary to natural justice, or
    (iv) exercised their discretion in an unreasonable manner, or
  (b) where the decision is to take any of the steps mentioned in subsection (4), that the step taken is disproportionate in all the circumstances.
(4) Those steps are-
  (a) at a review hearing in respect of a premise licence-
    (i) issuing a written warning to the licence holder,
    (ii) revoking or suspending the licence, or
    (iii) making a variation of the licence, or
  (b) making an order revoking, suspending or endorsing a personal licence.
(5) Where the sheriff principal or, as the case may be, sheriff upholds an appeal against a Licensing Board's decision under this section, the sheriff principal or sheriff may-
  (a) remit the case back to the Licensing Board for reconsideration of the decision,
  (b) reverse the decision, or
  (c) make, in substitution for the decision, such other decision as the sheriff principal or sheriff considers appropriate, being a decision of such nature as the Licensing Board could have made.
(6) In this section, "the appropriate sheriffdom" means the sheriffdom in which the principal office of the Licensing Board whose decision is being appealed is situated.

DEFINITIONS
"review hearing": see s.38(2) of this Act
"premises licence": see s.17 of this Act
"variation": see s.29(5) of this Act
"personal licence": see s.71 of this Act
"appropriate sheriffdom": see subs.(6)

GENERAL NOTE
The 1976 Act provides applicants, licence holders and objectors with a right of appeal against the majority of licensing board decisions. The most significant omission is in relation to applications for the regular extension of permitted hours (1976 Act, s.64): it was no doubt considered that extensions would only be sought very occasionally and in a limited range of circumstances and locations (Nicholson, Report, para.11.4). In the event, the grant of extended hours became the norm, rather than the exception.

Nicholson saw "no good reason" why all licensing board decisions, other than purely procedural ones, should not be open to appeal (Report, para.11.7). Schedule 5 of the Act, introduced by s.133(1), provides applicants and the holder of a personal licence with comprehensive rights of appeal. However, despite the Scottish Executive's determination to widen the scope for objections (see notes to s.22), objectors' appeal rights have all but disappeared.

The Executive's policy in this area appears to have shifted during the Bill's progress. At a meeting of the Local Government and Transport Committee on March 22, 2005, Margaret Smith MSP taxed the Scottish Executive's solicitor on the absence of objectors' appeal rights in the Bill as introduced: "Why is no provision made for objectors or personal licence holders to appeal?... Not having an appeal provision for objectors is slightly worrying". In response, the solicitor told the Committee that: "Objectors and applicants for reviews will be allowed to appeal" (Official Report, col.2214).

In the result, with two exceptions, no licensing board decisions are open to appeal by an objector. An appeal may be taken against the decision of a licensing board to grant an occasional licence, which will have a short life (note more than 14 days: s.56(4)) and could not practicably be reviewed during its currency. Paradoxically, because occasional licence applications are likely to be made in respect of events due to take place in a matter of weeks, an appeal against a decision to grant an application, even if disposed of expeditiously, is liable to prevent the event taking place.

Any person adversely affected by the conduct of the premises may initiate a procedure which could lead to the imposition of a sanction upon the licence holder (see ss.36-39). An applicant for review who is aggrieved by the board's decision in the matter may appeal to the sheriff principal. But the scope of that appeal is narrower than may first appear. An applicant for a premises licence review may appeal against "A decision under section 39(1) to issue a written warning to a premises licence holder, to make a variation of a premises licence, or to suspend or revoke such a licence" (Sch.5, Pt.1). In other words, the applicant may challenge the particular sanction imposed by the licensing board but not, it seems, a decision not to impose any sanction.

The Act's treatment of objectors was the subject of opprobrium when Sheriff Principal Gordon Nicholson addressed delegates at a Law Society of Scotland conference in September 2005. The following passage is taken from the text of his address reported at [2005] 32 SLLP 11:

> "There appears to be a view in some quarters, partly by reference to planning law and practice, that it would be a startling innovation to allow a right of appeal to objectors in cases where a licence application has been granted in the face of objections, but of course this would not be an innovation at all. As you are well aware, s.17(5) of the 1976 Act has always allowed a right of appeal to competent objectors. Moreover, when the Bill was considered a few months ago by the Local Government and Transport Committee, that Committee expressly recommended that unsuccessful objectors should have a right of appeal.
>
> Personally, I consider that it would be contrary to natural justice that an objector who had been unsuccessful, but whose objection had not been characterised as frivolous or vexatious, should be denied any right of appeal against a decision rejecting his or her objection...
>
> Moreover, it seems to me that... the consequence is likely to be that we will see a continuation of the present situation whereby certain licensing board decisions can only be challenged by the process of judicial review."

While provision is made for an appeal at the instance of an applicant against a decision to refuse a personal licence application, no express provision is made for an appeal against the refusal of an application to renew a personal licence. The expressions "personal licence application" and "personal licence renewal application" are the subject of separate definitions (ss.72(2) and 78(4) respectively). Section 78(5) provides that for the purpose of ss.73 (notification of application to chief constable) and 74 (determination of personal licence application) references to a personal licence application "are to be read as if they included reference to a personal licence renewal application". Presumably, by implication, the refusal of a personal licence application is to be equiparated with the refusal of a personal licence renewal application.

While a decision to refuse an application for a premises licence may be appealed by the applicant, a question arises as to whether that entitlement extends to the imposition of unwanted conditions. There are certain conditions which a licensing board must impose and which are plainly inviolable, namely, (a) the conditions set out in Sch.3 which a licensing board must impose (s.27(1)); and (b) in the case of "late-opening" premises, the conditions which are made mandatory by s.27(3), (4). However, on the basis of *Wolfson v Glasgow District Licensing Board*, 1981 S.L.T. 136 (following *Baillie v Wilson*, (1916) 2 S.L.T. 252) it would appear that an applicant may competently appeal against the attachment of a "pool" condition (s.27(5)) or a condition of the board's own devising in terms of s.27(6). In *Wolfson*, the Court considered competent an appeal against the grant of an off-sale licence which did not permit the sale of spirits, despite the lack of express provision for such an appeal in the 1976 Act.

Subsection (2)

Clayson's recommendation that appeals against licensing board decisions should proceed by way of stated case and be determined by the sheriff principal (Report, paras. 6.9, 6.17) was not adopted in the 1976 Act, which provides for an appeal to the sheriff by way of a summary application.

Nicholson noted that the present arrangements had been widely criticised by the Committee's consultees, who said that procedures before sheriffs are very slow, resulting in unacceptable delays in cases where a licence has been suspended but continues to be operable during the appeal process (Report, para.11.3).

The Committee considered that provision for the disposal of appeals by sheriff principals would result in them being disposed of very much more quickly than at present. (The prompt disposal of appeals will be particularly important under the new system: see notes to s.132(7).) The suggested creation of an appeal tribunal consisting of a legally-qualified chairman and two lay members was rejected having regard to the anticipated number of appeals and cost considerations (Report, para.11.6).

Read with Sch.5, this subsection provides that, with two exceptions, appeals will be considered by the sheriff principal. For reasons which are impossible to divine, an appeal against the refusal of a personal licence and against a decision to impose a sanction upon a personal licence holder are to be considered by the sheriff.

Appeals will proceed by way of stated case. Nicholson considered that the stated case procedure was better suited than the summary application procedure. It had the advantage of providing an opportunity for the body whose decision is being challenged to set out clearly the matters which it took into account and the reasons for its decision; and it ought to make it easier for the appellate court to focus on the question whether or not a ground of appeal has been established (Report, para.11.10). Continuing provision should also be made to allow a person dissatisfied with a licensing board's decision to request a statement of reasons prior to marking an appeal (Report, para.11.11; see also notes to s.51(2)).

Subsection (3)

Nicholson considered that the grounds of appeal set out in s.39(4) of the 1976 Act ought to be retained, but the "unreasonable exercise of discretion" ground of appeal (39(4)(d)) should be replaced with one which reflects the concept of proportionality developed in the jurisprudence of the European Court of Human Rights (Report, para. 11.14). The grounds of appeal set out here are identical to those contained in s.39(4) of the 1976 Act, save for the introduction of proportionality considerations in relation to certain decisions (see subs.(4)). For a case in which the proportionality of a (taxi) licence suspension was considered, see *Baird v Glasgow City Council* [2003] 25 S.L.L.P. 27.

Subsection (5)

The means by which the court may dispose of an appeal more or less replicate those contained in s.39(6) of the 1976 Act (as recommended by Nicholson: Report, para.11.17), save that the court may, instead of remitting the case to the board or reversing its decision, substitute a different decision of a nature which the board itself could have made.

132. Appeals: supplementary provision

(1) A Licensing Board whose decision is appealed under section 131 may be a party to the appeal.

(2) In considering the appeal, the sheriff principal or, as the case may be, sheriff may hear evidence.

(3) On determining the appeal, the sheriff principal or sheriff may make such ancillary order (including an order as to the expenses of the appeal) as the sheriff principal or sheriff thinks fit.

(4) A sheriff principal may authorise, whether generally or specifically, any other sheriff of the sheriff principal's sheriffdom to consider and determine an appeal made to the sheriff principal under section 131(2)(a).

(5) In this section and section 131, references to a sheriff principal include references to any sheriff authorised under subsection (4).

(6) Any party to an appeal under section 131 may appeal to the Court of Session on a point of law against the sheriff principal's or sheriff's decision on the appeal.
(7) A decision of a Licensing Board which is appealed under section 131 continues to have effect despite the appeal, subject to subsection (8).
(8) Where an appeal is taken against a decision of a Licensing Board to suspend or revoke a premises licence, the sheriff principal may-
   (a) on the application of the appellant, and
   (b) if satisfied on the balance of convenience that it is appropriate to do so,

recall the suspension or revocation pending determination of the appeal.
(9) Further provision as to the procedure in any appeal under section 131, including in particular provision as to the times by which such an appeal is to be made or determined, may be prescribed by Act of Sederunt.

DEFINITIONS
"premises licence": see s.17 of this Act

GENERAL NOTE
The 1976 Act provides that where a licensing board refuses to renew, or suspends, a licence, the licence nevertheless continues in effect on the dependency of an appeal against the decision. As explained in the notes to s.132(2), Nicholson considered that lengthy appeal procedures did not serve the public interest well; and the Report noted (para.7.10) that some licensing boards were apparently reluctant to make suspension orders (1976 Act, s.31) when, by the simple marking of an appeal, they could be rendered of no effect for a prolonged period.

This section addresses this unsatisfactory state of affairs by providing that the decision of a licensing board continues to have an effect despite an appeal, subject to the interim suspension of certain sanctions.

Subsection (1)

A licensing board may be a party to an appeal against its decision. Presently, a licensing board will invariably choose to defend its decision. Nicholson considered that there was "something of an anomaly in a situation where the body whose decision is the subject of an appeal is also permitted to be a party to that appeal"; but there was nevertheless advantage at present in having a contradictor to the arguments advanced by an appellant (Report, para.11.12). On the other hand, if an appeal proceeded by way of a stated case, setting out the board's findings-in-fact and the reasons for its decision, in future a licensing board need never feel obliged to appear as a party in an appeal. On balance, the Committee considered that a licensing board should continue to enjoy the choice afforded by s.39(2A) of the 1976 Act and be entitled to participate in an appeal if it so wished (Report, *ibid.*). It is likely that licensing boards will avail themselves of this option, although it is conceivable that, on occasions, they may be dissuaded from so doing by reason of cost considerations.

Subsection (2)

This subsection continues the present provision for the hearing of evidence by the appellate court (1976 Act, s.39(5)), despite a Nicholson recommendation to the contrary: in the Committee's view, as an accepted feature of the stated case procedure, findings-in-fact required to be accepted as accurate (Report, para.11.16).

Subsection (4)

An appeal made to the sheriff principal may be considered and determined by a sheriff. It is to be hoped that such a step will not normally be taken. As explained in the notes to s.131(2), the disposal of appeals by the sheriff principal is designed to eliminate the present delays in the procedure.

Subsection (6)

This provision retains the current right of appeal from the sheriff court to the Court of Session (1976 Act, s.39(8)).

Subsections (7) and (8)

A licensing board's decision will have immediate effect. The sheriff principal may, however, recall the suspension or revocation of a premises licence pending the determination of an appeal "if satisfied on the balance of convenience that it is appropriate to do so". The "balance of convenience test" is oddly chosen; and it may be considered that the matter ought to be approach on a consideration as to whether the appeal had a *prima facie* prospect of success. Giving evidence to the Local Government and Transport Committee, Sheriff Principal Gordon Nicholson imagined that the sheriff principal would say: "Does the appeal at least seem arguable rather than merely frivolous? Is there a reasonable case to make?" (Official Report, col.2240).

The provisions of these subsections are designed to address concerns that, under the current system, errant licence holders may trade for extended periods on the dependency of an appeal (see notes to s.131(2)). Putting the point sharply, Tommy Sheridan MSP told the Local Government and Transport Committee: "When I was a member of Glasgow City Council, there were a number of occasions over the years on which a publican cocked a snook at the board's decision because the appeals process allowed their premises to remain open for extraordinary lengths of time." (Official Report, col.2239).

According to the Policy Memorandum, Scottish Ministers considered the potential impact on small businesses; but they took the view that a licensing board's decision which resulted in the cessation of alcohol sales would not be taken lightly: the new system would require boards to give reasons for their decisions and to act in a proportionate manner. In addition, licence holders would have an opportunity "to remedy an emerging problem before suspension or revocation becomes an option". (Nicholson anticipated that many transgressions by licence holders would not come to the attention of the licensing board until informal attempts to secure compliance had failed (Report, para.7.12)).

There is, however, a real danger that, by virtue of the new provisions, the pendulum may swing too far in the other direction. In the first place, while Nicholson had in view the interim suspension of sanctions "involving the closure of licensed premises for any period, or a reduction in authorised hours" (Report, para.7.14), the temporary recall procedure does not extend to the variation of a premises licence, which could result in a truncation of the approved licensed hours (see s.39(2)(b), read with s.29(5)). Such a sanction could have an extremely damaging effect on many businesses if in place for a very short period. For example, a nightclub largely deriving its income from trading periods after, say, 11 pm, would, in effect, suffer a penalty of a magnitude similar to the suspension of the premises licence.

In the second place, and more disconcertingly, while appeals to the sheriff principal ought to be capable of speedy disposal, a further appeal to the Court of Session will result in considerable delays. By way of examples:

- In *Smith v North Lanarkshire Licensing Board*, 2005 S.L.T. 544, a licence was suspended on November 1, 2002. The sheriff upheld the board's decision. The licence holder appealed to the Court of Session. On March 3, 2005 an Extra Division upheld the appeal and directed the sheriff to quash the suspension decision. The appeal process thus extended over 27 months.

- In *J B Recreation Ltd. v City of Glasgow Licensing Board*, digested at [2006] 33 SLLP 25, the decision to refuse an application for the renewal of a licence was taken in March 2004. An appeal to the sheriff was head in March 2005. The sheriff's reversed the Board's decision and the Board appealed to the Court of Session. That appeal was withdrawn in or around June 2006 just before it was due to be heard.

(See further: "Delays in licensing appeals", 2003 S.L.T. (News) 233.)

Licensing (Scotland) Act 2005

Procedures, forms etc

133. Hearings

(1) Where a Licensing Board is to hold a hearing under any provision of this Act, the hearing must be held at a meeting of the Board.
(2) The Scottish Ministers may by regulations make provision as to the procedure to be followed at or in connection with any hearing to be held by a Licensing Board under this Act.
(3) Regulations under subsection (2) may, in particular, make provision-
   (a) for notice of the hearing to be given to such persons as may be prescribed in the regulations,
   (b) about the rules of evidence which are to apply for the purposes of the hearing,
   (c) about the representation of any party at the hearing,
   (d) as to the times by which any step in the procedure must be taken, and
   (e) as to liability for expenses.

DEFINITIONS
"prescribed": see s.147(1) of this Act

GENERAL NOTE
The 1976 Act provides little assistance as to the manner in which licensing boards should conduct their business, although they have a limited opportunity to supplement the statutory provisions by the making of regulations under s.37.

Subsection (1)
Where a hearing is required in terms of the act - for example, to consider an application for a premises licence (s.23(2)) - the hearing must take place at a board meeting. Paragraph 10(2) of Sch.1 sets out those functions of a licensing board which may not be delegated to a committee or the persons specified in para.10(1).

Subsection (3) (a)
Regulations may make provision for the rules of evidence which are to apply at a hearing of the board. A number of shrieval decisions under the 1976 Act suggested that a licensing board should not proceed simply on the basis of *ex parte* statements where material facts were in dispute (see Cummins, pp.345 et seq). However, in *JAE (Glasgow) Ltd v City of Glasgow District Licensing Board*, 1994 S.L.T. 1064, while the Lord Ordinary rejected the argument that a licensing board was not empowered to entertain evidence, oral or written, it was envisaged that applications "should be heard and disposed of expeditiously and with a minimum of formality". Boards had a discretion to proceed on any type of material which had a bearing on the questions which they had to decide; and while a licence holder or applicant should have a fair and equal opportunity to challenge information put before the board by an objector, he had no right "to insist that he do so by leading evidence". Equality of treatment could consist of allowing parties to make *ex parte* submissions.

More recently, in *Catscratch Ltd v City of Glasgow Licensing Board (No 2)*, 2002 S.L.T. 503; [2001] 20 SLLP 12, applicants argued that an objector's submissions amounted to evidence, but their agent had not been afforded an opportunity to examine him on that basis, nor had they been able to lead their own evidence. The conduct of the hearing accordingly breached the principles of natural justice as well as the applicant's rights under art.6 of the ECHR. The Lord Ordinary held that the applicant's common law arguments as to unfairness failed in the light of *JAE (Glasgow) Ltd, cit. supra*, since the hearing of evidence would be unnecessarily cumbersome in a relatively routine application where objection has been taken by local residents and was not essential to the concept of natural justice, provided that the applicant's case had been properly stated. The test for the purposes of art.6 raised the same issues and a similar conclusion required to be drawn.

In *Hamid v City of Glasgow Licensing Board* [1999] 14 SLLP 37, where a licence holder denied that alcohol had been sold to an under-age person and was refused an opportunity to challenge the chief constable's formal observations, the sheriff held that the Board had exercised their discretion unreasonably by proceeding on the basis of *ex parte* statements. In his opinion, this was a case in which the right to a fair hearing and the "equality of treatment" desiderated by the Lord Ordinary in *JAE (Glasgow) Ltd, cit. supra*, demanded the hearing of evidence. (*Hamid* is reported on appeal at 2001 S.L.T. 193; [2001] 18 SLLP 8, but the opinion of the Extra Division was confined to the issue as to whether the Board had a proper basis in fact for concluding that the licence holder was not a "fit and proper person".)

Although "convenience and justice are often not on speaking terms" (*General Medical Council v Spackman* (1943 A.C. 627 at 638, per Lord Atkin), the hearing of evidence by licensing boards (especially in the light of the much wider enfranchisement of objectors), would give rise to interminable licensing board sittings.

Subsection (3) (e)

This Act makes provision for the recovery of expenses by a licensing board where a notice of objection (ss.22(5), 58(4) or review application is rejected as "frivolous or vexatious" (s.36(7)). This is a step which is unlikely to be taken even in extreme cases. This subsection allows regulations to make wider provision for an award of expenses, possibly where the licensing board has agreed to the continuation of an application following a party's procedural failure (*cf* 1976 Act, s.13(2)).

134. Form etc. of applications, proposals, and notices

(1) The Scottish Ministers may by regulations prescribe-
  (a) the form of any application, proposal or notice under this Act,
  (b) the manner in which it is to be made or given,
  (c) the time by which it is to be made or given,
  (d) requirements as to the publicising of the making or giving of the application, proposal or notice,
  (e) the information to be contained in it (in addition to any required to be contained in it by virtue of any other provision of this Act), and
  (f) the documents which are to accompany it (in addition to any required to accompany it by virtue of any other provision this Act).
(2) Regulations under subsection (1) may provide that any application, proposal or notice made or given under this Act may be treated as not made or given if any requirement prescribed in the regulations in relation to it is not complied with.

DEFINITIONS
"prescribed": see s.147(1) of this Act

GENERAL NOTE

Regulations will make provision for the form and content of applications, proposals and notices; the manner in which they are to be made or given; time-limits; advertising requirements; and supporting documents.

Presently, each licensing board employs its own application forms. Nicholson considered that standardisation would be of assistance "for those applicants who may be seeking licences in different board areas" and that a standard form should be devised for use by objectors (Report, para.6.5). Provision should also be made to enable any notice or document to be served by fax or email, as well as by post (*ibid.*, para.14.52).

Licensing (Scotland) Act 2005 185

135. Power to relieve failure to comply with rules and other requirements

(1) A Licensing Board may relieve any applicant or other party to proceedings before the Board of any failure to comply with any procedural provision if-
   (a) the failure is due to mistake, oversight or other excusable cause, and
   (b) the Board considers it appropriate in all the circumstance to relieve the failure.
(2) Where a Board exercises the power under subsection (1), the Board may make such order as appears necessary or expedient to enable the proceedings to continue as if the failure had not occurred.
(3) In subsection (1), "procedural provision" means-
   (a) any requirement of regulations under-
      (i) section 133(2),
      (ii) section 134(1), or
      (iii) paragraph 12(4) of schedule 1,
   (b) any requirement of rules under paragraph 12(5) of that schedule, and
   (c) any other requirement imposed by virtue of this Act as respects the procedure to be followed in connection with applications made to, or other proceedings before, a Licensing Board.

GENERAL NOTE

The 1976 Act provides a very limited safety net for hapless applicants or objectors who have failed to observe its terms. Section 13(2) allows a licensing board to continue an application for the grant or renewal of a licence or for a new licence where the applicant or an objector has "through inadvertence or misadventure" failed to comply with any preliminary requirement. Otherwise, no dispensing power is available. This section allows a licensing board to grant relief in a wide variety of circumstances, not simply in relation to requirements imposed by the specified regulations and rules (subs.(3)(a), (b)), but also any other requirement arising by virtue of the Act in relation to application procedures and board proceedings.

136. Fees

(1) The Scottish Ministers may by regulations make provision for the charging of fees by Licensing Boards-
   (a) in respect of applications under this Act, and
   (b) otherwise in respect of the performance of functions by Licensing Boards, councils and Licensing Standards Officers under this Act.
(2) Regulations under subsection (1) may, in particular-
   (a) specify fees or provide for them to be determined by reference to such factors as may be specified in or determined under the regulations,
   (b) provide for annual or other recurring fees,
   (c) provide for the remission or repayment of fees in such circumstances as may be specified in or determined under the regulations.
(3) Before making any regulations under subsection (1) (other than regulations consolidating other regulations), the Scottish Ministers must consult-
   (a) such body or bodies as appear to them to be representative of the interests of-

(i) Licensing Boards,
(ii) councils, and
(iii) those likely to be affected by the regulations, and
(b) such other persons (if any) as they think appropriate.
(4) Where regulations under subsection (1) provide for a fee to be charged in respect of any application made to a Licensing Board under this Act, the Board need not consider the application unless and until the fee is paid.
(5) Any fee chargeable by a Licensing Board under any regulations made under subsection (1) is to be paid to the clerk of the Board.
(6) The clerk of a Licensing Board must pay any sums received under subsection (5) to the relevant council.

DEFINITION
"council": see s.147(1) of this Act

GENERAL NOTE
Fees prescribed by virtue of this section will reflect the Scottish Executive's intention to make the new system self-funding and are bound to reflect the cost of employing licensing standards officers. Regulations made under the 2003 Act provide for fees based on rateable value bands.
See further: "*Licensing (Scotland) Bill: Proposal and analysis of fee charging options*" (Scottish Executive, 2005).

Subsection (3) (a)
It is conceivable that this provision may result in fees being specified according to the primary use of premises. In England and Wales, higher fees are charged where premises are exclusively or primarily in the business of selling alcohol.

Subsection (3) (b)
Licences issued under the 1976 Act have a three-year currency. Under this Act, premises licences will remain in effect until revoked or surrendered. Provision will require to be made for an annual retention fee to ensure that the system is sufficiently resourced.

Miscellaneous

137. Inspection of premises before grant of licence etc

(1) In this section, "relevant proposal or application" means-
(a) a premises licence application,
(b) a premises licence variation application,
(c) a premises licence review proposal or application,
(d) an application under section 47(2) for a temporary premises licence,
(e) an occasional licence application, or
(f) an extended hours application.
(2) Any of the persons specified in subsection (3) may, at any reasonable time before the determination of a relevant proposal or application, enter the premises to which the proposal or application relates for the purposes of assessing-
(a) in the case of an application such as is mentioned in paragraph (a), (b), (d), (e) or (f) of subsection (1), the likely effect of the grant of the application on the licensing objectives, or
(b) in the case of a proposal or application such as is mentioned in paragraph (c) of that subsection, the effect which the selling of

alcohol in accordance with the premises licence is having on those objectives.
(3) The persons referred to in subsection (2) are-
   (a) a constable, and
   (b) a Licensing Standards Officer for the council area in which the premises are situated.
(4) A person exercising the power conferred by subsection (2) may if necessary use reasonable force.
(5) A person who intentionally obstructs a person exercising the power conferred by subsection (2) commits an offence.
(6) A person guilty of an offence under subsection (5) is liable on summary conviction to a fine not exceeding level 3 on the standard scale.

DEFINITIONS
"relevant proposal or application": see subs.(1)
"premises licence application": see s.20(3) of this Act
"premises licence variation application": see s.29(3) of this Act
"premises licence review proposal": see s.37(2) of this Act
"premises licence review application": see s.36(2) of this Act
"temporary premises licence": see s.47(4) of this Act
"occasional licence application": see s.56(4) of this Act
"extended hours application": see s.68(3) of this Act
"licensing objectives": see s.4(1) of this Act
"alcohol": see s.2 of this Act
"premises licence": see s.17 of this Act

GENERAL NOTE
This section affords the police and licensing standards officers the power to enter premises at any reasonable time for the purpose of assessing the likely effect of the grant of an application on the licensing objectives; or, for the purposes of a premises licence review proposal or application, the effect which the sale of alcohol is having on the those objectives.

This is a curious provision, since, in practice, those most likely to carry out premises visits are licensing board members; and sanctioning of "reasonable force" in the exercise of the powers conferred (subs.(4)) may well be considered *de trop*.

138. Police powers of entry

(1) A constable may at any time enter and inspect any licensed premises.
(2) A constable may-
   (a) if the condition in subsection (3) is satisfied, and
   (b) subject to subsection (4),
at any time enter and inspect any premises (other than licensed premises) on which food or drink is sold for consumption on the premises.
(3) The condition referred to in subsection (2)(a) is that the constable has reasonable grounds for believing that alcohol is being sold on the premises in breach of section 1(1).
(4) A constable below the rank of inspector may exercise the power conferred by subsection (2) only-
   (a) if the constable has obtained written authority to do so from a justice of the peace or a constable of or above the rank of inspector,
   (b) within the period of 8 days beginning with the date on which such authority is obtained, and

(c) at such time or times as is specified in the authority.
(5) A person who intentionally obstructs a constable exercising a power conferred by this section commits an offence.
(6) A person guilty of an offence under subsection (5) is liable on summary conviction to a fine not exceeding level 3 on the standard scale.

DEFINITIONS
"premises": see s.147(1) of this Act
"licensed premises": see s.147(1) of this Act
"alcohol": see s.2

GENERAL NOTE
This section effectively re-enacts, with modifications, the provisions of ss.85 and 86 of the 1976 Act.

Subsection (1)
Police rights of entry extend to all licensed premises, including members' clubs. (The 1976 Act provides only a limited right in relation to off-sale premises (s.85(1)) and no right in relation to clubs).
The power of entry and inspection is unqualified: no reason need be given.
For the powers of entry afforded to licensing standards officers, see ss.15 and 137.

Subsections (2)-(4)
In terms similar to s.86 of the 1976 Act, these subsections provide police with a right of entry to unlicensed premises on which food or drink is sold for consumption on the premises, provided a constable has reasonable grounds that alcohol is being sold in contravention of s.1(1) of this Act.
The power would appear to be exercisable in relation to exempt premises (s.124) which fall within the terms of subs.(2), but not trade premises used to sell alcohol for consumption off the premises (as to which see ss.1(2), 117, 147(2)).

Subsections (2)-(4)
An offence is committed where any person intentionally obstructs a constable exercising his right of entry. In *Hinchcliffe v Sheldon* [1955] 3 All ER 406, a licence holder's son shouted warnings to his father than police officers were outside hotel premises after closing time. After a delay of some eight minutes, the police were admitted and found no evidence of any offence having been committed. It was held that the officers had been wilfully obstructed in the execution of their duty.

139. Remote sales of alcohol

(1) This section applies where, in connection with any sale of alcohol, the premises from which the alcohol is despatched for delivery in pursuance of the sale is not the same as those where the order for the alcohol is taken.
(2) Where the premises from which the alcohol is despatched are in Scotland, the sale of the alcohol is, for the purposes of this Act, to be treated as taking place on those premises.
(3) The Scottish Ministers may by regulations make such provision as they consider appropriate for the purpose of regulating the taking of orders in Scotland for sales of alcohol in circumstances where-
　(a) the premises from which the alcohol is despatched for delivery in pursuance of the sales are not in Scotland, but
　(b) the place to which the alcohol is delivered is in Scotland.

(4) Regulations under subsection (3) may, in particular-
  (a) modify any provision of this Act,
  (b) apply any such provision with modifications, or
  (c) disapply any such provision.

DEFINITIONS
"sale": see s.147(1) of this Act
"alcohol": see s.2
"premises": see s.147(1) of this Act

GENERAL NOTE

To a limited extent, provision is made for alcohol sold remotely, for example, by means of telephone, fax or internet orders. Where the order is executed by despatch of the goods from Scottish premises, those premises will require to be the subject of a premises licence, rather than the premises at which the order was taken. The Scottish Executive considered this to be a "difficult area". The head of their licensing bill team told the Local Government and Transport Committee that:

> "We have gone as far as we can by ensuring that the place from where the sales are despatched is subject to a premises licence so that there is an opportunity for the board to apply licensing conditions" (Official Report, col. 2197).

The position is similar in England and Wales: s.190(2) of the 2003 Act provides that the sale of alcohol takes place where the alcohol is appropriated to the contract.

Presently, some call centres in Scotland used for the taking of alcohol orders are the subject of off-sale licences, although no alcohol is stored at the premises. Licences have also been obtained for warehouses used for order fulfilment. For the purposes of the 1976 Act, it is probably the case that the premises which require to be licensed are those at which the order is accepted, rather than the place from which the order is delivered: see *Guild v Freeman* (1898) 25 R(J) 106.

For a fuller consideration of the e-commerce aspects of alcohol sales, see Agnew and Baillie, p.39.

Subsections (3), (4)

These subsections allow Scottish Ministers to make provision for alcohol sales where the despatch of the goods takes place from premises outwith Scotland but delivery is to be made to a place in Scotland.

In their memorandum to the Subordinate Legislation Committee, the Scottish Executive explained that this power had been taken because internet sales "from overseas companies" were a "new and developing market" and Ministers wished to ensure that the sector "can be regulated appropriately in the future should the need arise".

Nicholson considered that there was currently no need for express provision in primary legislation in respect of sales arranged by telephone or through the internet; but the matter should be kept under review (Report, para.14.8).

140. Presumption as to liquid contents of containers

(1) This section applies for the purpose of any trial in proceedings for an alleged offence under any provision of this Act.
(2) Where-
  (a) liquid is found in a container (whether open or sealed), and
  (b) there is on the container a description of the liquid contents of the container,
the liquid found is to be presumed to be liquid of that description.
(3) Where an open container is found which-
  (a) contains-
    (i) no liquid, or
    (ii) an amount of liquid insufficient to allow analysis of it,

    (b) was sealed at the time it was sold or supplied, and
    (c) has on it a description of the liquid contents of the container,
the container is to be presumed to have contained, at the time it was sold or supplied, liquid of that description.
  (4) At the trial, any party to the proceedings may rebut the presumption mentioned in subsection (2) or (3) by proving that, at the time of its sale or supply, the liquid in the container was not of the description on the container.
  (5) However, a party may lead evidence for the purpose of rebutting the presumption only if the party has, not less than 7 days before the date of the trial, given notice of the intention to do so to the other parties.

GENERAL NOTE

This section more or less replicates the terms of s.127 of the 1976 Act.

Any liquid found in a container (sealer or open) is presumed to conform to the description on the container. A similar presumption applies where a container contains no liquid or its contents defy analysis: if the container was sealed when sold or supplied it is presumed to have contained at that time liquid matching the description.

Subsections (4), (5)

Any party to trial proceedings may rebut a presumption raised by subs.(2) or (3) if he gives not less than seven days pre-trial notice to the other parties of his intention so to do. Rebuttal will take place on the balance of probabilities: *Neish v Stevenson*, 1969 S.L.T. 229. Corroboration is not required:

> "Where... an assumption falls to be made unless the accused proves otherwise, it is, we consider, in accordance with principle that the evidence led by the accused for this purpose need not be corroborated: all that is required is that the court accepts the evidence led by the accused as being credible and reliable." (*King v Lees*, 1993, S.L.T. 1184 per the Lord Justice Clerk (Ross) at p.1187).

141. Offences by bodies corporate etc

  (1) Where-
    (a) an offence under this Act has been committed by-
      (i) a body corporate,
      (ii) a Scottish partnership, or
      (iii) an unincorporated association other than a Scottish partnership, and
    (b) it is proved that the offence was committed with the consent or connivance of, or was attributable to any neglect on the part of-
      (i) a relevant person, or
      (ii) a person purporting to act in the capacity of a relevant person,
  that person, as well as the body corporate, partnership or, as the case may be, unincorporated association, is guilty of the offence and liable to be proceeded against and punished accordingly.
  (2) In subsection (1), "relevant person" means-
    (a) in relation to a body corporate other than a council, a director, manager, secretary, member or other similar officer of the body,
    (b) in relation to a council, an officer or member of the council,
    (c) in relation to a Scottish partnership, a partner, and
    (d) in relation to an unincorporated association other than a Scottish partnership, a person who is concerned in the management or control of the association.

DEFINITIONS
"relevant person": see subs.(2)

GENERAL NOTE
This section deals with offences under the Act committed by companies, partnerships and unincorporated associations (cf 1976 Act, 67(5)). Certain persons responsible for their management or control share responsibility for offences committed with their consent or connivance or attributable to any neglect.

Subsection (1)
The reference to an unincorporated association is apt to include members' clubs.

General

142. Guidance

(1) The Scottish Ministers may issue guidance to Licensing Boards as to the exercise of their functions under this Act.
(2) The Scottish Ministers may modify any guidance issued by them under subsection (1).
(3) Each Licensing Board must, in the exercise of their functions under this Act, have regard to any guidance issued to them under subsection (1).
(4) Where a Licensing Board decides not to follow any guidance issued under subsection (1), the Board must give the Scottish Ministers notice of the decision together with a statement of the reasons for it.
(5) The first guidance to Licensing Boards under subsection (1) is not to be issued by the Scottish Ministers unless a draft of the guidance has been laid before, and approved by resolution of, the Scottish Parliament.
(6) The Scottish Ministers must lay any subsequent guidance issued by them under subsection (1) before the Parliament.

GENERAL NOTE
Scottish Ministers are empowered to issue guidance to licensing boards as to the exercise of their functions under the Act and to modify any such guidance. Where a licensing board elects not to follow Ministerial guidance, they must give notice of the decision and the reasons for it.

Subsection (5)
The first guidance must be laid before the Parliament before it is issued and is subject to the affirmation resolution parliamentary procedure.

143. Crown application

(1) This Act binds the Crown.
(2) No contravention by the Crown of any provision made by virtue of this Act makes the Crown criminally liable; but the Court of Session may, on the application of any public body or office-holder having responsibility for enforcing that provision, declare unlawful any act or omission of the Crown which constitutes such a contravention.
(3) However, any provision made by virtue of this Act applies to persons in the public service of the Crown as it applies to other persons.

144. Modification of enactments

Schedule 6, which modifies enactments, has effect.

145. Ancillary provision

The Scottish Ministers may by order make such incidental, supplemental, consequential, transitional, transitory or saving provision as they consider necessary or expedient for the purposes of or in consequence of this Act.

146. Orders and regulations

(1) Any power of the Scottish Ministers to make orders or regulations under this Act is exercisable by statutory instrument.
(2) Any such power includes power to make-
   (a) such incidental, supplemental, consequential, transitional, transitory or saving provision as the Scottish Ministers think necessary or expedient,
   (b) different provision for different purposes.
(3) An order under section 145 may modify any enactment (including this Act), instrument or document.
(4) A statutory instrument containing an order or regulations under this Act except-
   (a) an order under section 65(4), 123(6) or 150(2),
   (b) regulations under section 27(2) or 139(3), and
   (c) where subsection (5) applies, an order under section 145,

is subject to annulment in pursuance of a resolution of the Scottish Parliament.

(5) No-
   (a) order under section 65(4) or 123(6),
   (b) regulations under section 27(2) or 139(3), or
   (c) order under section 145 containing provisions which add to, replace or omit any part of the text of an Act,

is to be made unless a draft of the statutory instrument containing the order or regulations has been laid before, and approved by resolution of, the Parliament.

GENERAL NOTE

This extensive power, which may be used to modify any enactment, instrument or document (see s.146(3), (5)), will allow Ministers to make regulations relative to *inter alia* the transition to the new licensing system.

The Scottish Ministers' power to make orders or regulations under the Act is exercisable by statutory instrument. With certain exceptions, a statutory instrument containing an order or regulation is subject to annulment in pursuance of a resolution of the Parliament.

Certain orders and regulations cannot be made unless a draft of the relevant statutory instrument had been laid before, and approved by resolution of, the Parliament.

147. Interpretation

(1) In this Act-
   "alcoholic drink" means a drink consisting of or containing alcohol,
   "applicant", in relation to any application under this Act, means the person making the application,

"appropriate chief constable" means, in relation to a Licensing Board, the chief constable for the police area in which the area of the Board is situated,

"area" means-
- (a) in relation to a council, the local government area for which the council is constituted,
- (b) in relation to a Licensing Board or Local Licensing Forum, the council area or, as the case may be, licensing division for which the Board or Forum is established,

"capacity", in relation to licensed premises, means-
- (a) in relation to licensed premises (or any part of such premises) on which alcohol is sold for consumption on the premises (or, as the case may be, that part), the maximum number of customers which can be accommodated in the premises (or, as the case may be, that part) at any one time, and
- (b) in relation to licensed premises (or any part of such premises) on which alcohol is sold for consumption off the premises (or, as the case may be, that part), the amount of space in the premises (or, as the case may be, that part) given over to the display of alcohol for sale,

"child" means a person under the age of 16,

"community council" has the same meaning as in Part IV of the Local Government (Scotland) Act 1973 (c.65),

"council" means a council constituted under section 2 of the Local Government etc. (Scotland) Act 1994 (c.39),

"licensed premises" means premises in respect of which a premises licence or occasional licence has effect,

"liqueur confectionery" means confectionery which-
- (a) contains alcohol in a proportion not greater than 0.2 litres of alcohol (of a strength not exceeding 57%) per kilogramme of the confectionery, and
- (b) either consists of separate pieces weighing not more than 50 grammes or is designed to be broken into such pieces for the purposes of consumption,

"premises" means any place and includes a vehicle, vessel or moveable structure,

"prescribed" means prescribed by regulations made by the Scottish Ministers,

"railway vehicle" means a railway vehicle within the meaning of section 83 of the Railways Act 1993 (c.43) that is used in the provision of a railway service within the meaning of section 82 of that Act (excluding the wider meaning of "railway" given by section 81(2) of that Act),

"relevant council" means, in relation to a Licensing Board or Local Licensing Forum, the council-
- (a) for whose area the Board or Forum is established, or
- (b) in the case of a Board or Forum established for a licensing division, for the area of which the division forms part,

"sell", in relation to alcohol, includes barter and expose to or offer for sale, and related expressions such as "sale" are to be construed accordingly,

"senior police officer" means a constable of or above the rank of superintendent,

"strength", in relation to alcohol, is to be determined in accordance with section 2 of the Alcoholic Liquor Duties Act 1979 (c.4),

"subject premises" means, in relation to any application under this Act, the premises to which the application relates,

"vehicle" means a vehicle intended or adapted for use on roads,

"vessel" includes a ship, boat, raft or other apparatus constructed or adapted for floating on water,

"young person" means a person aged 16 or 17.

(2) In this Act, references to selling alcohol or other goods to trade are references to selling the alcohol or goods to a person for the purposes of the person's trade; and related expressions are to be construed accordingly.

(3) For the purposes of this Act, a person is, in relation to a partnership, a company, a club or other body (whether incorporated or unincorporated), a connected person if the person-
  (a) in the case of a partnership, is a partner,
  (b) in the case of a company-
      (i) is a director, or
      (ii) has control of the company,
  (c) in the case of a club, is an office bearer of the club,
  (d) in any other case, is concerned in the management or control of the body.

(4) For the purposes of subsection (3)(b)(ii) and this subsection, a person is taken to have control of a company if-
  (a) any of the directors of the company, or of any other company having control of the company, is accustomed to act in accordance with the person's directions or instructions, or
  (b) the person is entitled to exercise, or to control the exercise of, at least one third of the voting power at any general meeting of the company or of any other company having control of the company.

148. Index of defined expressions

The expressions in the left-hand column of the table are defined or otherwise explained by the provisions of this Act specified in the right-hand column.

Expression	Interpretation provision
alcohol	section 2
alcoholic drink	section 147(1)
applicant	section 147(1)
appropriate chief constable	section 147(1)
area	section 147(1)
capacity (in relation to licensed premises)	section 147(1)
	section 55

Expression	Interpretation provision
certified copy (of premises licence or summary)	
child	section 147(1)
closure order	section 97(3)
community council	section 147(1)
connected person	section 147(3)
council	section 147(1)
crime prevention objective	section 4(2)
emergency closure order	section 97(4)
excluded premises	section 123(2)
exclusion order	section 94(6)
exempt premises	section 124
expiry date (of a personal licence)	section 77(7)
extended hours application	section 68(3)
foreign offence	section 129(2)
layout plan	section 20(2)(b)(ii)
licensed hours	section 62(1)
licensed premises	section 147(1)
licensing objectives	section 4(1)
licensing policy statement	section 6(1)
licensing qualification	section 91(1)
licensing register	section 9(1)
liqueur confectionery	section 147(1)
locality	section 7(2)
operating plan	section 20(4)
occasional licence	section 56(1)
occasional licence application	section 56(4)
off-sales hours	section 62(2)(a)(ii)
on-sales hours	section 62(2)(a)(i)
personal licence	section 71
personal licence application	section 72(2)
personal licence renewal application	section 78(4)
premises	section 147(1)
premises licence	section 17
premises licence application	section 20(3)

Expression	Interpretation provision
premises licence review application	section 36(2)
premises licence review proposal	section 37(2)
premises licence variation application	section 29(3)
premises manager	section 19(1)
prescribed	section 147(1)
provisional premises licence	section 45(5)
provisional premises licence application	section 45(2)
railway vehicle	section 147(1)
relevant council	section 147(1)
relevant offence	section 129(1)
review hearing	section 38(2)
sell (and related expressions)	section 147(1)
selling to trade	section 147(2)
senior police officer	section 147(1)
strength (of alcohol)	section 147(1)
subject premises	section 147(1)
supplementary licensing policy statement	section 6(2)
temporary premises licence	section 47(4)
variation (of a premises licence)	section 29(5)
minor variation (of such a licence)	section 29(6)
vehicle	section 147(1)
vessel	section 147(1)
young person	section 147(1)

149. Repeals

The enactments mentioned in the first column in schedule 7 are repealed to the extent specified in the second column.

150. Short title and commencement

(1) This Act may be cited as the Licensing (Scotland) Act 2005.
(2) This Act (other than this section and sections 145 to 148) comes into force on such day as the Scottish Ministers may by order appoint.

Licensing (Scotland) Act 2005

SCHEDULES

SCHEDULE 1

LICENSING BOARDS

(introduced by section 5(8))

1. Membership

(1) A Licensing Board is to consist of such number (being not fewer than 5 and not more than 10) of members as may be determined by the relevant council.
(2) The members of a Licensing Board are to be elected by the relevant council from among their councillors.
(3) In the case of a Licensing Board for a licensing division, not less than one third of the total number of members of the Board must be councillors for wards within the division.

2. Election of members

(1) Each council must, at their first meeting after each ordinary election of the council, hold an election of members to-
   (a) the Licensing Board for the council's area, or
   (b) if that area is divided into licensing divisions, each of the Licensing Boards for those divisions.
(2) Where a council makes a determination under section 5(2) to divide their area into divisions, the council must-
   (a) at the meeting at which that determination is made, or
   (b) at the first meeting of the council after that meeting,
hold an election of members to the Licensing Board for each division.
(3) Where, under section 5(4), a council revokes a determination dividing their area into divisions, the council must-
   (a) at the meeting at which the determination is revoked, or
   (b) at the first meeting of the council after that meeting,
hold an election of members to the single Licensing Board for the council's area.
(4) Where there is a vacancy in the membership of a Licensing Board, the relevant council must, at their first meeting after the vacancy arises, hold an election to fill the vacancy.

3. Disqualification from membership

(1) A councillor is disqualified from election as, and from being, a member of a Licensing Board if the councillor is-
   (a) a premises licence holder,
   (b) an employee of a premises licence holder and works as such in licensed premises,
   (c) whether alone or in partnership with another person, engaged in the business of producing or selling alcohol,
   (d) a director or other officer of a company so engaged, or
   (e) an employee of any person so engaged and works as such in that business.
(2) A councillor who knowingly acts or purports to act as a member of a Licensing Board at a time when the councillor is disqualified from being such a member by virtue of sub-paragraph (1) commits an offence.
(3) A person guilty of an offence under sub-paragraph (2) is liable on summary conviction to a fine not exceeding level 5 on the standard scale.

4. Tenure of office etc

(1) A member of a Licensing Board-
   (a) holds office as such, subject to the following provisions of this paragraph and to paragraph 11(4), during the period-
      (i) beginning on the day after the member's election, and
      (ii) ending on the day on which the next election of members of the Board is held in accordance with paragraph 2(1),
   (b) is eligible for re-election as a member,
   (c) may, at any time, resign by giving notice to the clerk of the Board, and
   (d) ceases to hold office-
      (i) on ceasing to be a councillor of the relevant council, or
      (ii) on becoming disqualified from being a member of a Licensing Board.

(2) The clerk must give the relevant council a copy of any notice received under subparagraph (1)(c).

5. Removal of members from office

The relevant council may remove a member from office if the member is unfit by reason of mental or physical inability.

6. Convener

(1) A Licensing Board must, at their first meeting after each election of members of the Board held in accordance with paragraph 2(1), (2) or (3), elect one of their members as convener of the Board.
(2) Where there is a vacancy in the office of convener, the Board must, at their first meeting after the vacancy arises, elect one of their members to fill the vacancy.
(3) The convener of a Licensing Board-
   (a) holds office as such for the period-
      (i) beginning on the day after the convener's election, and
      (ii) ending with the day on which the next election of a convener is held in accordance with sub-paragraph (1),
   (b) is eligible for re-election as convener of the Board,
   (c) may, at any time, resign by giving notice to the clerk of the Board, and
   (d) ceases to hold office on ceasing to be a member of the Board.
(4) The clerk must give the relevant council a copy of any notice received under subparagraph (3)(c).
(5) If the convener is for any reason unable to chair any meeting of the Board, the Board must, at the meeting, elect another of their members to chair that meeting.
(6) If, at any meeting of the Board, there is an equality in the votes of members on any matter, the member chairing the meeting has a casting vote.

7. Removal of convener

(1) The convener of a Licensing Board may be removed from office by the Board.
(2) A decision of a Board to remove the convener is valid only if the number of members voting in favour of the decision exceeds one half of the total number of members of the Board.

8. Administrative support

(1) In relation to each Licensing Board, the relevant council must-
   (a) appoint, on such terms and conditions as they may determine, a clerk of the Board, and
   (b) provide the Board and the clerk, or ensure they are provided, with such other staff, property and services as are required for their purposes.
(2) A clerk appointed under sub-paragraph (1)(a) must be an advocate or solicitor.

9. Committees

A Licensing Board may establish committees for or in connection with the exercise of any of their functions.

10. Delegation of functions

(1) A Licensing Board may authorise (whether generally or specifically)-
   (a) any member of the Board,
   (b) any committee established by the Board,
   (c) the clerk of the Board, or
   (d) any member of staff provided under paragraph 8(1)(b),
to exercise on behalf of the Board any of the Board's functions under this Act, other than the functions mentioned in sub-paragraph (2).
(2) Those functions are-
   (a) determining the Board's policy for the purposes of a licensing policy statement or supplementary licensing policy statement,
   (b) determining, for the purposes of any such statement, whether there is overprovision of licensed premises, or licensed premises of any particular description, in any locality,
   (c) determining a premises licence application,
   (d) determining a premises licence variation application where the variation sought is not a minor variation,

Licensing (Scotland) Act 2005 199

      (e) determining an application for the transfer of a premises licence where the applicant has been convicted of a relevant offence or a foreign offence,
      (f) determining-
          (i) a personal licence application, or
          (ii) a personal licence renewal application,
      where the applicant has been convicted of a relevant offence or a foreign offence,
      (g) conducting a hearing under this Act (including taking any of the steps mentioned in sub-paragraph (3) at, or as result of, the hearing),
      (h) making a closure order,
      (i) refusing an application for confirmation of a provisional premises licence.
  (3) The steps referred in sub-paragraph (2)(g) are-
      (a) at a review hearing in respect of a premises licence-
          (i) issuing a written warning to the licence holder,
          (ii) revoking or suspending the licence, or
          (iii) making a variation of the licence, or
      (b) making an order revoking, suspending or endorsing a personal licence.
  (4) A Licensing Board may, under sub-paragraph (1), delegate to the clerk of the Board the function of granting an occasional licence application only where there is no notice of objection or representations in relation to the application, or no notice from the appropriate chief constable recommending refusal of the application.

11. Training of members

(1) Each member of a Licensing Board must, no later than one month after the expiry of each 3 month period, produce to the clerk of the Board evidence that the member has, during the period, complied with such requirements as to the training of members of Licensing Boards as may be prescribed.

(2) In sub-paragraph (1), "3 month period" means, in relation to a member of a Licensing Board-
      (a) the period of 3 months beginning on the day on which the member is elected, and
      (b) if the member is re-elected, the period of 3 months beginning with the day on which the member is re-elected.

(3) A member of a Licensing Board must not take part in any proceedings of the Board until the member has produced the evidence required by sub-paragraph (1).

(4) If a member of a Licensing Board fails to comply with sub-paragraph (1), the member ceases to hold office as a member of the Board.

(5) Regulations under sub-paragraph (1) prescribing training requirements may, in particular-
      (a) provide for accreditation by the Scottish Ministers of-
          (i) courses of training, and
          (ii) persons providing such courses,
      for the purposes of the regulations,
      (b) prescribe different requirements in relation to different descriptions of members, and
      (c) require that any person providing training or any particular description of training in accordance with the regulations holds such qualification as may be prescribed in the regulations.

12. Proceedings

(1) The quorum for a meeting of a Licensing Board is one half of the number of members (but in any case not fewer than 3).

(2) Subject to sub-paragraph (3), meetings of a Licensing Board must be held in public.

(3) The members of a Licensing Board may, before the Board decides any matter, conduct their deliberations on the matter in private.

(4) The Scottish Ministers may by regulations make further provision about the proceedings of Licensing Boards including, in particular, provision as to-
      (a) the times by which applications to a Board under this Act, and other business to be considered by a Board, are to be determined or considered,
      (b) the publicising of meetings of a Board, and
      (c) public access to any agenda and record of, and other information concerning, a meeting of a Board.

(5) Subject to-
      (a) the other provisions of this paragraph, and
      (b) any regulations made under sub-paragraph (4),
the arrangements for meetings of a Licensing Board, and other matters relating to proceedings of the Board, are to be such as the Board may by rules provide.

(6) A Licensing Board must ensure that any rules made by them under sub-paragraph (5) are published.

13. Validity of proceedings

The proceedings of a Licensing Board are not affected by-
    (a) any vacancy in the membership of the Board,
    (b) any defect in the election of any member of the Board, or
    (c) the disqualification of any councillor from being a member of the Board.

14. Transitional and transitory provision

(1) Until the end of the day of the first election of members of a Licensing Board in accordance with paragraph 2(1), the members of the Board are to continue to be those who were, immediately before the coming into force of section 5, the members of the Board established under section 1 of the Licensing (Scotland) Act 1976 (c.66) for the same area or, as the case may be, division.
(2) Paragraph 4(1)(a) does not apply to a person who is a member of a Licensing Board by virtue of sub-paragraph (1) of this paragraph.
(3) In the application of paragraph 11 to such a person-
    (a) sub-paragraph (1) has effect as if for "each 3 month period" there were substituted "such period as the Scottish Ministers may direct", and
    (b) sub-paragraph (2) is treated as if it were omitted.

GENERAL NOTE

This schedule makes detailed provision for the constitution of licensing boards and the exercise of their certain functions; and requires licensing board members to undergo prescribed training.

SCHEDULE 2

Local Licensing Forums

(introduced by section 10(4))

1. Introductory

In this schedule, "Forum" means a Local Licensing Forum established under section 10.

2. Membership

(1) A Forum is to consist of such number (being not fewer than 5 and not more than 20) of members as the relevant council may determine.
(2) The Scottish Ministers may by order substitute another number for the minimum or maximum number of members for the time being specified in sub-paragraph (1).
(3) At least one of the members must be a Licensing Standards Officer for the council's area.
(4) The other members are to be individuals appointed by the relevant council on such terms and conditions as the relevant council may determine.
(5) In appointing members of a Forum, the relevant council must seek to ensure so far as possible that the membership of the Forum is representative of the interests of persons or descriptions of persons who have an interest which is relevant to the Forum's general functions.
(6) Those persons include-
    (a) holders of premises licences and personal licences,
    (b) the chief constable for the police area in which the Forum's area is situated,
    (c) persons having functions relating to health, education or social work,
    (d) young people,
    (e) persons resident within the Forum's area.

3. Convener

(1) At their first meeting in each calendar year, a Forum must elect one of the members of the Forum to be the convener of the Forum.
(2) The convener holds office, on such terms and conditions as the relevant council may determine, until the next election under sub-paragraph (1).

(3) Meetings of the Forum are to be chaired by the convener.
(4) If the office of convener is vacant or the convener is for any reason unable to act, a meeting of the Forum may be chaired by any other member present.

4. Administrative support

A council must provide each Forum established by them, or ensure each such Forum is provided, with such staff, property and services as the council considers are required for the Forum's purposes.

5. Meetings and proceedings

(1) Each Forum must, in each calendar year, hold at least 4 meetings.
(2) The quorum for a meeting of a Forum is one half of the number of members (but in any case not fewer than 3).
(3) Meetings of a Forum must be held in public.
(4) Otherwise, the arrangements for meetings of a Forum and other matters relating to proceedings of the Forum, are to be such as the Forum may determine.
(5) The proceedings of a Forum are not affected by-
   (a) any vacancy in the membership of the Forum, or
   (b) any defect in the appointment of a member of the Forum.

GENERAL NOTE

Local licensing forums require to be established by virtue of the provisions of s.10. A forum is to consist of not fewer than five and not more than 20 members, one of whom must be a licensing standards officer for the area. The membership requires to be, so far as possible, representative of the interests of persons (or descriptions of persons) who have an interest relevant to the forum's functions, including the persons specified in subs.(6).

The forum's functions are set out in s.11; and a licensing board's duties in relation to forums in s.12.

Paragraph 5

Each forum must hold at least four meetings in each calendar year. In addition s.10(3) requires a licensing board to hold a joint meeting with the local forum during that period.

SCHEDULE 3

Premises Licences: Mandatory Conditions

(introduced by section 27(1))

1. In this schedule, "the premises" means, in relation to any premises licence, the premises specified in the licence.

2. (1) Alcohol is to be sold on the premises only in accordance with the operating plan contained in the licence.
   (2) Nothing in sub-paragraph (1) is to be read as preventing or restricting the doing of anything referred to in section 63(2).

3. Any other activity to be carried on in the premises is to be carried on only in accordance with the operating plan contained in the licence.

4. (1) Alcohol is not to be sold on the premises at any time when-
   (a) there is no premises manager in respect of the premises,
   (b) the premises manager does not hold a personal licence,
   (c) the personal licence held by the premises manager is suspended, or
   (d) the licensing qualification held by the premises manager is not the appropriate licensing qualification in relation to the premises.
   (2) In sub-paragraph (1), "appropriate licensing qualification" in relation to any licensed premises means any licensing qualification prescribed as such in relation to licensed premises of that description in regulations under section 91(2)(d).
   (3) Nothing in sub-paragraph (1) or paragraph 5 is to be read as requiring the premises manager to be present on the premises at the time any sale of alcohol is made.

5. Every sale of alcohol made on the premises must be authorised (whether generally or specifically) by-
    (a) the premises manager, or
    (b) another person who holds a personal licence.

6. (1) No person (other than a person who holds a personal licence) is to work in the premises in the capacity mentioned in sub-paragraph (2) unless that person has complied with such requirements as to the training of staff as may be prescribed for the purposes of this paragraph.
(2) That is a capacity (whether paid or unpaid) which involves the person-
    (a) making sales of alcohol, or
    (b) where alcohol is sold on the premises for consumption on the premises, serving such alcohol to any person.
(3) Regulations under sub-paragraph (1) prescribing training requirements may, in particular-
    (a) provide for the accreditation by the Scottish Ministers of-
        (i) courses of training, and
        (ii) persons providing such courses,
    for the purposes of the regulations,
    (b) prescribe different training requirements in relation to different descriptions of persons,
    (c) require that any person providing training or any particular description of training in accordance with the regulations hold a personal licence or such other qualification as may be prescribed in the regulations, and
    (d) require training to be undergone again at such intervals as may be prescribed in the regulations.

7. Where the price at which any alcohol sold on the premises is varied-
    (a) the variation (referred to in this paragraph as "the earlier price variation") may be brought into effect only at the beginning of a period of licensed hours, and
    (b) no further variation of the price at which that or any other alcohol is sold on the premises may be brought into effect before the expiry of the period of 72 hours beginning with the coming into effect of the earlier price variation.

8. (1) An irresponsible drinks promotion must not be carried on in or in connection with the premises.
(2) Subject to sub-paragraph (3), a drinks promotion is irresponsible if it-
    (a) relates specifically to an alcoholic drink likely to appeal largely to persons under the age of 18,
    (b) involves the supply of an alcoholic drink free of charge or at a reduced price on the purchase of one or more drinks (whether or not alcoholic drinks),
    (c) involves the supply free of charge or at a reduced price of one or more extra measures of an alcoholic drink on the purchase of one or more measures of the drink,
    (d) involves the supply of unlimited amounts of alcohol for a fixed charge (including any charge for entry to the premises),
    (e) encourages, or seeks to encourage, a person to buy or consume a larger measure of alcohol than the person had otherwise intended to buy or consume,
    (f) is based on the strength of any alcohol,
    (g) rewards or encourages, or seeks to reward or encourage, drinking alcohol quickly, or
    (h) offers alcohol as a reward or prize, unless the alcohol is in a sealed container and consumed off the premises.
(3) Paragraphs (b) to (d) of sub-paragraph (2) apply only to a drinks promotion carried on in relation to alcohol sold for consumption on the premises.
(4) The Scottish Ministers may by regulations modify sub-paragraph (2) or (3) so as to-
    (a) add further descriptions of drinks promotions,
    (b) modify any of the descriptions of drinks promotions for the time being listed in it, or
    (c) extend or restrict the application of any of those descriptions of drinks promotions.
(5) In this paragraph, "drinks promotion" means, in relation to any premises, any activity which promotes, or seeks to promote, the buying or consumption of any alcohol on the premises.

9. (1) The conditions specified in this paragraph apply only to the extent that the premises licence authorises the sale of alcohol for consumption on the premises.
(2) Tap water fit for drinking must be provided free of charge on request.
(3) Other non-alcoholic drinks must be available for purchase at a reasonable price.

10. (1) The condition specified in sub-paragraph (2) applies only in relation to a premises licence in respect of which an annual or other recurring fee is to be paid by virtue of regulations under section 136(1).

(2) The fee must be paid as required by the regulations.

GENERAL NOTE

Except as otherwise provided here, in the interests of national consistency every premises licence must be subject to the conditions set out in the Schedule (s.27(1)). These conditions may be added to by regulations (s.27(3)); but they may not be varied by a licensing board (s.29(5)).

Paragraph 2(1)

This paragraph appears to create what has been termed a "duty to trade": in other words, an obligation to remain open for the sale of alcohol throughout the hours set out in an operating plan: see General Note to s.63.

Paragraph 2(2)

Section 63(2) sets out the circumstances in which alcohol may be sold, consumed or taken away from licensed premises outwith the licensed hours.

Paragraph 4

Alcohol is not to be sold on premises where there is no premises manager, the premises manager does not hold a personal licence or his licence is suspended or the licensing qualification held by the premises manager is not the appropriate qualification.

Section 31 makes provision for the deemed variation of a premises licence so as to substitute a new premises manager, helping to obviate the potential closure of the premises by virtue of para.4(1)(a).

Paragraph 5

Every sale of alcohol must be authorised (whether generally or specifically) by the premises manager or another personal licence holder.

This provision may well give rise to difficulty. While para.4(3) of this Schedule eliminates the requirement for a *premises manager* to be present on premises at any time when alcohol is being sold, it could by implication lead to the view another holder of a personal licence does require to be present. Indeed, it is difficult to see how alcohol sales could, in any meaningful sense, be "authorised" by an absent licence holder.

Section 19(3) of the 2003 Act provides as a mandatory licence condition that "every supply of alcohol... must be made or authorised by a person who holds a personal licence".

That subsection has, in certain parts of England, been interpreted by police forces and licensing authorities as requiring the physical presence of a personal licence holder at all times when alcohol is being sold, with the result that police have required the closure of premises when the owner of a business (and the sole personal licence holder) has absented him on holiday.

(While the absence of any personal licence holder on premises may (on the police interpretation of s.19(3)) amount to a breach of a licence condition, it is difficult to detect any statutory authority for the closure of premises. In one English case, the closure was ordered under s.19 of the Criminal Justice and Police Act 2001, on the basis that the premises *in quo* had been used for the unlicensed sale of intoxicating liquor.)

By way of response, the DCMS Guidance states that:

> "'Authorisation' does not imply direct supervision of each sale by a personal licence holder. The question arises as to how sales can be authorised in circumstances where the personal licence holder is absent for longer periods, such as when taking a holiday. In the Government's view it is not possible to state categorically how the requirement of authorisation is satisfied as the facts and circumstances of each case will differ. Whether or not authorisation has been given within the meaning of the Act or whether the frequency and length of absence meant that the personal licence holder could not, in fact, have authorised the sale would, ultimately, be a matter for a court to determine on the evidence before it when the issue arose.
>
> Nevertheless, it seems reasonable to expect that the courts would require

the authorisation to be meaningful and properly carried out and not involve any abdication of responsibility. In our view, the following factors might be relevant in considering whether there was any real authorisation:
- the person(s) authorised to sell alcohol should be clearly identified;
- the authorisation should have specified the acts which may be carried out by the person being authorised;
- there should be an overt act of authorisation, for example, a specific oral or written statement given to the individual(s) being authorised; and
- there should be in place sensible arrangements for monitoring by the personal licence holder of the activity authorised by him or her on a reasonably regular basis."

It remains to be seen whether a similar approach will be adopted in Scotland; but, even if sales may be "authorised" by an absent personal licence holder, there may well be difficulty in holding the licence holder accountable for sales which constitute an offence under the Act. In terms of s.103 "any responsible person" (who, for present purposes, will normally be the premises manager) commits an offence if he "knowingly allows" alcohol to be sold to a child or young person. As more fully explained in the notes to s.103, it appears that an offence is not committed where "knowingly" is of the essence unless there is actual personal knowledge on the part of the accused (*Noble v Heatly*, 1967 J.C. 5; 1967 S.L.T. 26).

It seems that this difficulty may not arise in England and Wales because of the doctrine of "delegation" excluded from Scots Law by *Noble* (see Gordon, para.8.56). In *Howker v Robinson* [1973] Q.B. 178; [1972] 3 W.L.R. 234 the holder of a licence was charged with knowingly allowing the sale of intoxicating liquor to a person under the age of 18 (Licensing Act 1974, s.169(1)). The defendant had no actual knowledge of the sale, but he was nevertheless convicted: "knowingly" was to be construed so that the licence holder could not escape his responsibilities by delegating the control of the premises to another person: the knowledge of the delegate was imputed to the licence holder, whether or not he was present on the premises. (See also *Linnet v Metropolitan Police Commissioner* [1946] K.B. 290; [1946] 1 All E.R. 380 and *R v Winston* [1969] 1 Q.B. 371; [1968] 2 W.L.R. 113; cf *Vane v Yiannopoullos* [1965] A.C. 486; and *Thornley v Hunter*, 1965 S.L.T. 206, which paved the path to *Noble*.)

On the line of English authorities, the 2003 Act's approach to authorisation, if correctly interpreted by the DCMS Guidance, does no violence to the principle that a licence holder bears criminal responsibility for the conduct of premises even while he is absent; but the translation of such an approach to Scotland may, standing the decision in *Noble*, prove impossible. (Indeed, the successful prosecution of a "responsible person" under s.103 may be an awkward matter even when he was present on the premises at the time of the offence but bereft of actual knowledge of its commission.) Perhaps the accountability of premises managers and other "responsible persons" for the actions of staff will require to rest on the Act's provisions for the review of premises licences (see ss.36-39).

Paragraph 6

Those involved in the sale or service of alcohol will require to undergo training, the nature of which will be prescribed by regulations. According to the Policy Memorandum, the majority of respondents who took part in the consultation following publication of the White Paper "agreed that casual staff need not undertake training but... there should be a clear definition of 'casual' to avoid licensees using this as a loophole". The Scottish Executive's memorandum to the Subordinate Legislation Committee indicated that casual staff were likely to be given "basic instruction" by the designated personal licence holder; and that 'casual staff' would be considered to be those staff working in the trade in any post for a total of four months or less, ie, the four month period is cumulative (sic)." Such an approach is broadly consistent with that proposed by Nicholson (Report, para.4.23).

Paragraph 7

As part of the Act's attempt to curb the irresponsible promotion of alcohol (as to which see also the notes to para.8), the pricing of alcohol, whether sold for consumption on or off the premises, may not vary in any 72-hour period.

Paragraph 8

In recent years, the irresponsible promotion of alcohol, which leads to binge drinking and alcohol misuse, has been a source of considerable concern to licensing boards. Although it may well be considered that those members of the licensed trade who seek to attract business with offers such as "Drink all you like for £10" ought to be regarded as unfit to hold a licence, the 1976 Act provides no means of pricing control.

In *Mitchells and Butlers Retail Ltd v Aberdeen City Licensing Board*, 2005 S.L.T. 13; [2005] 30 SLLP 24, the Lord Ordinary held that the Board had acted *ultra vires* by implementing a policy providing for minimum alcohol prices. It is probable that this Act could adopted such an approach, standing the nature of the licensing objectives and the wide condition-attaching powers afforded to licensing boards: see Scott Blair, "'Happy hours' controls: are they lawful?" [2004] 28 S.L.L.P. 24; and Philip Kolvin, "Minimum pricing: An English Perspective" [2004] 29 SLLP 18. However, although no Competition Law issues would have been likely to arise, the Executive has chosen to prohibit price variations (para.7); and to introduce further controls in this paragraph (on the view, as expressed in the Policy Memorandum, that it was also necessary to strike at "upselling" (see below) and promotions involving "all you can drink" for a fixed amount and free drinks linked to entry fees).

The original provisions contained in the Bill did not embrace the sale of alcohol for consumption off the premises. According to the Policy Memorandum, there was "no concrete evidence to suggest that purchasing a large quantity of alcohol in an off-licence is linked to immediate consumption and binge drinking": but that approach was not well received in many quarters, and, in the result, the Act contains at least some controls on off-sales promotions.

Paragraph 8(2)(c) is designed to suppress the practice of "upselling", that is to say, providing customers with an incentive to purchase a larger measure of a drink at a commensurately lower price than the one originally ordered: for example, where the purchaser of 25 ml of spirits at a price of, say, £1.25, is offered a 50 ml measure for the price of £1.75, rather than £2.50. Some alcohol suppliers are known to be concerned that this provision imposes "linear pricing": if a 25 ml measure of spirits costs £1.25, a 50 ml measure must be priced at £2.50. However, on the example given, there would appear to be nothing which prohibits the pricing of a 50 ml measure at £1.75 where such a measure is requested by the customer: he has not been supplied with an extra measure on the purchase of a smaller measure. Put another way, the reduced price of the extra measure does not begin with the purchase of the smaller measure. George Lyon, Minister in charge of licensing, gave the Local Government and Transport Committee an assurance that "linear pricing" was not the Executive's intention: "The provisions are directed specifically at promotional activity, not pricing activity. We have chosen to prevent the irresponsible promotions that are listed in schedules 3 and 4 from being carried out in licensed premises, but we have not chosen and do not intend to dictate the prices at which any alcohol or measure of alcohol is to be sold." (Official Report, col.2687.)

Paragraph 9

Where alcohol is sold for consumption on the premises, tap water fit for drinking must be available without cost on request and other non-alcoholic drinks must be available "at a reasonable price". It is doubtful whether the later requirement will be capable of enforcement: in many cases it will be impossible to determine whether a price is "reasonable".

SCHEDULE 4

Occasional Licences: Mandatory Conditions

(introduced by section 60(1))

1. In this schedule, "the premises" means, in relation to any occasional licence, the premises specified in the licence.

2. (1) Alcohol may be sold on the premises only in accordance with the terms of the licence.
   (2) Nothing in sub-paragraph (1) is to be read as preventing or restricting the doing of anything referred to in section 63(2).

3. Any other activity to be carried on in the premises may be carried on only in accordance with the description of the activity contained in the licence.

4.—(1) The condition specified in sub-paragraph (2) applies only to an occasional licence issued to the holder of a premises licence or personal licence.
(2) Every sale of alcohol made on the premises to which the licence relates must be authorised (whether generally or specifically) by the holder of a personal licence.

5.—(1) The condition specified in sub-paragraph (2) applies only to an occasional licence issued to a representative of a voluntary organisation.
(2) Alcohol may be sold on the premises only at an event taking place on the premises in connection with the voluntary organisation's activities.

6. Where the price at which any alcohol sold on the premises is varied-
   (a) the variation (referred to in this paragraph as "the earlier price variation") may be brought into effect only at the beginning of a period of licensed hours, and
   (b) no further variation of the price at which that or any other alcohol is sold on the premises may be brought into effect before the expiry of the period of 72 hours beginning with the coming into effect of the earlier price variation.

7.—(1) An irresponsible drinks promotion must not be carried on in or in connection with the premises.
(2) Subject to sub-paragraph (3), a drinks promotion is irresponsible if it-
   (a) relates specifically to an alcoholic drink likely to appeal largely to persons under the age of 18,
   (b) involves the supply of an alcoholic drink free of charge or at a reduced price on the purchase of one or more drinks (whether or not alcoholic drinks),
   (c) involves the supply free of charge or at a reduced price of one or more extra measures of an alcoholic drink on the purchase of one or more measures of the drink,
   (d) involves the supply of unlimited amounts of alcohol for a fixed charge (including any charge for entry to the premises),
   (e) encourages, or seeks to encourage, a person to buy or consume a larger measure of alcohol than the person had otherwise intended to buy or consume,
   (f) is based on the strength of any alcohol,
   (g) rewards or encourages, or seeks to reward or encourage, drinking alcohol quickly, or
   (h) offers alcohol as a reward or prize, unless the alcohol is in a sealed container and consumed off the premises.
(3) Paragraphs (b) to (d) of sub-paragraph (2) apply only to a drinks promotion carried on in relation to alcohol sold for consumption on the premises.
(4) The Scottish Ministers may by regulations modify sub-paragraph (2) or (3) so as to-
   (a) add further descriptions of drinks promotions,
   (b) modify any of the descriptions of drinks promotions for the time being listed in it, or
   (c) extend or restrict the application of any of those descriptions of drinks promotions.
(5) In this paragraph, "drinks promotion" means, in relation to any premises, any activity which promotes, or seeks to promote, the buying or consumption of any alcohol on the premises.

8.—(1) The conditions specified in this paragraph apply only to the extent that the occasional licence authorises the sale of alcohol for consumption on the premises.
(2) Tap water fit for drinking must be provided free of charge on request.
(3) Other non-alcoholic drinks must be available for purchase at a reasonable price.

GENERAL NOTE

This Schedule adapts the provisions of Sch.3 to occasional licences granted to the holders or premises and personal licences and voluntary organisations.

Licensing (Scotland) Act 2005

SCHEDULE 5

APPEALS

(introduced by section 131(1))

PART I

APPEALS TO THE SHERIFF PRINCIPAL

Decision	*Persons who can appeal*
A decision to refuse a premises licence application	The applicant
A decision to refuse a premises licence variation application	The applicant
A decision to refuse an application under section 33(1) or 34(1) for transfer of a premises licence	The applicant
A decision to refuse an application under section 35(1) for a variation of a premises licence	The applicant
A decision under section 39(1) to issue a written warning to a premises licence holder, to make a variation of a premises licence, or to suspend or revoke such a licence	The premises licence holder or, where the decision is taken in connection with a premises licence review application, the applicant
A decision to refuse an application under section 40 to revoke a variation or suspension of a premises licence	The applicant
A decision to refuse an application under section 45(7) to extend the provisional period in relation to a provisional premises licence	The applicant
A decision to refuse an application under section 46(4) to confirm a provisional premises licence	The applicant
A decision to refuse an application under section 47(2) to issue a premises licence for temporary premises	The applicant
A decision to refuse an application under section 47(6) to extend the period for which a temporary premises licence has effect	The applicant
A decision to refuse an occasional licence application	The applicant
A decision to grant an occasional licence application	Any person who has given a notice of objection under section 58(1)
A decision to refuse an extended hours application	The applicant

Part 2

Appeals to the Sheriff

Decision	Persons who can appeal
A decision to refuse a personal licence application	The applicant
A decision to make an order under section 83(9), 84(7), or 86(3) revoking, suspending or endorsing a personal licence	The personal licence holder

GENERAL NOTE

See the notes to ss.131 and 132 in relation to the Act's appeal provisions.

SCHEDULE 6

Modification of Enactments

(introduced by section 144)

1. Children and Young Persons Act 1963 (c.37)

In section 37(2)(b)(ii) (restriction on persons under 16 taking part in public performances within licensed premises) of the Children and Young Persons Act 1963, for "1976) or in respect of which a club is registered under that Act" substitute "2005 (asp 16))".

2. Countryside (Scotland) Act 1967 (c.86)

In section 78(1) (interpretation) of the Countryside (Scotland) Act 1967, in the definition of "refreshments", for "alcoholic liquor within the meaning of the Licensing (Scotland) Act 1976" substitute "alcohol within the meaning of section 2 of the Licensing (Scotland) Act 2005 (asp 16)".

3. New Towns (Scotland) Act 1968 (c.16)

(1) The New Towns (Scotland) Act 1968 is amended as follows.
   (2) In section 18(2) (disposal of land by development corporations), in the proviso, for "alcoholic liquor" substitute "alcohol".
   (3) In section 47(1) (interpretation), for the definition of "alcoholic liquor", substitute the following definition-
      ""alcohol" has the meaning given by section 2 of the Licensing (Scotland) Act 2005 (asp 16);".

4. Water (Scotland) Act 1980 (c.45)

In section 50(1)(b) (power to require supply by meter to certain premises) of the Water (Scotland) Act 1980, for "1976" substitute "2005 (asp 16)".

5. Local Government, Planning and Land Act 1980 (c.65)

In section 146 (disposal of land by urban development corporation) of the Local Government, Planning and Land Act 1980, for subsection (6) substitute-
      "(6) In this section, "alcohol" has the meaning given by section 2 of the Licensing (Scotland) Act 2005 (asp 16).".

6. Civic Government (Scotland) Act 1982 (c.45)

(1) The Civic Government (Scotland) Act 1982 is amended as follows.
   (2) In section 41(2)(f) (exclusion of licensed premises from definition of place of public entertainment)-
      (a) for "1976" substitute "2005 (asp 16)", and
      (b) for "the permitted" substitute "licensed".
   (3) In section 42(4)(a) (late hours catering licence not required in respect of licensed premises), for "1976" substitute "2005 (asp 16)".

7. Criminal Law (Consolidation) (Scotland) Act 1995 (c.39)

(1) The Criminal Law (Consolidation) (Scotland) Act 1995 is amended as follows.

(2) In section 22 (presumption as to contents of container), for "Section 127 of the Licensing (Scotland) Act 1976 (presumption as to contents of container)" substitute "Section 140 of the Licensing (Scotland) Act 2005 (asp 16) (presumption as to liquid contents of containers)".

(3) In section 23 (interpretation of Part II), for the definition of "alcohol", substitute the following definition-

"alcohol" has the meaning given in section 2 of the Licensing (Scotland) Act 2005 (asp 16);".

8. Crime and Punishment (Scotland) Act 1997 (c.48)

(1) Section 61 (confiscation of alcohol from persons under 18) of the Crime and Punishment (Scotland) Act 1997 is amended as follows.

(2) In subsection (1)-
   (a) in paragraph (b), for "alcoholic liquor, within the meaning of the Licensing (Scotland) Act 1976" substitute "alcohol", and
   (b) for "that liquor" substitute "the alcohol".

(3) In subsection (2), for-
   (a) "alcoholic liquor", and
   (b) "liquor" in each place where that word appears,
substitute "alcohol".

(4) In subsection (6), for "1976" substitute "2005 (asp 16)".

(5) After subsection (6) insert-
"(7) In this section, "alcohol" has the meaning given in section 2 of the Licensing (Scotland) Act 2005 (asp 16).".

9. Scottish Public Services Ombudsman Act 2002 (asp 11)

In paragraph 10 of Part 1 of schedule 2 (authorities not amendable by Order in Council) to the Scottish Public Services Ombudsman Act 2002, for "within the meaning of the Licensing (Scotland) Act 1976 (c.66)" substitute "continued in existence by or established under section 5 of the Licensing (Scotland) Act 2005 (asp 16)".

10. Freedom of Information (Scotland) Act 2002 (asp 13)

In paragraph 23 of Part 3 of schedule 1 (local government) to the Freedom of Information (Scotland) Act 2002, for "constituted in accordance with the provisions of section 1 of the Licensing (Scotland) Act 1976 (c.66)" substitute "continued in existence by or established under section 5 of the Licensing (Scotland) Act 2005 (asp 16)".

SCHEDULE 7

REPEALS

(introduced by section 149)

Enactment	Extent of repeal
The Revenue Act 1889 (c.42)	Section 26
The Children and Young Persons (Scotland) Act 1937 (c.37)	Section 16
The Methylated Spirits (Sale by Retail) (Scotland) Act 1937 (c.48)	The whole Act
The Finance Act 1970 (c.24)	Section 6
The Local Government (Scotland) Act 1973 (c.65)	Paragraph 36 of Schedule 24 Paragraph 17 of Schedule 25
The Licensing (Scotland) Act 1976 (c.66)	The whole Act

Enactment	Extent of repeal
The Alcoholic Liquor Duties Act 1979 (c.4)	Section 77(6)
The Licensed Premises (Exclusion of Certain Persons) Act 1980 (c.32)	The whole Act
The Law Reform (Miscellaneous Provisions) (Scotland) Act 1980 (c.55)	Section 21 Paragraphs 9 to 11 of Schedule 2
The Local Government, Planning and Land Act 1980 (c.65)	In section 146(3), the words "or alcoholic liquor"
The Local Government (Miscellaneous Provisions) (Scotland) Act 1981 (c.23)	Paragraphs 4 and 5 of Schedule 2
The Roads (Scotland) Act 1984 (c.54)	Paragraph 77 of Schedule 9
The Transport Act 1985 (c.67)	Paragraph 18 of Schedule 7
The Law Reform (Miscellaneous Provisions) (Scotland) Act 1985 (c.73)	Section 53
The Housing (Scotland) Act 1987 (c.26)	Subsection (3) of section 5
The Food Safety Act 1990 (c.16)	Paragraph 19 of Schedule 3
The Licensing (Low Alcohol Drinks) Act 1990 (c.21)	The whole Act
The Law Reform (Miscellaneous Provisions) (Scotland) Act 1990 (c.40)	Part III Schedule 5 In Schedule 8, Part I
The Finance Act 1991 (c.31)	In paragraph 1(a) of Schedule 2, the words "or the Licensing (Scotland) Act 1976,"
The Licensing (Amendment) (Scotland) Act 1993 (c.20)	The whole Act
The Local Government etc. (Scotland) Act 1994 (c.39)	Section 46 Paragraphs 23 and 106 of Schedule 13
The Criminal Law (Consolidation) (Scotland) Act 1995 (c.39)	In section 19(2), the words from "Notwithstanding" to "but"
The Criminal Procedure (Consequential Provisions) Act 1995 (c.40)	Paragraph 29 of Schedule 4
The Licensing (Amendment) (Scotland) Act 1996 (c.36)	The whole Act
The Access to Justice Act 1999 (c.22)	Paragraph 94 of Schedule 13
The Powers of Criminal Courts (Sentencing) Act 2000 (c.6)	Paragraph 60 of Schedule 9
The Licensing Act 2003 (c.17)	Paragraph 74 of Schedule 6
The Courts Act 2003 (c.39)	The unnumbered paragraph (which amends the Licensed Premises (Exclusion of Certain Persons) Act 1980) immediately following paragraph 200 of Schedule 8

INDEX

References are to sections

ACCESS TO JUSTICE ACT 1999,
   repeal of section, Sch.7
ADULTS WITH INCAPACITY (SCOTLAND) ACT 2000, 28, 34
ALCOHOL,
   certain supplies to be treated as sales, 3
   consumption by young person, 106
   delivery by young person, 108
   delivery from vehicles, 119
   delivery to young person, 108
   duty to display notice barring young people from purchasing, 110
   meaning of, 2
   offences relating to sale to trade, 117
   permitting sale to young person, 103
   power to prohibit sale off ferries, 128
   power to prohibit sale on trains, 127
   prohibition of late-night deliveries, 120
   prohibition of unauthorised sale, 1
     on moving vehicles, 118
   prohibition outside licensed hours, 63
   purchase for young person, 105
   remote sales, 139
   sale to young person, 102
   sending young person to collect, 109
   unsupervised sale by young person, 107
ALCOHOLIC LIQUOR DUTIES ACT 1979, 2, 147
   repeal of section, Sch.7
AMENDMENTS,
   Children and Young Persons Act 1963, Sch.6
   Civic Government (Scotland) Act 1982, Sch.6
   Countryside (Scotland) Act 1967, Sch.6
   Crime and Punishment (Scotland) Act 1997, Sch.6
   Criminal Law (Consolidation) (Scotland) Act 1995, Sch.6
   Freedom of Information (Scotland) Act 2002, Sch.6
   Local Government, Planning and Land Act 1980, Sch.6
   New Towns (Scotland) Act 1968, Sch.6
   Scottish Public Services Ombudsman Act 2002, Sch.6
   Water (Scotland) Act 1980, Sch.6
ANTISOCIAL BEHAVIOUR ETC (SCOTLAND) ACT 2004, 21, 65
APPEALS, 131, Sch.5
   provisions, 132
   to sheriff principal, Sch.5 Pt.1
   to the sheriff, Sch.5 Pt.2

APPLICANTS,
   attempting to influence Board members, 8
APPLICATION FORMS, 134
APPROPRIATE LICENSING BOARD,
   meaning, 18

BOARD MEMBERS,
   applicants attempting to influence, 8
BODIES CORPORATE,
   offences by, 141
BRITISH SUMMER TIMES,
   effect on licensed hours, 66
BUILDING (SCOTLAND) ACT 2003, 45, 47, 50
BUILDING STANDARDS,
   certificates, 50

CERTIFICATES,
   building standards, 50
   food hygiene, 50
   planning, 50
CHANGE OF ADDRESS,
   notification, 88
   updating of premises licence, 48
CHANGE OF NAME,
   notification, 88
   updating of premises licence, 48
CHIEF CONSTABLE,
   notification of application for occasional licence to, 57
CHILDREN AND YOUNG PERSONS ACT 1963,
   amendments, Sch.6
CHILDREN AND YOUNG PERSONS (SCOTLAND) ACT 1937,
   repeal of sections, Sch.7
CIVIC GOVERNMENT (SC0TLAND) ACT 1982,
   amendments, Sch.6
CLOSURE ORDERS, 97
   extension of emergency, 99
   interpretation, 101
   regulation, 100
   termination, 98
CLUBS,
   special provision for certain, 125
COMMENCEMENT, 150
CONTAINERS,
   liquid contents, 140

CONVICTIONS,
  duty to notify Licensing Board of licence holder, 42, 81
COUNTRYSIDE (SCOTLAND) ACT 1967,
  amendments, Sch.6
COURT,
  duty to notify Licensing Board of convictions of licence holder, 42, 81
COURTS ACT 2003,
  repeal of section, Sch.7
CRIME AND PUNISHMENT (SCOTLAND) ACT 1997,
  amendments, Sch.6
CRIMINAL LAW (CONSOLIDATION) (SCOTLAND) ACT 1995,
  amendments, Sch.6
  repeal of section, Sch.7
CRIMINAL PROCEDURE (CONSEQUENTIAL PROVISIONS) ACT 1995,
  repeal of section, Sch.7
CRIMINAL PROCEDURE (SCOTLAND) ACT 1995, 96
CROWN APPLICATION, 143
CUSTOMS AND EXCISE MANAGEMENT ACT 1979, 124

DEFINED EXPRESSIONS,
  index, 148
DETERMINATIONS,
  notification, 51
DISORDERLY CONDUCT, 115
DISPLAY NOTICE,
  duty barring young persons buying alcohol, 110
DRUNKEN PERSONS,
  entering or in premises which sells alcohol, 111
  obtaining alcohol, 112
  sale of alcohol to, 113

ENACTMENTS,
  modification of, 144, Sch.6
ENDORSEMENTS,
  expiry, 85
  suspension of licence after multiple, 86
EXCLUDED PREMISES, 123
EXCLUSION ORDERS, 94
  breach of, 95
  provision, 96
EXEMPT PREMISES, 124

FEES, 136
FERRIES,
  power to prohibit sale of alcohol, 128
FINANCE ACT 1970,
  repeal of section, Sch.7

FINANCE ACT 1991,
  repeal of section, Sch.7
FOOD HYGIENE,
  certificates, 50
FOOD SAFETY ACT 1990, 50
  repeal of section, Sch.7
FORM OF APPLICATIONS, 134
FORM OF NOTICES, 134
FORM OF PROPOSALS, 134
FREEDOM OF INFORMATION (SCOTLAND) ACT 2002,
  amendments, Sch.6

GRANTING OF LICENCES,
  inspection of premises, 137
GUIDANCE, 142

HEARINGS, 133
HOUSING (SCOTLAND) ACT 1987,
  repeal of section, Sch.7

INSPECTION OF PREMISES,
  before granting licence, 137
INTERPRETATION, 147

LATE-NIGHT DELIVERIES,
  prohibition of alcohol, 120
LAW REFORM (MISCELLANEOUS PROVISIONS) (SCOTLAND) ACT 1980,
  repeal of section, Sch.7
LAW REFORM (MISCELLANEOUS PROVISIONS) (SCOTLAND) ACT 1985,
  repeal of section, Sch.7
LAW REFORM (MISCELLANEOUS PROVISIONS) (SCOTLAND) ACT 1990,
  repeal of sections, Sch.7
LICENCE HOLDER,
  duty of court to notify Licensing Board of convictions of, 42
  duty to notify court of premises licence, 41
  duty to notify Licensing Board of convictions, 43, 82
  duty to produce licence, 3
  duty to undergo training, 87
  suspension of licence after multiple endorsements, 86
  transfer of premises licence on application of, 33
  transfer of premises licence on application of person other than, 34
  variation on transfer of premises licence on application of person other than, 35
LICENCE HOLDER PREMISES LICENCE,
  transfer on application of person other than licence holder, 34

WATER (SCOTLAND) ACT 1980,—*cont.*
Courts Act 2003, Sch.7
Criminal Law (Consolidation) (Scotland) Act 1995, Sch.7
Criminal Procedure (Consequential Provisions) Act 1995, Sch.7
Finance Act 1970, Sch.7
Finance Act 1991, Sch.7
Housing (Scotland) Act 1987, Sch.7
Law Reform (Miscellaneous Provisions) (Scotland) Act 1980, Sch.7
Law Reform (Miscellaneous Provisions) (Scotland) Act 1985, Sch.7
Law Reform (Miscellaneous Provisions) (Scotland) Act 1990, Sch.7
Licensing Act 2003, Sch.7
Local Government etc (Scotland) Act 1994, Sch.7
Local Government (Miscellaneous Provisions) (Scotland) Act 1981, Sch.7
Local Government, Planning and Land Act 1980, Sch.7
Local Government (Scotland) Act 1973, Sch.7
Powers of Criminal Courts (Sentencing) Act 2000, Sch.7
Revenue Act 1889, Sch.7
Roads (Scotland) Act 1984, Sch.7
Transport Act 1985, Sch.7
REVENUE ACT 1889,
repeal of sections, Sch.7
REVIEW HEARING,
premises licence, 38
ROADS (SCOTLAND) ACT 1984, 123
repeal of section, Sch.7
RULES,
power to relieve failure to comply with, 135

SALES,
certain supplies of alcohol to be treated as, 3
SCOTTISH PUBLIC SERVICES OMBUDSMAN ACT 2002,
amendments, Sch.6
SHERIFF,
appeals to, Sch.5 Pt.2
SHERIFF PRINCIPAL,
appeals to, Sch.5 Pt.1
SHORT TITLE, 150
SMUGGLED GOODS,
keeping, 121
SUMMER TIME ACT 1972, 66

TEMPORARY PREMISES LICENCE, 47
TRADE SALES OF ALCOHOL,
offences, 117
TRAINS,
power to prohibit sale of alcohol on, 127
TRANSPORT ACT 1985,
repeal of section, Sch.7
TWENTYFOUR HOUR LICENCES,
granted only in exceptional circumstances, 64

UNLICENSED SALE,
prohibition of sale of alcohol, 1

VEHICLES, 126
delivery of alcohol from, 119
VESSELS, 126
VIOLENT OFFENDERS,
exclusion orders, 94

WATER (SCOTLAND) ACT 1980,
amendments, Sch.6

OCCASIONAL LICENCES, 56—*cont.*
representations, 58
OFF-SALES,
licensed hours, 65
OFFENCES,
by bodies corporate, 142
effect of appeal against conviction for foreign, 130
effect of appeal against conviction for relevant, 130
foreign, 129
interpretation, 122
relevant, 129
ORDERS, 146
OVERPROVISION,
duty to assess, 7

PERSONAL LICENCE, 71
application, 72
determination of application, 74
duty to notify court of convictions, 80
duty to notify Licensing Board of convictions, 75
issue of, 76
loss of, 92
notification of application to chief constable, 73
period of effect, 77
renewal, 78

notification of determinations, 79
theft of, 92
PLANNING,
certificates, 50
POLICE POWERS OF ENTRY, 138
POWER,
to relieve failure to comply with rules, 135
POWERS OF CRIMINAL COURTS (SENTENCING) ACT 2000,
repeal of section, Sch.7
POWERS OF ENTRY,
Licensing Standard Officers, 15
POWERS OF INSPECTION,
Licensing Standard Officers, 15
PREMISES,
refusal to leave, 116
PREMISES LICENCE, 17
applicant s duty to notify Licensing Board of convictions, 24
application, 20
after refusal of application, 25, 32
for review, 36
to vary, 29
certified copies, 55
conditions, 27, Sch.3
determination of application, 23

PREMISES LICENCE, 17—*cont.*
determination of application to vary, 30
duration, 28
duty of Licensing Board to update, 49
duty to display, 52
duty to keep, 52
duty to produce, 52
issue of, 26
loss of, 53
notification of application, 21
notification of change of name or address, 48
objections, 22
provisional, 45
provisional confirmation, 46
representations, 22
review hearing, 38
review on Licensing Board's initiative, 37
temporary, 47
theft of, 53
transfer on application of licence holder, 33
PREMISES MANAGER, 19
death of, 54
dismissal of, 54
resignation of, 54
variation to substitute, 31
PREMISES STAFF,
not to be drunk, 114
PROHIBITION,
unlicensed sale of alcohol, 1
PROPOSAL FORMS, 134
PROVISIONAL PREMISES LICENCE, 45
confirmation, 46
PROVISIONS, 145
PUBLIC REGISTER,
duty of Licensing Board to keep, 9

RAILWAYS ACT 1993, 127, 147
REGULATIONS, 146
REMOTE SALES OF ALCOHOL, 139
REPEAL OF ACTS,
Licensed Premises (Exclusion of Certain Persons) Act 1980, Sch.7
Licensing (Amendment) (Scotland) Act 1993, Sch.7
Licensing (Amendment) (Scotland) Act 1996, Sch.7
Licensing (Low Alcohol Drinks) Act 1990, Sch.7
Licensing (Scotland) Act 1976, Sch.7
Methylated Spirits (Sale by Retail) (Scotland) Act 1937, Sch.7
REPEAL OF SECTIONS,
Access to Justice Act 1999, Sch.7
Alcoholic Liquor Duties Act 1979, Sch.7
Children and Young Persons (Scotland) Act 1937, Sch.7

LICENCE HOLDER PREMISES LICENCE,—*cont.*
variation on transfer on application of person other than licence holder, 35
LICENCE,
occasional, 56
LICENSED HOURS, 62
effect of British Summer Time, 66
off-sales, 65
prohibition of alcohol outside, 63
LICENSED HOURS EXTENSIONS,
applications, 68
determination of application, 70
notification of application, 69
power of Licensing Board to grant, 67
LICENSED PREMISES (EXCLUSION OF CERTAIN PERSONS) ACT 1980,
repeal of Act, Sch.7
LICENSING ACT 2003,
repeal of section, Sch.7
LICENSING (AMENDMENT) (SCOTLAND) ACT 1993,
repeal of Act, Sch.7
LICENSING (AMENDMENT) (SCOTLAND) ACT 1996,
repeal of Act, Sch.7
LICENSING BOARDS, 5, Sch.1
duty in relation to Local Licensing Forums, 12
duty of applicant to notify of convictions, 24
duty of court to notify of convictions of licence holder, 42, 81
duty of licence holder to notify of convictions, 43, 82
duty of to notify of convictions, 75
duty to keep public register, 9
duty to update licence, 89
duty to update premises licence, 49
power on review, 39
power to grant extensions to licensed hours, 67
power to specify which to exercise functions, 90
procedure on receiving notice of conviction, 83
review of decision to vary or suspend licence, 40
review of premises licence by, 37
LICENSING (LOW ALCOHOL DRINKS) ACT 1990,
repeal of Act, Sch.7
LICENSING OBJECTIVES, 4
inconsistent conduct, 84
LICENSING POLICY,
statements, 6

LICENSING QUALIFICATIONS,
power to prescribe, 91
LICENSING (SCOTLAND) ACT 1976,
repeal of Act, Sch.7
LICENSING STANDARDS OFFICERS, 13
functions of, 14
notification of application for occasional licence to, 57
powers on inspection, 15
powers of entry, 15
training of, 16
LIQUEUR CONFECTIONERY,
sale to young person, 104
LIQUID CONTENTS,
of containers, 140
LOCAL GOVERNMENT ETC (SCOTLAND) ACT 1994, 5
repeal of sections, Sch.7
LOCAL GOVERNMENT (MISCELLANEOUS PROVISIONS) (SCOTLAND) ACT 1981,
repeal of section, Sch.7
LOCAL GOVERNMENT, PLANNING AND LAND ACT 1980,
amendments, Sch.6
repeal of section, Sch.7
LOCAL GOVERNMENT (SCOTLAND) ACT 1973, 147
repeal of section, Sch.7
LOCAL GOVERNMENT (SCOTLAND) ACT 1994, 147
LOCAL LICENSING FORUMS, 10, Sch.2
duties of Licensing Boards, 12
functions, 11

METHYLATED SPIRITS (SALE BY RETAIL) (SCOTLAND) ACT 1937,
repeal of Act, Sch.7
MOVEABLE STRUCTURES, 126
MOVING VEHICLES,
prohibition of unauthorised sale of alcohol, 118

NEW TOWNS (SCOTLAND) ACT 1968,
amendments, Sch.6
NOTICE FORMS, 134

OCCASIONAL LICENCES, 56
conditions, 60, Sch.4
determination of application, 59
notification of determinations, 61
notification of application to chief constable, 57
notification of application to Licensing Standards Officer, 57
objections, 58

INDEX

References are to sections

ADVICE, 4
AGREEMENTS,
  between designated bodies, 79
  between Secretary of State and designated bodies, 78
  with local authorities, 84
  maximum duration, 82
  provisions, 85
AGRICULTURAL ACT 1967, 91
AGRICULTURAL BOARDS, Sch.8
  permissible functions of, 89
  permissible purpose of, 88
  power to establish, 87
  provisions, 90
AGRICULTURAL COMMITTEES,
  abolition of certain, 101
AGRICULTURAL MARKETING ACT 1958, 101
  amendments, Sch.11 Pt 1
  repeal of sections, Sch.12
AGRICULTURAL MARKETING (NORTHERN IRELAND) ORDER 1982 (SI 1982/1080 (NI 12)), 101, Sch.11 Pt 1
  revocation of sections, Sch.12
AGRICULTURAL OPERATIONS,
  notification in National Parks, 63
AGRICULTURE ACT 1967,
  amendments, Sch.11 Pt 1
  repeal of sections, Sch.12
AGRICULTURE ACT 1986,
  amendments, Sch.11 Pt 1
AGRICULTURE ACT 1993,
  amendments, Sch.11 Pt 1
AGRICULTURE (NORTHERN IRELAND) ORDER 1993 (SI 1993/2665 (NI 10)),
  revocation of sections, Sch.12
AMENDMENTS, 105
  Agricultural Act 1967, Sch.11 Pt 1
  Agricultural Marketing Act 1958, Sch.11 Pt 1
  Agriculture Act 1986, Sch.11 Pt 1
  Agriculture Act 1993, Sch.11 Pt 1
  Animal Health Act 1981, Sch.11 Pt 1
  British Waterways Act 1983, Sch.11 Pt 2
  British Waterways Act 1995, Sch.11 Pt 2
  Cereals Marketing Act 1965, Sch.11 Pt 1
  Channel Tunnel Act 1987, Sch.11 Pt 1
  Channel Tunnel Rail Link Act 1996, Sch.11 Pt 1
  Civil Contingencies Act 2004, Sch.11 Pt 1
  Conservation of Seals Act 1970, Sch.6, Sch.11 Pt 1

AMENDMENTS, 105—*cont.*
  Countryside Act 1968, Sch.11 Pt 1
  Countryside and Rights of Way Act 2000, 71, Sch.11 Pt 1
  Deer Act 1991, Sch.6, Sch.11 Pt 1
  Derelict Land Act 1982, Sch.11 Pt 1
  Destructive Imported Animals Act 1932, Sch.6, Sch.11 Pt 1
  Electricity Act 1989, Sch.11 Pt 1
  Environment Act 1995, 61, Sch.11 Pt 1
  Freedom of Information Act 2000, Sch.11 Pt 1, Sch.11 Pt 2
  General Consumer Council (Northern Ireland) Order 1984 (SI 1984/1822 (NI 12)), Sch.11 Pt 1
  Government of Wales Act 1998, Sch.11 Pt 1
  Greater London Authority Act 1999, Sch.11 Pt 1
  Highways Act 1980, Sch.11 Pt 1
  Hill Farming Act 1946, 101, Sch.11 Pt 1
  House of Commons Disqualification Act 1975, Sch.11 Pt 1, Sch.11 Pt 2
  Industrial Organisation and Development Act 1947, Sch.11 Pt 1
  Inheritance Tax Act 1984, Sch.11 Pt 1
  Import of Live Fish (England and Wales) Act 1980, Sch.11 Pt 1
  Land Drainage Act 1991, Sch.11 Pt 1
  Local Government Act 1974, Sch.11 Pt 1
  Local Government and Housing Act 1989, 65
  Manoeuvres Act 1958, Sch.11 Pt 1
  Miscellaneous Financial Provisions Act 1983, Sch.11 Pt 1
  National Assembly for Wales (Transfer of Functions) Order 1999 (SI 1999/672), 103
  National Heritage Act 1983, Sch.11 Pt 1
  National Parks and Access to the Countryside Act 1949, 59, 60, 62, Sch.11 Pt 1
  Norfolk and Suffolk Broads Act 1988, 64, Sch.11 Pt 1
  Parliamentary Commissioner Act 1967, Sch.11 Pt 1
  Protection of Badgers Act 1992, Sch.6, Sch.11 Pt 1
  Public Appointments and Public Bodies etc (Scotland) Act 2003, Sch.11 Pt 1
  Public Records Act 1958, Sch.11 Pt 1
  Race Relations Act 1976, Sch.11 Pt 1, Sch.11 Pt 2

AMENDMENTS, 105—*cont.*
  Road Traffic Regulation Act 1984, 72, Sch.11 Pt 1
  Scottish Public Services Ombudsman Act 2002, Sch.11 Pt 1
  Sea Fisheries Regulation Act 1966, Sch.11 Pt 1
  Superannuation Act 1965, Sch.11 Pt 1
  Superannuation Act 1972, Sch.11 Pt 1
  Transport Act 1968, 74, 75, 76, 77, Sch.11 Pt 2
  Transport and Works Act 1992, Sch.11 Pt 1
  Water Act 2003, Sch.11 Pt 1
  Water Resources Act 1991, Sch.11 Pt 1
  Wildlife and Countryside Act 1981
  Wildlife and Countryside Act 1981, 47, 48, 49, 50, 51, 54, 55, 56, 57, 58, 63, 69, 70, Sch.5 Pt 1, Sch.6, Sch.11 Pt 1
ANIMAL HEALTH ACT 1981,
  amendments, Sch.11 Pt 1
APPROPRIATE AUTHORITY,
  meaning of, 96
ASSISTANCE,
  financial and other, 6

BIOCIDAL PRODUCTS REGULATIONS 2001 (SI 2001/880), 43
BIODIVERSITY,
  duty to conserve of wildlife, 40
  lists and action,
    England, 41
    Wales, 42
BIRDS,
  protection of nests, 47
  re-population programme release into the wild, 48
  registration of captive, 49
BOARDS,
  dissolution of, 93
  functions which may be assigned to, Sch.9
  power to dissolve, 92
  provisions relating to, Sch.10
BRITISH WATERWAYS ACT 1983,
  amendments, Sch.11 Pt 2
BRITISH WATERWAYS ACT 1995,
  amendments, Sch.11 Pt 2
BROADS,
  functions in relation to, 64
BROADS AUTHORITY,
  functions of, 64
BYELAWS,
  relating to land drainage, 100

CEREALS MARKETING ACT 1965,
  amendments, Sch.11 Pt 1
  repeal of sections, Sch.12

CHANNEL TUNNEL ACT 1987,
  amendments, Sch.11 Pt 1
CHANNEL TUNNEL RAIL LINK ACT 1996,
  amendments, Sch.11 Pt 1
CIVIL CONTINGENCIES ACT 2004,
  amendments, Sch.11 Pt 1
CODES OF PRACTICE, Sch.5 Pt 3
COMMENCEMENT, 107
COMMISSION FOR RURAL COMMUNITIES, 17, Sch.2
  advice, 19
  information services, 21
  monitoring, 19
  power to charge for services, 22
  powers, 23
  purpose of, 18
  representation, 19
  research, 20
COMPANIES ACT 1985, Sch.10
COMPANIES (NORTHERN IRELAND) ORDER 1986 (SI 1986/1032 (NI 6)), Sch.10
CONSERVATION BODIES, 32
  advice from joint committee, 35
  functions, 34
    with respect to wildlife, 36
  powers, 37
  purpose of functions, 33
CONSERVATION OF SEALS ACT 1970, Sch.5 Pt 2
  amendments, Sch.6, Sch.11 Pt 1
CONSTITUTION, 1
CONSULTANCY SERVICES, 10
COUNTRYSIDE,
  natural beauty, 99
COUNTRYSIDE ACT 1968,
  amendments, Sch.11 Pt 1
  repeal of sections, Sch.12
COUNTRYSIDE AND RIGHTS OF WAY ACT 2000, 67
  amendments, 71, Sch.11 Pt 1
  repeal of sections, Sch.12
CRIMINAL JUSTICE ACT 2003, 43
CRIMINAL PROCEEDINGS,
  power to bring, 12
CROWN LAND, 102

DEER ACT 1991, Sch.5 Pt 2
  amendments, Sch.6, Sch.11 Pt 1
DEREGULATION AND CONTRACTING OUT ACT 1994, 85
DERELICT LAND ACT 1982,
  amendments, Sch.11 Pt 1
DESIGNATED BODIES, 80, Sch.7
  agreements, 79
    between Secretary of State and, 78

DESIGNATED BODIES, 80, Sch.7—*cont.*
  maximum duration, 82
  with local authorities, 84
  powers of, 83
  provisions with respect to agreements, 84
  reserved functions, 81
DESTRUCTIVE IMPORTED ANIMALS ACT 1932, Sch.5 Pt 2
  amendments, Sch.6, Sch.11 Pt 1
DEVELOPMENT COMMISSION (TRANSFER OF FUNCTIONS AND MISCELLANEOUS PROVISIONS) ORDER 1999 (SI 1999/416),
  revocation of sections, Sch.12
DIRECTIONS, 38, 95
  power of Secretary of State to give, 16, 25

ELECTRICITY ACT 1989,
  amendments, Sch.11 Pt 1
ENFORCEMENT POWERS,
  in connection with wildlife, Sch.5
ENGLAND,
  functions of Inland Waterways Advisory Council, 76
ENGLISH NATURE AND COUNTRYSIDE AGENCY,
  transfers on dissolution of, 26
ENVIRONMENT ACT 1995,
  amendments, 61, Sch.11 Pt 1
ENVIRONMENT PROTECTION ACT 1990,
  amendments, Sch.11 Pt 1
EXPERIMENTAL SCHEMES, 8
EXTENT, 108

FINANCIAL ASSISTANCE, 6, 98
  emergency, 65
FINANCIAL PROVISIONS, 106
FOOD AND ENVIRONMENT PROTECTION ACT 1985, 43, 45, 46
FORESTRY ACT 1967, 7
FREEDOM OF INFORMATION ACT 2000,
  amendments, Sch.11 Pt 1, Sch.11 Pt 2

GENERAL CONSUMER COUNCIL (NORTHERN IRELAND) ORDER 1984 (SI 1984/1822 (NI 12)),
  amendments, Sch.11 Pt 1
  revocation of sections, Sch.12
GOVERNMENT OF WALES ACT 1998, 72
  amendments, Sch.11 Pt 1
GRANTS, 94
  power of Secretary of State to give, 14, 24
GREATER LONDON AUTHORITY ACT 1999,
  amendments, Sch.11 Pt 1

GUIDANCE,
  power of Secretary of State to give, 15

HIGHWAYS ACT 1980, 67
  amendments, Sch.11 Pt 1
  repeal of sections, Sch.12
HILL FARMING ACT 1946,
  amendments, 101, Sch.11 Pt 1
  repeal of sections, Sch.12
HOUSE OF COMMONS DISQUALIFICATION ACT 1975,
  amendments, Sch.11 Pt 1, Sch.11 Pt 2
  repeal of sections, Sch.12

IMPORT OF LIVE FISH (ENGLAND AND WALES) ACT 1980,
  amendments, Sch.11 Pt 1
INDUSTRIAL ORGANISATION AND DEVELOPMENT ACT 1947, 91
  amendments, Sch.11 Pt 1
INFORMATION SERVICES, 9
INHERITANCE TAX ACT 1984,
  amendments, Sch.11 Pt 1
INLAND WATERWAYS, Sch.11 Pt 2
INLAND WATERWAYS ADVISORY COUNCIL, 73
  Constitution of, 74
  functions in England and Wales, 76
  functions in Scotland, 76
  procedure, 75
  terms of office, 75
INTERPRETATION, 30, 39, 46, 71, 86
INTERPRETATION ACT (NORTHERN IRELAND) 1954, 97

JOINT NATURE CONSERVATION COMMITTEE, 31, Sch.4

LAND DRAINAGE,
  byelaws relating to, 100
LAND DRAINAGE ACT 1991,
  amendments, Sch.11 Pt 1
LEVY BODIES,
  dissolution of, 93
  power to dissolve, 91
LICENCES,
  power to charge for, 11
LOCAL AUTHORITIES,
  agreements with designated bodies, 84
LOCAL GOVERNMENT ACT 1974,
  amendments, Sch.11 Pt 1
LOCAL GOVERNMENT ACT 2000, 84, 86
LOCAL GOVERNMENT AND HOUSING ACT 1989,
  amendments, 65

MANAGEMENT AGREEMENTS, 7
MANOEUVRES ACT 1958,
   amendments, Sch.11 Pt 1
MINISTERS OF THE CROWN ACT 1975, 30, 40
MISCELLANEOUS FINANCIAL PROVISIONS ACT 1983,
   amendments, Sch.11 Pt 1
   repeal of sections, Sch.12

NATIONAL ASSEMBLY FOR WALES (TRANSFER OF FUNCTIONS) ORDER 1999 (SI 1999/672),
   amendments, 103
   revocation of sections, Sch.12
NATIONAL HERITAGE ACT 1983,
   amendments, Sch.11 Pt 1
   repeal of sections, Sch.12
NATIONAL PARK AUTHORITIES,
   expenditure by, 62
   members, 61
NATIONAL PARKS,
   criteria for designating, 59
   notification of agricultural operations on moor and heath, 63
   procedure for orders designating, 60
   traffic regulation, 72
NATIONAL PARKS AND ACCESS TO THE COUNTRYSIDE ACT 1949, 7
   amendments, 59, 60, 62
   repeal of sections, Sch.11 Pt 1, Sch.12
NATURAL BEAUTY,
   in countryside, 99
NATURAL ENGLAND, Sch.1
NATURE CONSERVANCY COUNCIL ACT 1973,
   repeal of sections, Sch.12
NORFOLK AND SUFFOLK BROADS ACT 1988,
   amendments, 64, Sch.11 Pt 1

ORDERS,
   procedure, 97

PARLIAMENTARY COMMISSIONER ACT 1967,
   amendments, Sch.11 Pt 1
   repeal of sections, Sch.12
PESTICIDES,
   codes of practice, 45
   enforcement powers, 44
   possession harmful to wildlife, 43

PLANT PROTECTION PRODUCTS REGULATIONS 2005 (SI 2005/1435), 43
POISONS ACT 1972, 43
POWERS, 13
PROPOSAL ACTION, 5
PROTECTION OF BADGERS ACT 1992, Sch.5 Pt 2
   amendments, Sch.6, Sch.11 Pt 1
PROTECTION OF NESTS,
   for birds which re-use nests, 47
PROVISION,
   power to make, 104
PUBLIC APPOINTMENTS AND PUBLIC BODIES ETC (SCOTLAND) ACT 2003,
   amendments, Sch.11 Pt 1
   repeal of sections, Sch.12
PUBLIC RECORDS ACT 1958,
   amendments, Sch.11 Pt 1
   repeal of sections, Sch.12
PURPOSE, 2

RACE RELATIONS ACT 1976,
   amendments, Sch.11 Pt 1, Sch.11 Pt 2
   repeal of sections, Sch.12
RE-POPULATION PROGRAMME,
   birds released into the wild, 48
REGIONAL DEVELOPMENT AGENCIES ACT 1998, 26
REGISTRATION,
   of captive birds, 49
REPEAL OF SECTIONS,
   Agricultural Marketing Act 1958, Sch.12
   Agriculture Act 1967, Sch.12
   Cereals Marketing Act 1965, Sch.12
   Countryside Act 1968, Sch.12
   Countryside and Rights of Way Act 2000, Sch.12
   Highways Act 1980, Sch.12
   Hill Farming Act 1946, Sch.12
   House of Commons Disqualification Act 1975, Sch.12
   Miscellaneous Financial Provisions Act 1983, Sch.1
   National Heritage Act 1983, Sch.12
   National Parks and Access to the Countryside Act 1949, Sch.12
   Nature Conservancy Council Act 1971, Sch.12
   Parliamentary Commissioner Act 1967, Sch.12
   Public Appointments and Public Bodies etc (Scotland) Act 2003, Sch.12
   Public Records Act 1958, Sch.12
   Race Relations Act 1976, Sch.12

REPEAL OF SECTIONS,—*cont.*
　Scottish Public Services Ombudsman Act
　　2002, Sch.1
　Superannuation Act 1965, Sch.12
　Superannuation Act 1972, Sch.12
　Transport Act 1968, Sch.12
　Water Act 2003, Sch.12
　Wildlife and Countryside Act 1981, Sch.12
RESEARCH, 3
REVIEW, 3
REVOCATION OF SECTIONS,
　Agricultural Marketing (Northern Ireland)
　　Order 1982 (SI 1982/1080 (NI 12)),
　　Sch.12
　Agriculture (Northern Ireland) Order 1993
　　(SI 1993/2665 (NI 10)), Sch.12
　Development Commission (Transfer of
　　Functions and Miscellaneous
　　Provisions Order 1999 (SI 1999/416),
　　Sch.12
　General Consumer Council (Northern
　　Ireland) Order 1984 (SI 1984/1822
　　(NI 12)), Sch.12
　National Assembly for Wales (Transfer of
　　Functions) Order 1999 (SI 1999/672),
　　Sch.12
RIGHTS OF WAY,
　application under Wildlife and Countryside
　　Act 1981, 69
　dedication,
　　restricted byways, 68
　　under Wildlife and Countryside Act 1981,
　　　69
　ending of existing unrecorded public, 67
　restrictions on creation on new public, 66
　use by pedal cycles, 68
ROAD TRAFFIC ACT 1988, 71
ROAD TRAFFIC REGULATION ACT 1984,
　amendments, 72, Sch.11 Pt 1

SCOTLAND,
　functions of Inland Waterways Advisory
　　Council, 77
SCOTTISH PUBLIC SERVICES OMBUDSMAN ACT 2002,
　amendments, Sch.11 Pt 1
　repeal of sections, Sch.12
SEA FISHERIES REGULATION ACT 1966,
　amendments, Sch.11 Pt 1
SECRETARY OF STATE,
　agreement between designated bodies and, 78
　powers, 83
　　to give directions, 16, 25
　　to give grants, 14, 24
　　to give guidance, 15

SERVICES,
　power to charge for, 11
SHORT TITLE, 109
SITES OF SPECIAL SCIENTIFIC INTEREST,
　denotification, 56
　effect of failure to serve notices in
　　connection, 57
　notices and signs relating to, 58
　offences, 55
STATUTORY RULES (NORTHERN IRELAND) ORDER 1979 (SI 1979/1573 (NI 12)), 97
SUPERANNUATION ACT 1965,
　amendments, Sch.11 Pt 1
　repeal of sections, Sch.12
SUPERANNUATION ACT 1972, Sch.2
　amendments, Sch.11 Pt 1
　repeal of sections, Sch.12

TOWN AND COUNTRY PLANNING ACT 1990, 30, 40
TRAFFIC REGULATION,
　in National Parks, 72
TRAINING, 10
TRANSFER SCHEMES, Sch.3
　arrangements, 29
　on dissolution of English Nature and
　　Countryside Agency, 26
　power to make, 27, 28
TRANSPORT ACT 1968, 73
　amendments, 74, 75, 76, 77, Sch.11 Pt 2
　repeal of sections, Sch.12
TRANSPORT AND WORKS ACT 1992,
　amendments, Sch.11 Pt 1

WALES, 103
　functions of Inland Waterways Advisory
　　Council, 76
WATER ACT 2003,
　amendments, Sch.11 Pt 1
　repeal of sections, Sch.12
WATER INDUSTRY ACT 1991,
　amendments, Sch.11 Pt 1
WATER RESOURCES ACT 1991,
　amendments, Sch.11 Pt 1
WILDLIFE,
　duty to conserve biodiversity, 40
　enforcement powers, 52, Sch.5
　functions of conservation bodies, 36
　invasive non-native species,
　　codes of practice, 51
　　possession of harmful pesticides, 43
　　sale of invasive non-native species, 50

WILDLIFE AND COUNTRYSIDE ACT 1981, 7, 46, 67, 71, 72, 108
  amendments, 47, 48, 49, 50, 51, 54, 55, 56, 57, 58, 63, 69, 70, Sch.5 Pt 1, Sch.5 Pt 2, Sch.5 Pt 3, Sch.5 Pt 4, Sch.6, Sch.11 Pt 1
  repeal of sections, Sch.12

WILDLIFE INSPECTORS,
  extension of powers to certain other Acts, Sch.5 Pt 2
  search warrant powers extended to certain other Acts, Sch.5 Pt 4

WILDLIFE OFFENCES,
  time limit for proceedings, 53, Sch.6